BUILDING
THE
GOLDEN
GATE
BRIDGE

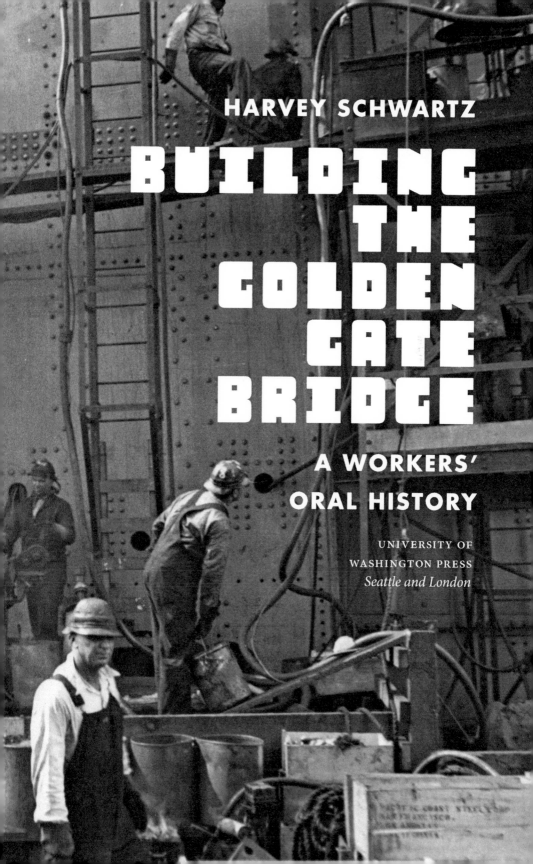

HARVEY SCHWARTZ

BUILDING THE GOLDEN GATE BRIDGE

A WORKERS' ORAL HISTORY

UNIVERSITY OF
WASHINGTON PRESS
Seattle and London

© 2015 by the University of Washington Press
Printed and bound in the United States of America
Design by Thomas Eykemans
Composed in Minion, typeface designed by Robert Slimbach
Display type set in Futura, designed by Paul Renner
18 17 16 15   5 4 3 2 1

UNIVERSITY OF WASHINGTON PRESS
www.washington.edu/uwpress

LIBRARY OF CONGRESS CATALOGING-IN-PUBLICATION DATA
Schwartz, Harvey.
    Building the Golden Gate Bridge : a workers' oral history / Harvey Schwartz. — First edition.
        p.   cm.
    Includes bibliographical references and index.
    ISBN 978-0-295-99506-9 (hardcover : alk. paper)
    1. Golden Gate Bridge (San Francisco, Calif.)   2. Construction workers—California—San Francisco—Interviews.   3. Structural steel workers—California—San Francisco—Interviews.   4. Construction workers—California—San Francisco—Biography.   5. Structural steel workers—California—San Francisco—Biography.
    6. San Francisco (Calif.)—Biography.   I. Title.
    TG25.S225S35   2015
    624.2'30979461—dc23   2015011452

The paper used in this publication is acid-free and meets the minimum requirements of American National Standard for Information Sciences—Permanence of Paper for Printed Library Materials, ANSI Z39.48–1984. ∞

FRONTISPIECE: Heaters and riveters at work on the Golden Gate Bridge (detail). Copyright Golden Gate Bridge, Highway, and Transportation District.

In memory of the eleven and others now gone,

and for M, D, and K

CONTENTS

BUILDING
THE
GOLDEN
GATE
BRIDGE

INTRODUCTION

I never met Joseph Strauss, the chief engineer, but I saw him around a lot of times. I never shook hands with him or nothing. I was out there working. We were busy. We couldn't leave and go shake hands with him. That was for the upper man. See, all the big shots were the ones that were doing all the hand-shaking. In fact, they should of come out and hand-shaked us. We were the ones doing the work.   **AL ZAMPA**

In 1936 Al Zampa, a thirty-one-year-old ironworker with a decade of bridge building behind him, landed a job on the Golden Gate Bridge construction project—an ambitious plan to span the mile-wide Golden Gate strait and connect San Francisco directly to Marin County and California's vast Redwood Empire to the north. Zampa considered himself lucky to find employment in the middle of the Great Depression, even though he knew full well the risks, mettle, and special savvy that were demanded in work as a high-steel "bridge man." But in October of that year his luck ran out. Zampa fell more than forty feet from one end of the partially completed bridge and broke his back in several places. Miraculously, he survived—and recovered. After a few years of light work, Zampa actually resumed his career as a high-steel bridge builder, an "ace" in the ironworkers' lingo. He was still performing that work when he retired in 1970. Zampa's return from the 1936 accident, his astonishing resilience, and his long career became legendary among construction workers.

This book is an oral history of Golden Gate Bridge ironworkers like Zampa, as well as equally dauntless construction people from other trades, who faced constant challenges between 1933 and 1937 to build one of the iconic structures of the United States. Their stories are not just about labor history—though most of the interviewees talk about unions and Depression-era politics—but also about the work itself, narrated sometimes in rather technical detail and often with vivid recollections of the physical conditions, small pleasures, hardships, and gruesome accidents of construction jobs on the Golden Gate Bridge. It is a deep description of working-class life and culture in a bygone era, told by a group of hardscrabble survivors of the Depression—former cowboys, "gandy dancers" (railroad workers), newsboys, fry cooks, loggers, and others—many of whom quit school and entered the working world when they were barely teenagers, equipped only with their pluck, adaptive instincts, strong values, sense of humor, and oversize fear of a "little bitty needle" (according to the two nurses who treated injured Golden Gate Bridge construction workers at St. Mary's Hospital in San Francisco).

On completion of any large undertaking like the Golden Gate Bridge, the "movers and shakers"—politicians, engineers, industry leaders—usually garner most of the attention and credit for the achievement. To be sure, newspapers briefly lionized Al Zampa in his time, and authors have written about some of the other workers quoted in this book. Still, the story of all great entrepreneurial enterprises demands the balance of full narratives by those who performed—and who continue to perform—the work. Speaking at the opening of the StoryCorps oral history booth in New York's Grand Central Terminal, the oral historian Studs Terkel proclaimed: "We're about to celebrate . . . the lives of the uncelebrated, of the working men and women of this country from the year one, who have made all the wheels go around. We're at the Grand Central Station now. We know there's an architect, but who hung the iron? Who were the brick masons? Who swept the floors? Who kept the trains going? These are the noncelebrated people. . . . They are the ones who have built this country."[1]

In this volume some of the workers who "hung the iron" and did other crucial jobs on the Golden Gate Bridge occupy center stage. Based predominantly on interviews I conducted with surviving bridge workers in 1987 for the fiftieth anniversary of the official opening of the span, the book presents the speakers' full stories to the public, many for the first time, more than seventy-five years after the completion of construction. Of the fourteen individuals represented, nine were bridge workers in the 1930s, a handful of survivors from an army originally numbering in the hundreds yet representing a variety of trades and exemplifying what historians generally know about the world of the American worker in the Depression. Rounding out their narratives are the testimonies of four women and one man whose life stories intersect with the bridge's history.

The Further Reading section describes the best books about the construction of "the Gate," or "the Gate Bridge," as many 1930s bridge workers called it. Most sources focus on the celebrity engineers, architects, and designers; the technological innovations and achievements; the pre-construction politics; and the exceptional beauty of what the California historian Kevin Starr pronounced "America's greatest bridge." A few mention the workers and their hardships. At least three volumes, published around the fiftieth anniversary of the bridge, give serious attention to the span's construction personnel.[2] But none of the major narratives consistently trains the spotlight on the workers and their lives beyond their daily labor.[3] This book lets the ones doing the work tell their life stories in depth and in their own words.

Who were these people? Where did they come from? What were their backgrounds? Not surprisingly, several bridge workers profiled in this book were children of the country's new immigrants, the many recently minted Americans who swelled the ranks of the U.S. labor force between 1880 and 1914. This flood of immigrants peaked between 1905 and 1914, when more than a million people arrived in each of six major waves. Thousands came from Russia, Poland, Austria-Hungary, the Balkans, and Italy. After 1914, the last of those peak years, World War I and subsequent changes in American immigration policy reduced the numbers coming to the United States for many decades. In 1914, however, nearly a million and a quarter people immigrated to the United States, a scant 13 percent from northern and western Europe and approximately 73 percent from southern and eastern European countries.[4] Thousands of these immigrants and their children became workers in America's manufacturing plants and heavy construction industries. Their immigrant origins significantly defined who they were and how they viewed their world.

Beyond their status as the children of new Americans, what did bridge builders say about their working conditions and the mid-1930s revitalization of unionism in the construction trades? What was work actually like on the bridge, in a climate that was often cold, wet, and windy? How did builders adapt their gear to survive the day safely and with as little discomfort as possible? How did they cope with the tragic accidents they describe here in harrowing detail? As members of the working class, did they view their tasks and the Golden Gate Bridge project differently from the way politicians, regional boosters, and the general public did? How, too, did they evaluate the wider politics and economics of their time? What did they think of the worker-friendly New Deal and the watershed union events of their day, such as the West Coast maritime and San Francisco general strikes of 1934?[5] Finally, what happened to them after the Golden Gate Bridge was finished? How did they reflect on their roles in the building of that world-famous landmark?

Oral history answers such questions with a vividness and drama rarely matched in traditional historical accounts, as exemplified by Evan "Slim" Lambert's tale of surviving a near-death ordeal. These first-person accounts offer us rare insights into the experience of workers who persevered through danger and hardship to build a bridge that became the internationally recognized symbol of San Francisco and all of Northern California.

The idea for this book grew out of a project undertaken in 1986–87 by Lynn A. Bonfield, founding director of the Labor Archives and Research Center (LARC) at San Francisco State University. Bonfield was at the time planning a celebration of the bridge's fiftieth birthday. She secured a grant from the California Council for the Humanities and hired me to interview veteran bridge workers while she and her staff collected historical photographs and other graphics. When the anniversary came in spring 1987, Bonfield staged a highly successful public event that featured speeches by union leaders, politicians, academics, and bridge workers; excerpts from my interviews; pictures; and a display of 1930s worker equipment.[6] I recognized even then the raw materials for a fascinating volume of oral history, even though I was unable to turn to the project until many years later.

Professional oral historians customarily define the interviews I intended to conduct as "full life histories," long the standard in the field.

Full life histories probe a person's recollections from early life through retirement. Most of the individuals quoted in this book sat for full life narratives. When I started the project in 1987, I had just finished a six-year research job that included interviews with 140 members of the International Longshore and Warehouse Union for a National Endowment for the Humanities–funded oral history project cosponsored by the ILWU and the Institute for the Study of Social Change at the University of California, Berkeley. Although I was originally trained in traditional document- and archive-based research at the University of California, Davis, by the labor historian David Brody, I had thus acquired substantial interview experience and had pored over the scholarly literature on oral history. Bonfield, herself an accomplished oral historian, also provided invaluable advice about interviewing priorities and questions on the bridge project.

The construction workers who sat for recordings, listed here with their Golden Gate Bridge jobs, included Fred Divita, a paint scraper and field engineer; John Noren, an elevator builder; Glenn McIntyre, Al Zampa, Walter Vestnys, and Joyce "Big J" Harris, ironworkers; John Urban, a cable spinner, which was a type of ironworker; Fred Brusati, an electrician; Martin Adams, a laborer; Evan C. "Slim" Lambert, a labor foreman; and Bert Vestnys, a truck driver. I also interviewed Alvina McIntyre, Glenn McIntyre's wife, as well as Sister Mary Zita Felciano and Patricia DeWeese, two nurses who had cared for seriously injured bridge men in the 1930s.

The roles of women have been largely omitted from histories of the bridge.[7] I have tried to add to the record. The reminiscences of the four women quoted in this volume include those of the two nurses; Glenn McIntyre's wife, Alvina; and Joyce Harris, an African American ironworker who performed maintenance on the bridge in the late 1990s and early 2000s.[8] Although no women builders and almost no African American men worked on the bridge's original construction, the crews required for ongoing maintenance have achieved a measure of diversity.[9] Thus Harris's recollections help to update the story.[10]

Except for two individuals, I interviewed all the people quoted in this book for the 1987 LARC project. The late Isabelle Maynard recorded the interview with Al Zampa in 1986. I interviewed Joyce Harris in 2008 for Jo Kreiter, founder and choreographer of Flyaway Productions, who was preparing a dance program in celebration of post-1960s women bridge workers. All interviews represented here were originally recorded on analog tape cassettes (now digitized by LARC) and are on permanent deposit at LARC in San Francisco, along with transcriptions of the recording sessions, which range from thirty to a hundred pages each. Several sessions were significantly longer than others because some interviewees spoke in great depth. Twelve of the interviews were full life; two were more limited in scope, owing to circumstances surrounding the tape sessions, but still added unique and valuable information.

Preparing recorded material for a book of oral histories always requires decisions about the extent of permissible editorial changes. Verbatim transcriptions of interviews are invariably too rambling and roughshod for unedited publication. I have thus made some adjustments in the transcripts, but always within strict guidelines. To emphasize the force and drama of the words of the quoted workers, I have eliminated my own questions and comments. I have also excised redundant and extraneous material, such as hesitations and irrelevant pleasantries. At times I have rearranged material or combined repeated accounts by the same person to improve continuity and clarity. To assess the accuracy of interviewees' memories before using material in this book, I compared several oral descriptions of the same events and consulted the existing written record. Only when absolutely necessary to avoid confusion have I added or corrected a name or date or inserted a small transitional detail. At all times, I have retained my subjects' style of speech, tone, and meaning in the knowledge that these give oral history its authenticity and credibility.

My goal has been to follow the advice of oral history authorities such as Sherna Berger Gluck and Donald A. Ritchie. "In editing," Gluck wrote about her own pathbreaking work in 1988, "care was taken to preserve each individual's speaking style and syntax. False starts and repetitions were removed—unless they revealed something about the interviewee or represented her speech pattern. Words or phrases were added only when necessary for clarity." Later Gluck added, "Although I tried to preserve the narrator's thought process, passages relating to the same topic were often drawn together from different places in the interview."[11] Writing seven years after Gluck, Ritchie—long held to be one of the leading arbiters of oral history methodology—observed, "Editing and rearranging interviews for clarification and cutting away tangential material are appropriate so long as the original meaning is retained."[12] These are the standards I have adhered to.

■　■　■

The idea of bridging the Bay to connect San Francisco and the counties to the north dates back to the nineteenth century. Joshua Norton, an eccentric San Franciscan and self-proclaimed "Emperor of the United States and Protector of Mexico," proposed such a project in 1869. "Emperor" Norton's suggestion did not stimulate serious action, but fifty years later San Francisco City Engineer Michael M. O'Shaughnessy initiated what would become the successful effort to build a bridge. About 1916 O'Shaughnessy, regionally known for championing construction of the dam in the Hetch Hetchy valley of Yosemite National Park to supply water to San Francisco, entered into conversations with Joseph B. Strauss, already a bridge engineer of national standing, about the feasibility of spanning the Golden Gate.

In the early 1920s, O'Shaughnessy and Strauss publicly cosponsored the idea of building a bridge after a design by Strauss that would have combined cantilever and suspension styles.[13] Many viewed this hybrid concept as unprepossessing, even ugly, but Strauss promoted the bridge idea vigorously. As San Francisco Bay ferryboat traffic became increasingly congested in the 1920s, owing to growing reliance on automobile transportation, Strauss attracted a following despite the military's doubts about the project and the opposition of the ferry companies.

The War Department, as it was then known, had the authority to block a bridge project that might interfere with military priorities. But after much hesitation, lengthy debate, and hearings, the military finally issued a building permit in 1924. The ferry companies, under the leadership of Southern Pacific Railroad (which owned a subsidiary ferry company), continued to fight the project in an effort to retain control of all transportation revenues. Local anti-bridge litigation also delayed progress until late 1928, when the California State Legislature finally created a Golden Gate Bridge and Highway District to oversee the span's design and construction.

The new Bridge District comprised the six counties that supported its founding, including San Francisco and, to the north, Marin, Sonoma,

Del Norte, and parts of Mendocino and Napa counties. In 1929 Strauss became the project's chief engineer. The following year, district residents voted to approve the financing of the bridge's construction through a $35 million bond measure. Unfortunately, the Depression had seriously undermined the bond market, and the Bridge District found few buyers for its bonds until A. P. Giannini of the Bank of America saved the threatened project by having his institution purchase a huge allotment.

The nearby mid-1930s Bay Bridge building project connecting San Francisco to Oakland benefited from much federal support. In contrast, the Golden Gate Bridge was completed without state or federal funding. The only federal money spent in connection with the Golden Gate project was for a New Deal Works Progress Administration (WPA) approach road at Sausalito in Marin County on the north side of the strait.

Many construction people who labored on the Golden Gate also helped build the Bay Bridge because work on the two structures was nearly concurrent. The Bay Bridge went up between May 1933 and November 1936. (The eastern segment of the Bay Bridge was replaced in 2013 by a new span designed to be more earthquake-resistant than the original crossing, but when workers in these interviews refer to the Bay Bridge, they are talking about the one finished in 1936.) An assortment of local and national contracting firms built the Golden Gate Bridge in stages between January 5, 1933, and May 27, 1937.[14]

Sometime before construction of the Golden Gate Bridge began, the graceful all-suspension concept that made the structure world famous replaced Strauss's ungainly design for a hybrid cantilever-suspension bridge. The exact moment of this decision is unclear. Nonetheless, Leon Moisseiff, a suspension-bridge expert engaged with others on a consulting panel set up by the new Bridge District, advocated strongly for the change.

The district panel consultant Charles A. Ellis, a former professor of engineering at the University of Illinois and a master of mathematical bridge design, was responsible for the complex calculations that made possible the 1.7-mile structure, which reigned for twenty-seven years as the longest single-span suspension bridge in the world. As an employee of Strauss's Chicago-based firm, Ellis also artfully designed the bridge's classical arch above Fort Point, installed to preserve that historically important pre–Civil War fortification, which today still stands on the

San Francisco shoreline underneath the span's southern end. Ellis never received the public credit he deserved for his role in the bridge's design and engineering success, largely because of disagreements he had with Strauss, who fired him from his firm in December 1931. Shortly before construction began, Strauss hired Russell Cone, a former student of Ellis's and himself an accomplished suspension-bridge engineer, as the project supervisor in charge of all work crews. For years Strauss got the credit for Ellis's calculations, although that honor sometimes gravitated to Clifford Paine, Strauss's second in command, who frequently assumed control in the chief engineer's absence.[15]

When completed, the great bridge would rise 220 feet above the water at midspan. Two soaring 746-foot steel towers with art deco lines designed by Irving F. Morrow, a Northern California architect and illustrator, would support its suspension system. Morrow also contributed to the choice of the bridge's ultimate color, an orange-vermilion called international orange, which added to the structure's beauty and harmonized with the earthy tones of the surrounding hills, opening dramatically to the sea. Fortunately, international orange won out over the urging of military leaders that the bridge should be painted with horizontal stripes for visibility—the navy wanted black and yellow stripes, while the army Air Corps favored orange and white. Curiously, the striking visual appeal of the bridge's red lead-based primer paint inspired the final color.

The building of the two massive towers progressed at quite different paces. The Marin tower to the north rose rather smoothly and quickly because it was set near the land's edge. Workers utilized a large cofferdam filled with tons of concrete to make a pier for the north tower, completed by mid-1933.[16] A little more than a year later, ironworkers finished erecting the Marin tower itself.

The San Francisco tower to the south, though, was situated more than a thousand feet offshore in dangerous tidal water, and work progressed more slowly there than on the north side. The south-side tower was to be constructed on a foundation anchored in the ocean by a huge caisson floated into place, sunk, and then filled with concrete to become part of the tower's pier.[17] Deep-sea divers entering the water from a barge searched the sea floor for places where wells could be dynamited to secure the foundation pier in bedrock. They worked between powerful tides in churning seas that rendered them almost blind because of sediment stirred up by the ocean's constant movement.

The floating caisson was towed into place successfully. Then bad luck intruded when in October 1934 a furious storm ruined the caisson beyond repair. Strauss had the caisson towed out to sea and sunk there. To replace it, workers enclosed a curved fender consisting of big concrete boxes that had been erected to protect the caisson, pumped the water out of the fender, filled it with tons of cement, and converted it into a foundation pier.

Construction of the south tower was also slowed by accidents and storms that repeatedly damaged an access trestle extending far out into the strait from the south shore. Workers had to rebuild substantial sections of it several times. Despite the many setbacks, the San Francisco-side foundation was finally done in January 1935. Six months later, ironworkers completed the San Francisco tower. During the summer of 1935, workers installed catwalks, or footpaths for access to the towers, so that cable spinning could begin.

The spinning of thousands of thin, exceedingly strong wires that would be compacted into the bridge's two giant main cables concluded in spring 1936. The cables passed over large saddles at the tops of the two towers. Huge eyebars sunk into previously built massive concrete-block structures to the north and south of the bridge's ends anchored the bases of these cables. With the main cables in place, installation of the bridge's vertical suspension system proceeded. That system, composed of strong wire suspender ropes hung from the main cables and designed to hold up the bridge's roadway, was scheduled for construction over the last half of the year.

From the beginning Strauss had insisted that Golden Gate Bridge workers wear hard hats—a new safety adaptation in the 1930s—at all times. During the summer of 1936, in what was a historically significant safety innovation at the time, Strauss also ordered his men to install a large, heavy-duty trapeze rope net below the area where the especially dangerous roadway steel construction work was taking place. Done for the most part over the ocean, roadway work progressed from each tower in the direction of midspan as well as toward the two shores. Bridge road builders had previously worked at great heights with nothing below them but air. Those who "fell into the hole," as the men put it, suffered grave injuries or died. On the Golden Gate Bridge job, where a fall along most of the span would be more than two hundred feet, death seemed all but certain without the net.

Fred Divita, whose testimony forms chapter 1, oversaw the safety net's installation. By late 1936, the net was up. At that point in the bridge's construction, only one worker had died: on October 21, just as the last wire suspender ropes were going in and the steel roadway was nearing completion, a moving derrick had fallen and killed Kermit Moore. Unfortunately, even the new net did not guarantee complete safety. On February 17, 1937, a huge timber scaffolding holding a work crew gave way and tore through the net, plunging the whole apparatus and twelve men into the sea below. Only two survived the fall. One was Slim Lambert, who recalls his harrowing experience here in chapter 7.

The ten workers who died that February were Fred Dummatzen (a man Lambert tried mightily to rescue), O. A. Anderson, Chris Anderson, Bill Bass, Orrill Desper, Terence Hallinan, Eldridge Hillen, Charles Lindros, Jack Norman, and Louis Russell. Balanced against this traumatic event, Strauss's net saved the lives of nineteen men who fell into it during the span's construction. Given an early twentieth-century business formula—one worker's death for every million dollars spent on bridge construction—the eleven lives lost on the $35 million Golden Gate project would have been judged a good safety record, especially compared with that of the concurrent Bay Bridge job, with no safety net and twenty-four deaths.

Despite the tragedy of February 17, 1937, and some investigations that followed, construction of the Golden Gate Bridge went ahead essentially as planned. That April the men finished paving the bridge's roadway. On May 27, the Golden Gate Bridge officially opened to the public with great regional fanfare and a celebratory walk across the span by thousands of people. The next day the new bridge received automobile traffic. Almost immediately the structure was acclaimed as one of the industrial and engineering wonders of the world.[18] The workers, though, still had stories of their own to tell. You will hear some of them in the testimonies that enliven the pages to come.

Fred Divita

FIELD ENGINEER

You could hear the riveting hammers going and the compressors going. Just noise. And here I am, a country hick, just coming in. I'd never been on a job like that in my life. I'm going up this elevator, up, up, up, getting more scared as we get up there.   **FRED DIVITA**

The son of Italian immigrants, Fred Divita was born in 1911 in the town of Fairfax, in Marin County, California. He graduated from the University of California, Berkeley, in 1934 with a degree in engineering. The only job Divita could find during the Great Depression was as a paint scraper on the Golden Gate Bridge. Later he labored on the San Francisco–Oakland Bay Bridge construction project. He returned to the Golden Gate as a field engineer in 1936 and supervised the installation of chief engineer Joseph Strauss's innovative safety net. When the net was no longer needed, Divita found other employment on the Golden Gate Bridge until its completion in 1937. In later years he pursued a career as a construction engineer. I interviewed Divita in San Anselmo, California, on March 15, 1987.

■ ■ ■

I was commuting to Cal from San Francisco during 1933 and 1934 when the bridges were going in.[1] Just riding the ferries I was getting an engi-

:ducation, looking at all the bridge foundations being built. It ̄ ₐₙy amazing to see. You could see things going in at the approaches on the Oakland side of the San Francisco Bay Bridge, from putting in a cofferdam to driving the pile to pouring the concrete. You could see all that going on because the train to Berkeley went right by there.

Going across on the ferry from San Francisco to Marin County, you could see the tower starting up and the foundations going in on the Golden Gate Bridge. By the end of my last year at Cal, you could see the two big cranes and red iron sticking up a little bit from the tower. Sometimes you could even see a piece being erected.[2] I hadn't the least idea then that I would soon be working on the Golden Gate Bridge myself.

I was born in Fairfax, California, in 1911.[3] I was fortunate enough to be born in such a gifted country. When my father came to America from Pisa, Italy, around 1905, he was fifteen years old and looking for some way to subsist.[4] He went to work in the East as a water boy on a railroad, made his way west, and got into setting marble in San Francisco.[5]

My mother was from a little town near Lucca. My parents were both very poor when they met in the city. After the earthquake and fire in 1906, they stayed in a tent at the San Francisco Presidio. Then they came to Marin County. My father loved Marin County, so he commuted to San Francisco by ferryboat for a couple of years after the earthquake. Then he found a job closer to home as a caretaker, chauffeur, and gardener for a steel fabricator. He worked for him from about 1918 to 1931 or 1932.

In 1917 I started attending a school in St. Regis Church of Fairfax. We spoke Italian until about the fifth grade, when I moved to Fairfax Men's School, where we were taught to talk English. My father and mother began to pick it up, so we gradually eliminated the Italian. I graduated from Fairfax Men's School in 1925. Then I commuted to high school on a steam train.

We were pretty primitive here until some time after the Golden Gate Bridge was built. The woods were beautiful in Fairfax in the 1920s, and we hunted for deer, quail, and pigeons. We used to fish for trout in streams that went right through town. We'd rely a lot on what we could catch and hunt.[6] There were five children and my father and mother. My father was a gardener, so my parents struggled, but we had good food on the table. During high school, I waited tables and washed dishes in local Italian restaurants. My sister did housework for these people that my father was the caretaker for.

There were many other Italian families in Fairfax that came to America at the same time as my father and mother. They were all in the same boat, struggling to stay alive. They had a little community of their own. If there was somebody building something, the other Italians would go help them do the work. I remember that every year we'd all go over to Simi's vineyard and help them pick grapes to make wine.[7]

Our family eventually built a little compound of our own up in Fairfax just like the Kennedys have. It's still there [in 1987], including the first house, built by my father in 1918. My sister lives next door, my brother and sister-in-law live next to that, and my other sister built the house behind us. Then we put up another house over there, so there are five houses. Five families lived there for a long time.

When I started high school, my family couldn't give me advice [about what to study]! They didn't have that kind of a background. But the trades were coming up, so I took machine shop for three years and worked in a machine shop for a while. Then it dawned on me that I could stay at home and go to Marin Junior College, which opened in 1926. I went there from 1929 to 1931. School came hard, and I really studied. My grades weren't the best, but I got enough to get into Cal and start there.

In 1931, when I was at Cal, my mother passed away. Things were breaking up. Money was hard to come by after the Depression hit in 1929. There were many students with me in the same hole. I left school for a year, then tried to recoup. I was going from hand to mouth. My older sister took over, took care of my little sister, and helped me. I even lived with her and my brother-in-law while they were in San Francisco, where he owned a restaurant on Broadway in North Beach. Otherwise I would never have gotten through school.

At Cal I majored in mechanical engineering. When I graduated in 1934, I tried my best to find a job, but I couldn't find anything. It was just fortunate that two students I'd started Cal with continued on and graduated a year ahead of me. Somehow or another they got jobs on the Golden Gate Bridge project with Bethlehem Steel.[8] One was a timekeeper and one was an engineer. When they heard they needed a laborer to help scrape paint, they told the foreman they knew a kid that just graduated from college. They asked if he could come over and try. That's how I got a job on the bridge.

I started scraping paint for the Bethlehem Steel paint superintendent.[9] A couple of painters signed up at the same time with me. When we went to work, we got in the Marin tower elevator. The tower was nearing completion at that time. The elevator was a wire cage operated on two cables that were about an inch in diameter on each side, and guides. You went up alongside the tower on the outside. The wind was blowing, the fog was coming in, and everything was dripping wet. As you went up, the wind pressure would push the elevator sideways.

Finally we were near the top. The travelers were still up there. A traveler is a movable construction rig with booms and stifflegs.[10] They would move it up the tower. I don't know if the last couple of steel pieces were in the tower, but all the construction equipment was there. The raising gang was still working. You could hear the riveting hammers going and the compressors going. Just noise. And here I am, a country hick, just coming in. I'd never been on a job like that in my life. I'm going up this elevator, up, up, up, getting more scared as we get up there.

The towers are 746 feet high. We were down near the bottom of the traveler strut. If the traveler top was at 746 feet, we would have been thirty feet lower, or about 710 feet. Then the elevator stopped. The elevator operator says, "This is where you get off." The two painters were with me. We looked out there. To get off, you had to step on a two-by-twelve that was cantilevered out from the bottom strut of the traveler.

The two painters started to go out. They looked over there and saw the two-by-twelve. They said, "Do we have to get out going across that?" The elevator operator said, "Well, that's the only way." The painters said, "No. Take me back down. I'm quitting." Then the elevator operator said to me, "How about you? Do you want to get off?" I thought a little bit. Then I says, "It's the only job I have. It's only three or four feet to walk out there. I can make that." So I braved it and went across.

When I got out, I looked up. There was the black steel of the travelers, the red steel of the towers, and hoses running in all directions. I was amazed at all the activity going on. I just couldn't picture it. I was in awe.

The paint superintendent's office or shack was up there. He assigned me to a foreman and told me the job was scraping inside the tower. I had a hard hat on with a light, a pair of overalls, and regular shoes. I don't think they had shoes with hard toes then. I couldn't afford 'em at that time anyway. There was some safety taken care of, with masks for

Heaters and riveters at work on the Golden Gate Bridge. The intense construction activity awed Fred Divita when he began his first day on the job in 1934. Photo by George Douglass. Courtesy of Labor Archives and Research Center, San Francisco State University. Copyright Golden Gate Bridge, Highway, and Transportation District.

the paint smell and safety belts. When I started to work, you could smell burning paint. The foreman gave me a scraper and a wire brush and told me what to do. There I was, scraping paint.

The towers were made of three-foot square cells.[11] Every ten feet or so there was a diaphragm and a ladder.[12] You went up the ladder. You got to the next diaphragm and you could stop and stand there. There were 103 of these cells starting out at the bottom of the tower. They ended up at the top with twenty-one cells.[13]

There were manholes that went from one cell to another. They couldn't be all in one position because that would weaken the tower. So they were

spaced. You'd go up five flights. You'd go in a manhole and maybe you'd have to go down another one to get into a certain cell. I later read there were twenty-three miles of ladders in those towers—that is, between the San Francisco tower and the Marin tower. I was in there for about four months, scraping the paint and cleaning it up.

I must say I really had admiration for those ironworkers. I'd hear them and watch 'em rivet. There would be the heater heating up the rivets and throwing 'em to the catcher, and the bucker-up trying to buck up the rivets.[14] And there would be the raising gang erecting these pieces. Some of those pieces were as much as eighty tons. They were erecting 'em thirty-five feet high raising the towers. They're just fascinating.

I got to know a lot of people in that four months scraping paint. Evidently I did a fairly good job because they sent me over to Alameda after that [to do a different job for the same company] when they were having trouble with the Golden Gate Bridge's San Francisco [south tower] foundation and there was a delay in that tower. They said something about four months' delay in the foundation. I read that the caisson they put in there wouldn't fit. It started to tip. They took it out and eventually towed it out in the ocean.[15] Then they built the foundation from the cofferdam that they built around it. So, during the delay, they sent me over to Alameda and I worked there for almost a year as a sandblaster. I was sandblasting the steel that went on the Bay Bridge.

Whenever they roll steel, there's a layer on there of mill scale. You could sandblast it, but on the Golden Gate Bridge they didn't do that. Somehow or another I think they wished they did to get it down to raw steel before they painted it. On the Bay Bridge, we had a new system of sandblasting using steel grit. This blasting was done inside a building and the grit could be used over and over. They got it down to raw steel before they painted it. Boy, it was really clean when they got through with that grit blasting. They would then take the steel outside and the painters would paint it. I don't know how many coats they would paint on the steel. Then they took it out to the Bay Bridge.

When the Bay Bridge was all sandblasted, I'd finally got to be a foreman on the sandblaster crew.

Workers on the Golden Gate Bridge's south tower with a view to the north, 1935. Divita described getting around in cells like these (*right*) when he became a paint scraper on the north tower in 1934. Photo by Ted Huggins. Courtesy of California Historical Society, Huggins Collection, CHS.Huggins.001.

I had five or six people. After we got through with the sandblasting, I got a job out on the Bay Bridge as a materials man. I would go to every foreman and ask him what he needed, whether it was slings, sledgehammers, cable clamps, or anything that was required out in a crew. Also, if the riveting gangs needed anything, I would be sure they got it. I had that job for quite a while. It must have been four to six months.

Then they ran out of work, so I went to work for American Bridge as a timekeeper on the Bay Bridge. I don't recall how I got that job. Jobs were really tough to get. I must have known somebody. A fellow by the name of Gage was the office manager. He was a rough, tough guy, but a hard worker.

Gage really worked us to death. I would catch a little boat and go all the way out to Yerba Buena Island from Pier 24 in San Francisco and I would take time on the people there.[16] They were just finishing up spinning the cable on the suspended span.[17] There was about two hundred people on that job that I had to keep time on. I'd go into the office and write down the time. Fortunately, there weren't as many fringe benefits in those days as there are now, because I had to get the time all lined up so we could have the payroll ready for 'em at the end of the week. It was a lot of work.

Then, in '36, they were gonna start the truss work for the suspended span of the Golden Gate Bridge. So they took me right back. I quit American Bridge and went to work for Bethlehem Steel as a field engineer. They knew I had graduated as an engineer and that I had worked on the Golden Gate Bridge before and knew a lot of the people on there. That was the first job I had with the title *engineer* in it. I was made responsible for installing the safety net under the suspended span as it was going out.[18]

When I began as a laborer on the Golden Gate Bridge, I made ninety cents an hour. When I worked as an engineer, I also got ninety cents an hour. It wasn't until I went to work as a rigger that I got $1.33 ⅓.[19] Fifty-five bucks a week. That was big money in those days. I was really in the Joe, really doing well then.[20] But in my Golden Gate Bridge days, I was tight with money. I didn't want to spend the money to go to those nightlife places. I'd been poor all my life and I would try to save my money if I could.

When I was working on the Bay Bridge, I was living with my sister. But as soon as I got back on the deck—that's what I called the Golden

Gate Bridge truss span—I went and lived with my father in Fairfax again. I went back and forth sometimes on the train. But my brother had a little Chevy coupe that he let me use and I would go back and forth on that, too. I'd park the car on the Marin side, walk up on the bridge, and walk out on it.

To build Strauss's safety net, we went up and put in a traveler net. First we had to erect some steel and then put up the net. It traveled on a top chord.[21] There were rollers near the bottom to keep it from tipping. It stuck out from the sides approximately ten feet beyond the widths of anywhere you'd go where the trusses were.

The mesh was six by six. It was half-inch Manila line with a six-inch mesh. It had some kind of a clip that held each section of the six inches in there. The net was in increments of fifty feet in length. That's how far we moved the traveler every time we wanted to move. We moved it in fifty-foot increments because the structural steel was erected in fifty-foot increments.

They'd hang the cables that were suspended, then the floor beams, the diagonals, and all the steel that was required for that section. Finally the stringers would go on and the erection traveler would move out ahead.[22] That's when the safety net traveler would move ahead the fifty feet. It cantilevered out beyond where the people were working so that when they erected steel they'd have a net underneath them all the time.

My responsibility was to see that they had all the material necessary for the next move and to see that it was installed as shown on the drawings. I'd be with the workers and sometimes I'd even help 'em make the ties. We were in the net all the time. Sometimes we wanted to get across to the other side and we would walk the net. There was nothing to it. It wasn't scary. It might be for somebody that hasn't seen it. I got used to it. I wasn't shaking like I was the first day on the job.

Building the net, I was more or less on my own. The chief engineer couldn't go around and bother looking at me all the time. Sometimes, when I was through with the net, I'd go up topside and watch 'em move the erection traveler and they'd ask me questions, like what was wrong. If there was something that wouldn't fit, I'd run down the drawings and try to find out what the errors were, just like a field engineer would be doing.

Once while I was responsible for the net being installed, for some reason I came up on the deck to where the traveler erecting the trusses

Chief engineer Joseph Strauss's innovative safety net, looking northward, 1936. Divita supervised the net's installation that year. Courtesy of Labor Archives and Research Center, San Francisco State University. Copyright Golden Gate Bridge, Highway, and Transportation District.

was. It was October 21, 1936. I was just going down and I heard this big bang. The traveler collapsed. It shook the bridge hard. I was shaking like that first day in there. I saw one man fall in the net. I went up there and Kermit Moore was decapitated, cut in two. Everybody called for stretchers and doctors. Then they locked up everything and everybody went home.[23] I wasn't there, though, when another accident tore the net and ten men died on February 17, 1937.

Unfortunately, on the Bay Bridge, I saw a man fall off a scaffold twenty feet and hit the ground. He was dead on impact. That was terrible to see. He was screaming when he was coming down. It made me sick. You couldn't do anything. There were no nets on the Bay Bridge. The Golden Gate Bridge started the nets with Strauss. When Kermit Moore was killed, that was the only fatality in twenty-four months. That was a record.

But you knew that there was some safety taken care of up there on the

Golden Gate Bridge. There were masks they put on for the paint smell, and there were the hard hats. That was the first time I ever saw a hard hat. Then they came up with the safety belts that you could tie yourself off with. They really started a good safety program there between Bethlehem Steel and the new Bridge District.

The thing for me was that on the Golden Gate job, I met all these top-notch riggers: Jack Turnipseed,[24] Ed Reed, the superintendent Slew Letterman, Chuck Letterman, and my friend Ed Stanley, who drove the first rivet on the bridge. He was the rivet superintendent on the truss span in addition to being the rivet superintendent on the towers. He was a very knowledgeable man in that field. I also met Grover McClain, a superintendent, and Harold McClain, who you sometimes read quite a bit about 'cause he worked all the way through the bridge.

Ed Stanley was called the Iron Horse. He could drive more rivets than anybody. Somebody told me that back east on one of the bridges he drove over a thousand rivets in one day. Now, if a crew could drive three hundred fifty to four hundred rivets a day, that's a pretty good day's work. Slew Letterman had been the superintendent for Bethlehem Steel on many other jobs. He was an expert on erecting and rigging. His brother, Chuck Letterman, was a foreman and a crackerjack bridge man. Jack Turnipseed had an Indian background. He came from those famous Indians back east that were steel erectors over there.[25]

When we got through with putting up the trusses on the Golden Gate Bridge, I got laid off. Bethlehem didn't have anything more. American Bridge didn't have anything more around there. But before the Golden Gate Bridge was opened in 1937, Ed Stanley gave me a job underneath the floor beams of the deck after the concrete was poured. They had some problems with the paint on the Marin side. Moist air had been coming up and had rusted all those beams.

So Stanley took me over there and we moved the scaffolds for the painters under the bridge. I did that for about four months. Fortunately, I didn't have to do the scraping and painting myself. But I did move the scaffolds for the painters who did the scraping, cleaning, and painting. The problem was only maybe a third of the way from the tower out. The paint was okay from there on.

Moving the scaffolds was physically hard. There were twenty-five-foot-long scaffold beams made of wood. They were six-by-eights and they were grade A-1 lumber. Then you had plywood decks that you'd put alongside each one of the floor beams. Painters could go in there and stand and scrape the paint. We would have to take all that scaffolding out each time the painters finished a panel of twenty-five feet and move it around for the next twenty-five feet.

You were standing on the bottom flange of the floor beam, trying to support one of these wood scaffold beams while moving ahead so you could put the plywood down. It was pretty difficult. I was five feet seven inches tall. In high school I weighed 117 pounds. I guess I got up to 130 by 1937. Being a small guy like I was, I did a lot of sleeping when I got home at night.

One of the things I wanted to tell you more about on the bridge was the weather. Some days it was really cold. I remember this particularly for the time when we were chaining that scaffolding for the painters onto the deck. The bridge had been completed and the fog would blow in through there and through the trusses. Water would be dripping. You'd think you were in a rainstorm. Your hands would get numb and you'd put on all the clothes you could trying to handle this heavy scaffolding.

But the worst part of cold weather was after I got in my car and started home. I was living in Fairfax. After being in that cold for eight hours a day and just freezing to death, I'd get up to Corte Madera and I would start picking up the heat of Marin County.[26] The temperature would get up to seventy, eighty, or maybe ninety degrees. My face would turn red as a beet and hurt, really hurt. Burn, burn, burn. It wouldn't be over until late that night when I really got used to the heat. It kind of worried me, but eventually it didn't affect my face too much.

I was also there when they drove the golden rivet on April something.[27] Ed Stanley drove the rivet. Ed Murphy, who was a friend of mine and a superintendent on the San Francisco side, bucked up the rivet. They'd slam it in there and buck it up and the driver would go in. All the dignitaries were around and I was standing there, watching.

They had the heater going, but they never heated the gold rivet because they thought it was malleable enough to drive in. The bucker-up got on the button head.[28] They had to hold it in. Stanley got on the driving side and drove the rivet. He drove and he drove and he drove and it wouldn't go. He kept driving it and got it halfway shaped and it fell off. It snapped off right between the shank and the partial head he was making with

Ed "Iron Horse" Stanley (*left*) attempting to drive a golden rivet during a ceremonial gathering just after the bridge's opening, April 28, 1937. Edward Murphy (*right*) served as bucker-up while Joseph Strauss (*middle*) helped. When Stanley's effort to drive the unheated rivet failed, Divita held on to the gold remnant for safekeeping. Courtesy of San Francisco History Center, San Francisco Public Library.

the rivet hammer. And it fell off. To this day, nobody knows what ever happened to that piece of gold.

I remember the rivet was a three-quarter by two and a half. If you take a steel rivet, it weighed 0.32 pounds per rivet. If you convert that to gold in specific gravity, you come up with a little under a pound and a half. At four hundred dollars an ounce in 1987, the rivet's worth about seventy-eight hundred dollars. Now, the rivet didn't stay there very long because everybody was trying to scrape some of that gold off. So they took it off and put in a steel rivet.

They gave the gold rivet to me. I looked like the only honest guy around there, I guess. I was a kid. When I got the rivet, I held it with Mr. Stanley. The next day we took it down to the shop on the Marin side and I threaded it. We brought it back up there and I put a steel nut on the gold rivet. Then we concreted the nut back in and put a chunk of concrete in there so nobody could take the nut off. But later somebody said they were scraping the head that was sticking out of there so they took it out completely. I kept the thread on the gold rivet for many years. But I moved around so much it got lost in the shuffle.

It was on the Golden Gate Bridge job that I met Mr. Pomeroy of the J. H. Pomeroy Company that I finally went to work for forever. Mr. Pomeroy used to go out on the Golden Gate Bridge approach span. He had a contract for the approach. I was in the office one day and A. F. McLane, the project manager for Bethlehem steel, came by. McLane was a terrific engineer and a very well educated man. He says, "Come on with me. I want you to go over and see what Pomeroy is doing over there." We went down and walked around the road to the backspan. There was Mr. Pomeroy, watching his people erect some new system of falsework for supporting the truss span over there.[29] So I met Mr. James Pomeroy and got to know him, or at least got introduced to him.

When he was through on the Golden Gate Bridge, Ed Stanley got a job with J. H. Pomeroy Company to be the rivet superintendent in Los Angeles on the federal building being constructed there. Stanley took me with him to L.A. in 1938. I worked as a field engineer there and we worked on several other jobs. On the Golden Gate Bridge as a laborer I wasn't in the union, but when I got down to Los Angeles and I got to know all these ironworkers, I joined the union.[30] I was very proud to be one of 'em. I didn't want to be an outsider. Even though I was working as an engineer, I wanted to be part of them.

When we were through in Los Angeles, Mr. Pomeroy didn't have anything to do. But I get ahold of Slew Letterman and they took me up through Grand Coulee and McChord Field and I worked there for a few years as an ironworker putting up bridges, steel buildings, or hangars. I advanced and was project manager of some things, but the ironworkers were always with me on part of one job or another. I only had admiration for 'em. From the background that I had on the Golden Gate Bridge and working with them, they were the kind of people I wanted to be.

During 1939 and '40, I came back to Mr. Pomeroy again when he was successful in getting a contract to build a pontoon bridge across Lake Washington. He took me up there to be the field engineer at the dock where we put the pontoons together. I was there from the start of the pontoon bridge until it was completed.[31] Then I worked for Pomeroy continually forever, I guess, on various jobs.

Mr. Pomeroy sent me to Oakland where I was a civil engineer for him when he was building a lot of warehouses for the army. From there, in 1941, just before we entered World War II, he sent me to Midway Island with Jack MacDonald, who had been an erection superintendent on the Golden Gate Bridge. Mr. Pomeroy was one of the naval air base contractors.

At Midway I became superintendent for putting up hangars and the big water tank. After their attack on Pearl Harbor in December 1941, the Japanese fired on us from cruisers and submarines. We had thirty or forty Marines protecting the island. I don't know how many four-inch guns they had. Once shots were going on all over. I jumped under a crawler crane in the yard and stayed there for a half hour until the shooting slowed. Then I ran for the gravel plant, which had a tunnel under it. I jumped in there and stayed until all the shooting was over. They had air raid warnings, too, that would go off three or four times a day. We'd drop everything and run down to foxholes on the beach. When the air raid warning rang at night, we'd run down and try to sleep in the foxholes. We never did get an air raid though. For days we thought the Japanese were going to land, but they never did.

In March 1942, a transport picked us up and took us to Pearl Harbor. We went right up the estuary where all of the battleships were stationed. You could just see the masts sticking up out of the water. Some of the ships were turned over. You could see the bottom of the shells in there. It was complete destruction. Those Japanese really dropped a lot of bombs. I just couldn't get over it.

During 1942 and '43, with the war still on, I worked as the superintendent of rigging and structural steel when we built these twenty big underground oil storage tanks at Red Hill near Honolulu. My wife, Mary, who was born in San Francisco, and I were married over there then.

In 1944, I worked in Alaska when Mr. Pomeroy got a contract to put up the structural steel on many of the river crossings on the Alcan Highway.[32] When he got a wartime contract to put the Canol Pipeline in from Norman Wells, Canada, to White Horse, Alaska, I was the pump station supervisor. Quite a bit later I was residential engineer of a big Alaskan project called Drift River, where we had to put a big platform a mile out in a hundred feet of water. I had to negotiate with the ironworkers over wages. The union's labor relations were done by Juel D. Drake, who now [in 1987] is the general president of the ironworkers' union. He came over and I negotiated with him. Jules was a really good, very fair negotiator. He made his point and everybody agreed. We set a rate and it seemed to work out pretty good even though I was a little afraid because I belonged to the union. That is, I was negotiating with Drake across the table and I was really scared that he'd say, "What are you doing fighting me? You're an ironworker!" But I was not getting paid as an ironworker at that time. I was getting paid as a resident engineer on that job, so I had to negotiate with him, although I had an ironworkers membership card and still do.

After the Second World War, I spent a lot of time in San Francisco as the vice-president in charge of domestic work for J. H. Pomeroy. We had quite a bit of work going on in San Francisco and along the Pacific Coast, but it wasn't necessary for me to be on the job continually. I would go from one job to another, trying to make it a day trip. Most of the time I tried to be home for the weekends. I was fortunate to have my wife, Mary, 'cause she could handle our five children when I traveled and she had to do it all. I retired in 1976.

Looking back, I want you to know that all these people I met on the Golden Gate Bridge set the pattern of my life. After I left the bridge, I met Jack MacDonald and C. T. Gutleben, who was a project manager on the bridge for J. H. Pomeroy. I worked with them for many years. You can see what the Golden Gate Bridge meant to me from there on out. I went from being just a kid that didn't know anything to meeting all these friendly and skillful people and getting all this information and all this education in construction. It just helped me all through my life. They were great people. And I was lucky enough to meet 'em all.

In those early days I voted all the time, but I didn't say I was in a political party. I didn't know the difference between the Republicans and the Democrats. I'm still not a politician and I don't follow politics too much. But I voted more Democratic then. Roosevelt came in during the heart of the Depression and right away put a stop order on the banks to close them so they wouldn't go broke. His WPA got a lot of people to work.[33] I think Roosevelt started the whole country getting back on its feet. It was he, or his party, that helped the country along. Later on, I thought his party went too far, so I got a little more on the conservative side and when Richard Nixon came around I voted for him.

I did a lot of work out in the Pacific over the years, and I would come in on an airplane and look down and see that beautiful bridge structure. Or when I came in on a boat several times, when you saw that Golden Gate Bridge, it was so beautiful. One of the things I admired so much is, when you look at the bridge from a side view, you get that fluted cowling on all of those struts rather than looking at the Bay Bridge and you see that X-bracing going up and down. The Golden Gate Bridge is just a marvelous, marvelous structure and it really looks like the Golden Gate. I was so proud of having worked on it. It was really something.

John Noren

ELEVATOR MAN

When the little elevator got overcrowded and there was no room for me, I would stand on what they call a crosshead, which was a small beam about ten feet above the elevator platform. You'd stand on that and hold on to the cables and ride up. I got used to it, but I still felt very much relieved when we hit the road at four-thirty and you'd stamp your feet on the ground. **JOHN NOREN**

John Noren was the son of immigrant parents from Norway and Sweden living in San Francisco. He was born in 1916. In early 1937 he needed a job. A former minor league professional baseball player with few marketable skills, he secured employment on the Golden Gate Bridge through his father, an elevator builders' union member. Noren worked as a mechanic's helper to an elevator installer until the bridge was nearly completed. He later had a long career in management as a field engineer for an elevator company. I interviewed Noren in San Carlos, California, on March 2, 1987.

■ ■ ■

Before World War I, the elevator constructors' union was a tightly knit group. You didn't do anything around an elevator in San Francisco without a union card.[1] My father, who was also named John, believed in union principles and was a good member for years. He retired as an honorary member of San Francisco's Local 8 of the International Union of Elevator Constructors [IUEC].[2]

My father sailed on fishing schooners off the East Coast before he came to California. Signe Noren was my mother's name. She worked in a seamen's boardinghouse. They met in Boston. He was from Sweden and she was from Norway. They came to San Francisco after the big earthquake and fire of 1906. I guess there was a lot of elevator work then, because he went into that business. He had a brother in the city who was the business agent for the carpenters' union.[3] The building trades was a natural thing for my father to follow. As a seaman, he was accustomed to rigging, using ropes, and working at heights—things that elevator constructors had to do.

I was born in San Francisco's Mission District in 1916. My wife and I graduated together from Mission High School in the city. We were educated in the public schools. I was in high school from 1930 to '33. Of course, money wasn't plentiful in the early thirties during the Depression. I got work occasionally as a night watchman when I was going to high school, which made life a little awkward because I'd be up all night. That job came through a friend of my uncle's who was a sea captain. I worked aboard ships up and down on the waterfront. This was from five o'clock in the afternoon till eight o'clock in the morning. I received five dollars, which was a lot of money in those days. I'd put out the kerosene lamps and help the drunken sailors aboard ship at night. I used to sleep whenever I could, which was against the rules, but otherwise you weren't in any shape to go to school.

My father was still an elevator constructor, but there was no work in the early '30s. There was absolutely nothing going on. So my father found his way to the waterfront and got a little work as a longshoreman now and then. He worked aboard ships assembling lumber and making loads that could be hoisted in and out. This was hard. It was all done manually. When things were tough, I told him I'd like to join the National Guard. I says, "I can go to camp, go to meetings, and pick up a few dollars." He said, "No, don't do it, John." This happened in early 1934, it must have been, because he says, "I think there is going to be a strike, and if that comes to pass, you'll be in the National Guard. They might call you out, and I'll be on the other side of the street." And he was right.[4] I never did join the National Guard.

In 1934, through a friend, I was alerted to a job opening coming up as an apprentice in the art department at Schmidt Lithograph, where they made large posters. These were printed from zinc plates. All the artwork was done by hand, and I loved to draw and print. Those men who worked there were remarkable, talented artists. I remember going down and being told, "Well, come back in a few months," that kind of thing. This was the closest thing I could come to as a steady job, so I kept going there every month. Finally Ben Schmidt says, "All right, I'm sick and tired of looking at you. I'll give you a thirty-day trial with the understanding that if you don't make it, you're going to be gone and don't come back." That sounded like a square deal to me. It worked out, but later the whole beautiful hand art process was replaced by the color photography method, so these men were just like blacksmiths. Their heart was gone and I with it.

I did have an offer to play professional baseball, not that I was any great shakes, but I loved the game and I wanted a fling at it. I signed a contract with the Saint Louis Cardinals. They assigned my contract to the Sacramento Senators of the old Pacific Coast League. Sacramento farmed me out to Albuquerque, New Mexico. Later I was sent to Midland, Texas. This was an experience because it was pretty down-to-earth. They talk about playing in bus leagues, but this was lower than that. We had three used cars. We tied everything to the roof and away we rambled from town to town.

I was a pitcher, but when you play in these Class X leagues, which is about as low as you can get, everybody's an outfielder in case somebody's hurt. And I hit pretty well. One day Branch Rickey, the very famous baseball owner, was there.[5] I was pitching, and when I came to bat I hit the ball about as hard as I could ever hit it. It hit up against the right center fence. At the end of the inning, Rickey came out to the pitcher's mound, took my glove away, and says, "Anybody that can hit a ball like that is not going to be a pitcher." They tried making a first baseman out of me, but I was a little awkward at the position. That just added to the fun I had.

Playing baseball was wonderful, but it was also my first exposure to racial prejudice in the South. Being from the Mission District, I grew up in a neighborhood of basically Italian and Irish people.[6] There was a smattering of Scandinavians, some Jewish and Greek people, but I'm telling you, to go to the South in the 1930s as a young kid from the Mission

District, it was really another world. You heard stories of the black people having to step off the sidewalk when you passed by, and that's exactly how it was. They also had those special separate areas in the theaters.

I remember one white woman down there who was everybody's picture of an ideal lovely grandmother. She was an elderly person. I saw her berate a black man who could have picked her up and broken her in half, but he just stood there saying, "Yes, ma'am." She just destroyed my image of her. I would never talk to a person like that, but that was the relationship in the South.

The black people in the South, too, loved baseball. When our park was idle, if we had off days, they made arrangements for the black teams to play each other. There were no games between the whites and the blacks. That was out. They wouldn't even consider that. But I'd go out and watch the blacks play, and I had to admire their skills and abilities. They were fine athletes, and the enthusiasm of both the fans and the players was infectious.

I came back to California and played with the Sacramento Senators again briefly. But I had to be honest with myself: I knew I wasn't going to be another all-star. It was time to settle down, make a career, or get into a trade or something. I went back home to San Francisco and looked for work everywhere. Things were tough. I couldn't find anything. It was early in 1937.

What happened then was the greatest coincidence in my life. One morning I wasn't even out of bed yet. I was sort of planning in my mind what I would do, where I would look, whose doorbell I would ring today. It occurred to me then that they were building this beautiful Golden Gate Bridge structure, and wouldn't it be interesting to be a part of that? At that moment, my mother came running upstairs. She said, "John, there's a man on the phone who wants to know if you want to go to work on the Golden Gate Bridge." Honestly, that was the greatest coincidence I can ever remember.

The man on the phone was Harry Melton, the business representative for Local 8 of the IUEC. He was a friend of my father's.[7] There were several things that made me uneasy about going out there. First, after I agreed to go, I was told, "One of the fellows got hurt and you'll be taking his place." I was there a long time and I never did dare to ask what happened to the guy. It could be anything under those conditions. I think I took the place of a man named Homer Widenback. This made me uneasy because I knew him to be a very strong, muscular, athletic, wrestler-type guy, and I thought, *Jesus, he got hurt and I'm just a 175-pound kid. I'll get killed out there.* It worked out, and the wages were $1.04 an hour, good for 1937. Elevator constructors were paid pretty well. But I didn't get to stay on the job very long. When the injured man recovered, I was out of work. By the time I left, though, the bridge was essentially complete.

Aside from the heights, I was also initially uneasy about the wind and the cold. Remember, this was my first time out. I had never been on a construction project. The work itself, too, as an elevator installer was unusual because of the configuration of the tower structures. So for me as a novice to be out there was stretching things. What was my background to go into a highly technical business? I'd played some baseball, worked in an art department, and been a night watchman. I had no idea what I was getting into.

Learning was strictly on-the-job. I was a young fellow, twenty at the time, but I knew how to use my hands and handle tools. This helped, and the mechanics to whom you reported did recognize your situation. Most of 'em took the time to say, "Try to understand what I'm doing and how you can help. That's what you're here for." Once in a while you'd run into somebody that would object to your coming on the job as a greenhorn. Jobs were hard to get, and maybe they didn't like the idea of a novice coming in. But it was up to you to overcome that.

On the job, there were just two of us, this mechanic, Frank Jorgensen, and me. I was the mechanic's helper. We were in the south tower. There was a similar crew in the north tower with Hank Beals and Paul Cooney. The elevator we used was not very large. It was a platform intended for the use of the painters and the maintenance people in bringing up their gear. It was what you would call a skip. It ran very slowly on temporary operation.

One of the other things that made me uneasy was this long Manila rope hanging down in front of the elevator skip platform. It ran from the top of the hoist all the way down to the bottom. I was afraid to ask what it was for. I got suspicious. I did have an idea of what it was there for, so finally, one day I says, "Frank, what's the rope there for?" He said, "Well, John, if this thing conks out, there's a power failure or something and we're stuck, we can just slide down that rope." I says, "No way. I ain't

John Noren, elevator installer mechanic's helper, near the top of the Golden Gate Bridge's south tower, 1937. Only twenty years old and a novice when he took a job on the bridge, Noren had to master highly technical skills quickly. Courtesy of Labor Archives and Research Center, San Francisco State University.

going to slide down that rope. I'll sit here until I rot. I'm not going to." He said, "Well, John, suit yourself. I like to go home at night. You can just sit here."

Fortunately, the lift kept going up and down. It was an interesting project because due to the height and the slow speed at which the skip ran, when you loaded up everything in the morning for whatever work assignment you had, you had to be sure you loaded all your materials and tools. This was true because if you got all the way up to the top and found you'd forgotten something in the lunchroom or something else, there was no way you'd be going back down. It would take too much traveling time. You could take your whole lunch hour going up and down. They had portable toilets, but they had 'em at the road level.[8] Still, it was no problem because I was young and could last a day. One of the things you would do along with taking all of your gear in the morning was to

be sure you were in good shape to go aloft for a long time. If worst came to worst, why, wherever you happened to be . . .

When the little elevator got overcrowded and there was no room for me, I would stand on what they call a crosshead, which was a small beam about ten feet above the elevator platform. You'd stand on that and hold on to the cables and ride up. I got used to it, but I still felt very much relieved when we hit the road at four-thirty and you'd stamp your feet on the ground.

In those days, too, we wore coveralls. The wind had a tendency to balloon you out and get under your sleeves. It blew like hell at the top and it was cold. I remember saying to Frank, "You know, this place is going to blow me away." He says, "You got to lean into the wind." I looked down and I said, "No way." But those men who could do that were like cats. I have to admire them, the fellows that really did the bread-and-butter construction stuff. I've seen pictures of them putting fabricated pieces together and bolting them, or welding one piece of steel to another, or standing on a load that was being lifted and then stepping off to the partially completed bridge, all without a safety belt. Nowadays, if you don't use safety gear, that's the first reason to let somebody go. You know, the Occupational Safety and Health Administration [OSHA] has come up with some pretty rigid requirements.[9] But the law was different in the 1930s in the construction world.

Installing the final elevator system included electrical work. We worked in dimly lighted areas with lights spaced here and there. It was almost like working in moonlight. We were running the wiring, which means feeding wires into conduits and wiring up the junction boxes and controllers and hanging what we call traveling cables, which were the flexible connections between junction boxes and the moving elevator. The elevator counterweights, one going up and one going down, consisted of a very long, thin system of weights. They ran the weights in a counterweight shaft that was like a very small honeycomb section. There was a ladder in there, but access to that shaft weight was through top and bottom doorways. They were very much like those on a submarine. You could step out of

Dignitaries visiting the bridge construction site, north tower. Noren recalled riding precariously outside the lift when he helped install the south tower's elevator in 1937. Photo by Ted Huggins. Courtesy of California Historical Society, Huggins Collection, CHS.Huggins.003.

the elevator and reach out and through one of these doors and into the conduit shaft. But you had to be in constant communication with the man running the elevator.

We through-bolted a lot of things. In other words, we'd have to drill through the plate of the bridge structure to fasten items. I'd be on one side of a plate with nuts. Each bolt had a nut. When I got into that shaft, the other man had to know where I was at all times. We signaled by hitting a hammer against the bulkhead, one up, two down. I wouldn't signal unless I'd positioned myself. Occasionally, there were little gussets you could stand on. These weights would pass by close to your person, so that if you were out of position, you could be smashed in there. That was a little hair-raising at times.

Practically all of our work was inside the Strauss safety net, too. The netting was all outside under the roadbed. So it didn't protect us. I came on the job shortly after the big accident of February 17, 1937, when the net broke and ten men died. I do remember seeing the net hanging in the water. It was laying there and it was a startling, grim thing to see.

The last thing I did on the bridge was starting to put the elevator cab on. I thought, *Gee, this is fine. At least I'm going to have something to stand in and not fall out of.* Before, there were big voids between elevator stops, and there was a big void from the front of the elevator on out. So there was plenty of room to fall. But we got the cab assembled and bolted together, and at that time I was taken off the job. That's when I lost my job there. I didn't go back into the elevator business until several years later.

After the bridge I got a little deal where I got twenty-five dollars for pitching for Hollister's baseball club down in what we called the Lettuce League, around Hollister and Watsonville, California. There were several young fellows trying to find work in the lettuce shacks there. Then they played baseball for the town team. I didn't work in the lettuce, I just got paid for pitching on Sunday through the summer. Getting five dollars a week was pretty good for 1937.

Then the fellow who steered me into pitching for Hollister asked me if I wanted to go to work for the Bank of America. The bank was very sports-minded. They had an organization called the Bank of America Club, which sponsored excellent basketball and baseball teams. I started work at the bank posting the Christmas Card account, registering twenty-five-cent deposits and things like that, and balancing the bank's savings machines. Then I became a teller. Banking wasn't for me, though. It was a livelihood, but it was just a job. Basically I had no feeling of ambition for the whole thing. The people at the bank weren't very well paid. I started at about seventy-five or eighty-five dollars a month. The bank employees weren't organized into a union. But they had a certain spirit and they thought highly of the bank, although they knew they were underpaid by a lot of standards. I worked there until I got married.[10]

Then I had a chance to go back into the elevator business. World War II had started in 1939 in Europe, the economy was picking up, the military was building up the naval supply depot in Oakland, the army was leasing out warehouse spaces, and elevator repair and rehabilitation was part of the scene. So I went back into the elevator business and stayed with it for forty-two years.

I was still relatively inexperienced in elevator work, but they were looking for men. I applied and got a call. As I got further along into it, I got exposed to elevator controls and found a talent I didn't realize I had. I could understand automatic circuitry like I could read a book. That was something that stymied a lot of experienced elevator men. They just didn't understand it. They would rather do the nuts-and-bolts work; but when I was exposed to it, it was like a piece of cake. That really helped me. I became a service mechanic with an elevator route. Being of service to people always appealed to me and it felt like my route was my own business. I owned it. Those were my elevators and the customers were my friends.

The first time I voted was in the 1940 election. I voted for President Franklin Roosevelt. I didn't hear much about politics until Roosevelt came in. Of course, he was admired very much for his reforms and for what he proposed to do and what he did. Before, I didn't know very much about politics. My folks didn't really follow politics much.

In those days I was in Local 8 of the IUEC. One year in the early 1940s, I was proposed as a candidate for the executive board. I was elected for a one-year term. I was a regular mechanic at the time. During the latter part of the term, I was asked by Westinghouse if I wanted to go on salary as part of management. Westinghouse became quite a factor in the elevator business. They had a beautiful line of equipment. This was a point of decision for me. Tom Fitzgerald was the Local 8 business agent. I had worked as his helper when he had a service route in Oakland. When he was appointed one of the union's international vice-presidents, he had to leave for the East. He said he would support me for business agent. I had to make up my mind whether to follow the labor movement or get into management. Both appealed, except on the labor side when you got into office, you had to run for reelection every year. It's true that getting a salary in management was no guarantee, either, but I opted to go that way and it worked out.

I became a field engineer and traveled around to hospitals, hotels, and office buildings dealing with special problems when new Westinghouse elevator equipment appeared on the market. This was because I had a field background, while many other managers, who were fine engineers, were absolutely unfamiliar with the workings of an elevator. We'd be assigned a novice salesman as a helper and a van and we'd go to work. I stayed at Westinghouse until I retired in the early 1980s.

My relationship with the union stayed generally successful. I had an edge and an advantage in that people who subsequently got into leadership positions with the union, including business representatives, were men I had worked with and knew on a personal basis. So there wasn't the hostility that you might associate with a relationship like that. Sometimes, when there was a union member who was hard to place, the business rep would call me and say, "John, I got so-and-so available." I knew the man and his background and problems. I'd say, "Okay, send him down and I'll find something for him." Then when I needed a favor, it was give and take. That's the way it should be.

There were three strikes at five-year intervals in the 1970s through the early 1980s.[11] Normally you could get inside the hoist way and you'd be out of sight [of the picketing workers], or up in the elevator machine room. One time when I arrived with the van, though, there was already a picket line around the building. But I'd made my decision which way I was going to go and I wasn't going to kick my career out the window. See, if you tell your company, "I'm sorry, you're going to have to keep these elevators running using somebody else," what are your chances? So I just grit my teeth and kept on walking, although it wasn't pleasant.

Over time I don't think anybody ever held my choice to go management against me. I still see my old mechanics and helpers at the company picnics and Christmas parties. I can tell it's just genuine friendship there.

Eventually at Westinghouse I became a regional sales manager and had the whole Pacific Coast as my responsibility.

Reflecting back as a native San Franciscan, I can say I've always admired the Golden Gate Bridge as one of the most beautiful structures I've ever seen. I have a great sense of pride for the relatively small part that I had in its completion. But I can't help admiring the designers, the planners, the engineers, the coordinators, the people who scheduled things, and above all the men who put the bridge together, who did the nuts and bolts of it. When you consider the times and the working conditions out there, you have to admire everyone who had anything to do with that structure.

In retirement I like to paint, and the bridge is one of my subjects. I can sit down and paint a picture of it out of my head.

Glenn McIntyre

IRONWORKER

I went over to an ironworker one day and I says, "How could you join the union?" He says, "You think you can make an ironworker? You may make one, but you'll never be one." That made my determination more.

GLENN McINTYRE

Born in 1912 and raised in Washington State, Glenn McIntyre came to California with his brother in 1928. After the Great Depression hit a year later, he held a series of survival jobs, including a stint as a gandy dancer (railroad worker) near the California-Oregon border while still a teenager. McIntyre was working as a fry cook in San Francisco when he found employment on the San Francisco–Oakland Bay Bridge project, where he became a skilled ironworker. He got hired to practice his new skill on the Golden Gate Bridge in 1936. McIntyre remained an ironworker for the rest of his career. I interviewed him in Saratoga, California, on April 4, 1987, and in Cupertino, California, two days later.

Alvina McIntyre, Glenn McIntyre's wife, was born circa 1913. Here she provides brief but insightful comments from her own perspective on the dangers inherent in her husband's job and how she coped with them. Sometime after the Golden Gate Bridge was built, Glenn McIntyre entered military service and Alvina McIntyre found employment with the Marine Corps. I interviewed her in Saratoga, California, on April 4, 1987.

Whatever the engineer designed, I was ready to build. I wasn't trained as an engineer, it was just bred into me. My father was the engineer for Yakima County in the state of Washington.

McIntyre comes from an Irish spelling, but we were considered Scotch because we were run out of Ireland in denouncing the Catholic church. We were Presbyterians. We migrated over here to America on the *Mayflower* on my mother's side. My father's side came over at approximately the same time. My grandparents on my mother's side migrated from Maine into Minnesota, North Dakota, and South Dakota in pioneer days.

I was born in 1912 on a small ranch that was two blocks outside the Yakima city limits. I went to school in Yakima, but thought it was time to leave the thing when I was about fifteen years old. My older brother was coming to California and I says, "I'm going with you." We came down here in 1928 and ended up in San Francisco. I lived there and worked there most of the time until retirement.

When we got to San Francisco, it was a Saturday. Monday morning my brother gave me a dollar and says, "Good-bye." There I was, only fifteen years old. The first place I headed for was Postal Telegraph because I had worked for 'em in my hometown during schooltime. I got fitted right away for a uniform. I hadn't thought I was going to get a job that first day. I worked at Postal Telegraph as a messenger boy until they caught up with me and wanted to put me in part-time high school.

So I took a hike and went to work as a gandy dancer on the Northwestern Pacific Railroad up near Eureka, California.[1] Of course, them days, gandy dancers, they never had a union. I stayed up there about fourteen months. I'd go work with the train operator at night. I'd help him and he'd teach me how to fire up the work engine. When he'd go in to Eureka on the weekend, he'd say, "Mac, you think you can take care of it?" I'd say, "Sure." I'd be running the engine up and down the siding. I was working it then with a steam shovel outfit. I ran the work engine until I run it into the cook shack. Then, son-of-a-bitch, the Chinese cook was going to throw me into a pot of soup and make soup out of me. So I didn't run the old work engine anymore. But by the end they was ready to send me in as an engineer because I could run anything. I even learned to run the big seventy-ton Syracuse steam shovel. There wasn't anything on the railroad I couldn't run.

I'll never forget the time the road master come out to inspect the track. They'd always call me to be the chauffeur because I could run the speeder.[2] We ran all the way up to Willits and had dinner with all the big shots and came back. I tried to show off a little too good for them and I jumped the track with the old speeder. Then I says, "It looks like we have a repair job here." We got the speeder back on the track and we came in.

I used to run the speeder against trains, but I didn't have a watch [to warn me when a train was due]. So I made myself a sundial. I'd put a stick down and watch the shadows. One time I looked behind my shoulder and here the old passenger train was right behind me. I laid the speeder over, the train went on by, and I just put the speeder back on the track again and come a-pumping in. The worst thing I did was I come a-pumping in right behind the passenger train. Of course, the engineer told the assistant road master what had happened. The assistant road master asked me, "Let's see your watch." I says, "I don't have it. I left my stick out on the riverbank." He says, "That's all you got? Get in to town and get yourself a watch." That weekend I went in to Eureka. I came back with a Pocket Ben.[3] A dollar ninety-five was a hell of a lot of money in them days.

The road master asked me to see the watch. I showed him. He says, "That isn't a railroad watch." I said, "Well, it will do for me. I ain't a railroad man." Once our section foreman borrowed my watch when we had to use the speeder to beat a damn train out of a mile-and-a-half-long tunnel. He had a railroad watch and he actually borrowed my watch. After that, anybody had a Pocket Ben, they was really appreciated.

I ended up having quite an experience, but gee whiz, it'd be pouring, I was just a kid and they'd say, "It's your night to go out and patrol track." I'd go out with all the rattlesnakes. Of course, it was raining, there wasn't any worry about them. But we'd put a box of dynamite on the back of the speeder. There was a guy that taught me how to put dynamite caps around the band of my hat. You'd have a whole band full of these caps around your head. If you ever fell off the speeder, all you had to do is blow. You wouldn't have to worry anymore.

The job was that if there was a big rock or something in our way, you'd take a stick of dynamite, get some mud and plaster, put a fuse in there, light it, and go on. Finally I'd had enough of this and of the wintertime rain around Eureka and I came back to San Francisco.

I went to work in a small planing mill in the city. The old guy there wouldn't even give you time to go to the restroom. Once I was doubled up sick and he wouldn't let me go. So I just took a piece of wood and give it a twist. I bent his saw and they run me off.

I ended up going to work for an office and business furniture company, M. G. West. I didn't like their kind of work too well. I didn't like anything where I felt penned in. I left M. G. West and got restaurant work as a dishwasher and busboy for the old Foster's Lunch System.[4] When the cook says, "You're a cook," I said, "Christ, I can't even fry eggs." He said, "Don't worry. You'll learn." I learned. I never knew people ate so many eggs in all the different ways they had of frying them there.

When I was out of work, I'd hustle sheets for old Randolph Hearst.[5] I had a camel-haired top coat, a Stetson hat, and Florsheim shoes.[6] I was the best-dressed sheet hustler there ever was. I wouldn't stand on the street corner and wait. I'd jump in the front end of a streetcar, go through the thing selling, and go out the back end of the car on the run. I did fairly well, too. I was the only sheet hustler smoking tailor-made cigarettes. Everybody else rolled their own.

Before I heard about the Golden Gate Bridge, the Bay Bridge was being built. I'd kept looking at it while I was working at Foster's Lunch. I said, "God darn, I want to see how that thing is built." At the bridge there was thirteen stairways and thirteen steps on the stairs. I always remembered that thirteen steps was the way to go to your gallows. I walked all of them up there and asked who the foreman was. A man says, "That fellow over there." I went over and I said, "I'm Glenn McIntyre. Could you use a good man?" He says, "Well, McIntyre, my name is McIntyre, too. You're hired. You got a pair of gloves?" I said, "No." He says, "Get down there, get yourself a pair of gloves, get back up here, and go to work."

The job was with a company pouring cement for the decks. I started walking a beam to get to the crew and I'll never forget looking down over the Embarcadero.[7] I seen them cars below and I says, "Oh, my God," and I froze on it. Here I was, sitting there, tears in my eyes, thinking, *I'll never make it.* A guy come along and he says, "What's the matter, kid?" I said, "I'm scared." He says, "Don't worry. Just scoot along and get over to the side. The gang is out toward the middle." I decided I'd never let McIntyre [the foreman] know I was scared, so I went out there.

We were going to lay the rail for the dinkey to haul the cement.[8] A guy says, "We're stringing the rail now. Grab ahold of that." I was right on the front. I was leading everybody else, but they didn't know that they was carrying me. I'd been so scared walking that darned old beam, but I says, "God durn it, I don't want to worry about it anymore. Hell, if I can lead them, I can lead anybody." And I kept on going.

That started my career. Two days later I was carrying timbers over to the dinkey with another young fellow. He got scared in the middle, threw his end, and I went off backwards. When I fell, I threw the timber, too. You want to know where I ended up? Hanging on to the dinkey car with my fingertips. And the six-by-six I was carrying that I threw was on top of my fingers. If that won't make you believe in the Lord, boy, nothing else will.

I started running and jumping from beam to beam. The beams on the Bay Bridge were four feet across. When I got back, the boss says, "What's the matter, you gone crazy?" I said, "No, I didn't want to lose my nerve." Two days later, I was a gang foreman. The boss says, "Anybody that can be as crazy as that needs to be leading 'em." I run the cement vibrator after that, too, all the way through the upper and lower decks.

Once I was carrying a settling tank on my shoulder.[9] It could be windier than hell. This night a God darn gust hit me. There was a ferry-boat under there, but I said, "It's either me or you." I jumped to the next beam and let the settling tank go. It was aimed just like a bomb heading for that ferryboat. I prayed while it went all the way down. Then it leveled out, went right over the boat, and missed it. There's another case where the Lord had his hand in. When they dredged the bay for BART, they probably picked up that tank with everything else.[10]

One time I went to the doctor's office when I was still working on the Bay Bridge. I had to get a cement burn doctored up. There was a call for the doctor to get to Pier 6 in San Francisco. The doctor says, "Sit there and wait until I come back." He come back and said, "Swept him up in a basket." [After he'd treated me] I went up on the job and says, "Where's my partner?" A guy said, "Down in the hole." It was him that they swept up. He'd gotten scared. They was riding a dinkey out and they was coming up on another dinkey like they was going to run into it. He thought it was going to hit, jumped, missed the beam, and went straight down and landed on Pier 6. That was the end of my buddy. But as an ironworker, you kept on going. You never lost your nerve. God darn, you didn't give a damn what it was, the job had to go on. The next day you come back to work.

I went over to an ironworker one day and I says, "How could you join the union?" He says, "You think you can make an ironworker? You may make one, but you'll never be one." That made my determination more. So when we finished the cement on the Bay, I went down to the ironworkers' Local 377 union hall. I said, "I was one of the laborers up there on the Bay Bridge. I'd like to join the union."

I asked for an apprentice card. But they'd been watching me. The man there says, "You don't need no apprentice card. Take a journeyman's card and be happy." I was still working when the one that said, "You may make a bridge man, but you'll never be one," was laid off. And I made a pretty good bridge man, because afterwards I worked on the Golden Gate Bridge right up in Jack Turnipseed's gang, right up in the front point.[11]

With them old-time ironworkers like Dago Frank, Steve Carter, Hook-nose Smitty, and Tobacco George, if you could work into their gang, God darn, boy, you was all right. You had to be all right to work in their gang. Otherwise, they had tricks of getting rid of you. If they didn't like you, they'd urinate in the coal bin for the heater.[12] When they threw that coal in the forge, you was going down the road. You'd give up quick. I don't think there's anything this side of a slaughterhouse that smells any worse.

You didn't know what modern sanitation was back then. There were some bucket latrines, but I don't remember ever using one. You could slide down a column and if there was no ferryboats going under you, you went. On the Bay Bridge, they didn't, because the ferryboats is going by and there's hundreds of people looking up. But when there was no ferryboat, you didn't worry. It wasn't going nowhere, just in the bay. Usually you'd have an old newspaper or something in your pocket. As a man, you didn't have no problem with that. Hell, there was no women, especially on the Golden Gate Bridge. I never ever saw one. We never had black workers, either. In them times, we didn't have too many black ironworkers that I can recall. I don't remember ever seeing one on the bridge.[13]

When they sent me out to the Golden Gate Bridge, the first place they put me I didn't have a net under me. That was before they stretched the safety net. In the raising gang on the Golden Gate, you didn't have nothing under you but the water. It was still quite strict on your safety there, though. We used to count the guys that would go down on the Bay Bridge.[14] It did give you a good feeling on the Golden Gate to have that net under there once it went in.

We'd jump down in the net and clean it out of any debris like rivets so that if we ever did fall, you wouldn't hit something. Running around in that net seemed like you was climbing uphill all the time, and you was going downhill. I didn't see anybody actually fall into the net. You didn't see everything that went on during the day. You was working. If you was watching it for everything else, you'd get run off the job for sure.

In driving rivets on the Golden Gate Bridge, you had a riveter and a bucker. Bucking, you'd stick the rivet and put your bucking bar on it. A bucking bar is solid steel with a little gooseneck on it so you can get the rivet in in different positions. The gooseneck had a die the size of the rivet. Whatever size rivets you'd be driving, why, you'd try to get the bar [with the right size of die] for them. With a rivet in place, the riveter would start driving with a hammer.

The forge was full of hot rivets. They'd have 'em stacked around the rim of the coals, preheated. They was heated to a cherry red. You'd take one off just like you was serving hamburgers. They'd throw the rivet and a man would catch it in a catch can. He'd hand it to you and you'd stick it in the hole. Sometimes they'd start driving ahead of time before you fumbled the rivet in. Then you'd catch hell. Them old guys, they didn't want to lose a rivet 'cause they had to heat another one then to take its place.

If a bad rivet cooled down too much, you'd have to take after it and use the hell dog on it. That's a 120-pound pressure gun. They're the same as a riveting gun, only it's a big one. A riveting gun had 90 pounds of pressure on there. With the hell dog, you'd drive the rivet back out. Sometimes it'd come out of there just like it was coming out of a shotgun.

At that time, the gloves that I used to wear was goatskin. They were more expensive, but you could get a burn on one and you could rub it and it would come back soft again. The old mule-skin gloves got hard as rocks after you had a few burns on 'em. The goat-skinned gloves were pliable. It was the mark of a good ironworker if he was wearing those. It was just according to what you could afford and how much you wanted to spend

Workers in Strauss's safety net, 1936. "It did give you a good feeling on the Golden Gate to have that net under there once it went in," Glenn McIntyre remembered. The net saved the lives of nineteen men who fell into it. Courtesy of San Francisco History Center, San Francisco Public Library.

on gloves, because you wore 'em out quick, especially in the connecting gang. You'd never ever see a connector wearing a pair of canvas gloves.

If some of the scale from a hot rivet got into your bib overalls or your boot, like when you was in a squatting position and your boots is open, you didn't dare lose that rivet. Sometimes the scale would go in your shirt and go down your stomach. You'd be there trying to wiggle away from that heat. But you'd stay there and burn. You'd never ever give that rivet up. You'd try to turn the scale loose with one hand, but that didn't usually work. You'd stay there, and there's quite a few scars over that. It'd leave a mark on you.

To work on bolts, we had old-fashioned power vane wrenches that were air-driven.[15] They was dangerous things. Usually two men worked one. If you didn't get a nut right with it, the other fellow would take it with his crescent wrench and turn it so it would go into the nut. Then, if the first man happened to hit the power vane trigger about the time you got it on the nut, the crescent wrench was gone. I lost a crescent wrench out into the Golden Gate somewhere that way. It cost a $1.95 for the best crescent wrench then. I still have the crescent wrench I bought to replace the one that I lost out there. I never lost another one. You'd usually always have a crescent wrench for emergency and for small stuff. You carried it in your back pocket or had it hanging on your belt. We had harness snaps and we'd have our crescent hanging on that. I used that crescent wrench all these years until I quit ironworking. Gee whiz, it cost $1.95. You wouldn't want to lose that.

Once on the Golden Gate, I was in the front point on the Marin side getting the nuts off of bolts. I felt the bridge shudder. The boom was swaying back and forth. Finally it went over the side. I looked for my buddy, who was hooking on. He was right under the headache ball and it hit him in the head. That was the end of him. I ate lunch with him at noon, and at two o'clock I went out and swept his brains into the Golden Gate.[16]

With things like my buddy's death, you'd leave your tools and go home.[17] I got hell that time. I left the one impact-style wrench we had on the Marin side.[18] Now everybody carries one; but not in those days. I said, "I don't give a damn what one costs. I lost my buddy." Still, you went back to work the next day. You couldn't be temperamental working there. An ironworker goes home for the day in respect, but the next day he comes back and he's supposed to have forgot about it. The show's got to go on. But things like that you never forget.

One time on the Golden Gate Bridge when I was with the Marin-side raising gang, my partner was putting pins in. I was laying on the diagonal and sticking the pins. My partner started missing his blows and he missed all right. He come bull's-eye right between my eyes with that eight-pound beater [mallet]. He didn't come down to help me or nothing. I decided I didn't want to work with him no more! I stayed there and shook the stars out. When I got 'em all out, I climbed up by myself and went to see the superintendent. He says, "Let's run you to Sausalito [where the ferries that ran between Marin and San Francisco were docked]." The ferryboat was waiting for us there. I never had treatment like that where they were holding a ferryboat for me. All the time I was wanting to get back on the job. They thought I was delirious.

We got to San Francisco. An ambulance took us to St. Luke's Hospital. Same thing over there. I wanted to get back on the job. It took three nurses and four doctors to get me into bed. But they finally did and hid my clothes. I had to stay. The next morning I was glad I was there because I had to feel about two feet out to try to find my head. I had a couple of good black eyes, but three days and I was back on the job. One man at the hospital said, "Hell, you're better off working than you are here."

ALVINA McINTYRE

The time Glenn was hit in the head by a hammer someone drove me to St. Luke's Hospital in San Francisco. I went right past the door when they told me the number of the room he was in. I walked back to the desk and I says, "He's not in there. I saw a fellow laying there all swollen up." She says, "Well, that's him." This nurse at the desk took me to the door. She says, "Right in there." I didn't recognize him.

When my husband Glenn kissed me good-bye in the morning to go to work on the Golden Gate Bridge, I never knew if he was coming home for dinner. That was my feeling the whole time that he worked there. If he'd leave the house a few minutes later than usual, then I knew he would have to speed up and run like hell up to those girders, and that was another thing that bothered me. I was always glad to see him when it was time for him to come home. You had to have strength and bear with it. You have children. You can't break yourself down. You got to keep on going.

GLENN McINTYRE

In those days, we didn't have respirators or anything to protect us from the lead. Still, we never thought nothing of that until we'd get cramps. Then the doctor would tell you, "Go home and drink some milk and get back on the job." That happened to me one time. After that, I was pretty much aware of the problem. Still, they didn't give you any protection in those days. You depended on the wind! They didn't care. It was, "Get the job done."[19]

Hard hats were required at all times on the Golden Gate, though. The ones we used was like the old miner's hat. It was like the old-time fireman's hat, actually, with a smaller bill on it. It was made of fiber, but it was hard, not pliable, and it was very strong. They was easier to get around in than the ones we used on the Bay Bridge.[20] They were surrey black. Some of the pushers or the superintendent might have some silver, red, or anything painted on to let 'em know he was the boss. But the hats were black originally and the ones we wore was the black ones. That was what they furnished you with. The hat had a specification of safety. You couldn't wear your own hat too much. There wasn't too many that owned their own hat in them days anyway. You had a string on there because sometimes you'd get 'em knocked off. It was easy to be working there and bump something and get 'em knocked off and heck, it was a long way down. They could go right through the safety net, too.

I imagine there was controversy about the color the Golden Gate Bridge was painted, but that was for other people. I don't think it mattered a hell of a lot to the ironworkers themselves. It may have been important with the politicians to have something to say, one against the other. But the ironworkers didn't care what color it was. Payday and five o'clock was what they was looking for. The color didn't make no difference as long as the green got in your pocket.[21]

Working on the Golden Gate, we was going from the Marin side to the San Francisco side. We met in the middle. She come right together just the way they planned on. From there, we'd start adjusting the suspender cables that hold up the roadbed. You had to get the proper tension on a cable. We had to use big water[-operated] jacks to jack the suspenders either one way or the other. That jack was monstrous. It was powered by water and air.

When I was working on the bridge I lived in San Francisco. They had an old fishing boat that would take us across the bay to Sausalito on the Marin side in the morning. It would be so foggy you couldn't see your hand before you. One time when we was going out, everybody started to holler at the skipper, "God darn, you're going the wrong way." He was out there, the fog horns was blowing, and hell, we was going out in the ocean instead of going to Sausalito. Finally he turned back. Sometimes coming from there at night, we'd end up missing our pier in San Francisco. We'd find it after a while.

Installing the last girder on the Golden Gate Bridge, November 19, 1936. "She come right together just the way they planned on," McIntyre recalled. Courtesy of San Francisco History Center, San Francisco Public Library.

Workers attaching suspender cables to one of the main cables, October 1936. McIntyre remembered adjusting the suspender cables using huge water-powered jacks. Courtesy of San Francisco History Center, San Francisco Public Library.

I often wondered afterwards how the heck I ever worked in that cold. Out in the breeze, you had a sweater underneath your regular hickory shirt. I always wore the old hickory, the one with the gray and black stripes. That was the old days and you got the most durable shirt. And it was warmer. They was more of the heavy denim type of shirt than most.

Sometimes you had three pair of bib overalls on. You wore them old denim overall jumpers. The ones that was more prosperous had a pair of big heavy denim Carhartt's [overalls]. They were like heavy canvas. They would retard burns better, they had padded knees on 'em, and they lasted longer. I never cared for 'em too much. They was too heavy for bending up and down. But they was warm. The farmer's blue denims were cheaper, 98 cents some days. You'd break the bank when you'd go down and they raised the price to a dollar and a half.

Them old fellows would have newspapers wrapped around them inside to break the wind. I don't know if any of the old buggers had a little mickey [bottle of liquor] on 'em, too. Some of 'em worked better when they were half swacked. If you was fortunate enough to have an old pair of wool dress pants, you'd have them under there, too. Sometimes you wondered how you could move. We didn't have thermals in them days. We had one-piece union suits with three holes—one for your neck and the others for front and back.

As a rule, you didn't have to take anything off out there. You was always looking for some more clothes to wear. That old-fashioned union suit underwear kept you from getting pneumonia because you got so hot working inside the bridge's steel chords, with the hot rivets and the sweat coming off you, and then you'd come out of there and you'd be out in that wind that would cut right through you. In the winter, there was icicles hanging up on there. In any case, the bosses never complained about how many clothes to wear. They just said, "Get the job done." That's all they were worried about.

You'd dress warm above, but you'd still be cold and your feet would be freezing. We'd use wool boot socks. Wool wouldn't burn as quick as cotton if you got hot scale down there. We had a mule-skinned boot, what we used to call the bridge man's boot. It was laced right to the toe. That way you could slip 'em on easier if you had extra socks on. They withstood any chance of getting a rivet burn and they was tough and comfortable.

We always used rubber soles. You'd break your neck out there with leather soles, especially when you was climbing and you had your eight-pound beater stuck in your belt and your wrenches hanging on you. The soles would usually be smooth. I never liked the ones that had bottoms like automobile tires because you was too apt to trip with them. You'd also rather have them smooth and flexible because sometimes when you was coming down, you'd wedge your heel into the flange so you wouldn't slide too fast.

Rain could trip you, too. You'd look out the window in the morning. If it looked like rain, you wouldn't even go to work. Not if you wanted to stay alive. The ones that would go to work we used to call "hungry." Of course, if it's just a shower, you'd duck out. But in those days they used oil in the paint, and that old red lead paint was full of oil. Step on that in the rain and it was like stepping in grease. You could work, but you had to be more cautious, and it wasn't advisable. You always lived a little longer if you didn't take those kinds of chances. I'd rather lose a day than my life.

Building the Golden Gate Bridge, you wouldn't feel an earthquake. With the wind and everything that's always blowing there, you wouldn't know if there was one or not. But it was a good job. We was well paid. We got eleven dollars a day for eight hours. That was good wages in those days. The bricklayers was the only ones in the crafts that made more than the ironworkers at that time. On the Golden Gate, we didn't get much of any overtime. It was an eight-hour day and you was glad of it. Laborers were getting only about five dollars a day. If you went up from five to seven, that was a good day's pay.

After the structural work on the bridge was finished, we were laid off. I went home to see my mother and the family in Washington over the Christmas of 1936. Then I went back to the ironworkers' Local 377 hall and got sent out to work at Treasure Island in San Francisco Bay where they were building a hangar for a Clipper flying boat. Once I was off of the Golden Gate and working somewhere else, I never gave it much thought. I don't even remember where I was at the opening day of it in May 1937. I was working some job. I wasn't about to take a day off.

ALVINA McINTYRE

It was a gala affair, opening day. I was there. They had concessions. I bought these hats on the bridge. You could buy candy and ice cream.

Everybody seemed happy. They were laughing and everything. I had my kid there. He was only seven. He was so excited. Not once did he say he was tired. Oh, I had such a proud feeling because my husband worked on there as a high climber. It was a great bridge for sightseers, too. Everybody that came to visit us wanted to see the Golden Gate Bridge. So off to the Golden Gate Bridge we went.

GLENN McINTYRE

Treasure Island was the only job that was going then and we had a lot of extra ironworkers around after the Gate was finished.[22] But while we were building the Golden Gate, ironworkers was like millionaires. You could walk in anyplace with your hard hat on and your face black as soot, and they would always acknowledge you there. They wouldn't run you out even if it was a classy restaurant and you walked in dressed that way. They knew that eleven dollars a day was a good scale. While I was working on the Golden Gate, I finally bought a newer car. It was a 1931 Chevrolet convertible. When I went to work, I only had a little old Ford.

After the Clipper hangar job, I followed steel and worked on the Pitt River Bridge in Northern California. We used that same net they pulled out of the bay after ten men died on the Golden Gate when the safety net tore in 1937. Some of it got torn up, but they cut the good section out. I jumped into the net on the Pitt River job once to help Elmer Olson when he got knocked into it and broke his leg.[23]

The Pitt River Bridge was five hundred feet above the river. You looked down and the river looked like a crick down there. They said Elmer fell a hundred feet, but I didn't see where it was that far or I wouldn't think I'd been crazy enough to do what I did. I didn't recall jumping, but I asked the fellows afterwards. I said, "Jesus, how the hell did I get down there to get him?" They said, "You damn fool, you jumped into the net a hundred feet down." The net drooped way down there. That kind of weight, you couldn't stretch it too tight. They said, "You jumped, you never ever thought anything of it." Elmer was close to the edge, close to rolling out. By my hitting the net, he was thrown back in. Then some of the others got down there and got him into a basket to bring him back up.

Years later I worked on BART. I was always interested in getting something operating and I wanted to make sure to get that thing running. So

Alvina McIntyre and her son at the Golden Gate Bridge's opening celebration, May 27, 1937. Approximately two hundred thousand elated people walked across the bridge that day. Courtesy of Labor Archives and Research Center, San Francisco State University.

I went over there with the structural gang. I trained all these kids and then taught them to drive heavy maintenance equipment. One night I had my helper there. We were working on the tunnel under the bay. I says, "You will probably never meet anybody with my experiences." He said, "How is that?" I says, "Now I'm working on BART. I've ate my lunch two hundred feet above, and now I'm eating my lunch two hundred feet below the bay."[24]

John Urban

CABLE SPINNER

They handed me the end of this galvanized wire to take to this tower top. The wire was just a little bit smaller than the lead in a lead pencil. That's the way that cable is built. . . . That first day, I looked at the catwalk and up to the top of the tower and I says, "Am I going up there or not?" I gritted my teeth and said, "Here goes," and I took off. I went up to the tower top. **JOHN URBAN**

John Urban was the son of Lithuanian immigrant parents living in Oregon. Born in 1910, he labored in the northwest woods as a youth. He came to San Francisco from Oregon early in the Great Depression. Urban did stints in a restaurant and as a truck driver before becoming an apprentice ironworker on the Golden Gate Bridge in 1935. On the bridge he initially worked as a cable spinner. Although he was seriously injured in 1936 while unloading steel, he returned to the Golden Gate project and was employed there through the spring of 1937, when the bridge job finished. Urban remained an ironworker until retirement. I interviewed Urban in San Francisco, California, on April 15, 1987.

■ ■ ■

My dad was gung-ho against war. He was an orphan from Lithuania who took off to get away from the czar's army. That was the day the Russians conscripted everybody. This was before the First World War.[1] Dad was pretty young to be taken into the army and he didn't want any of that. So he went to Canada and got into this country from there. He ended up in Oregon.

One time we went over to the St. Helens Pulp and Paper Company mill looking for jobs for my brother and me. The superintendent says, "We need another war to kill off all the young people so we'll have enough jobs for the ones that are left." My dad got mad after we got out of there. He said, "That kind is crazy. Who wants war?" That was the attitude some people had. They didn't want war, they didn't want to go in the army. That's the way I feel about things now [1987]. I don't blame some of these kids for protesting.

My mother was also from Lithuania. She came through Ellis Island just to go to America. My parents met in Oregon City. Dad worked in the sawmills there. I was born in Portland, Oregon, on December 26, 1910. When I was in the first grade of school, my parents moved into what I call the stump ranch. They bought a logged-off piece of land near Scappoose in rural Oregon. He cleared it and they made a living. My dad started out with a little small house. Then he built a bigger house with three bedrooms upstairs and one downstairs. He built a barn, had cows, raised his own hay, and grew vegetables and potatoes.

Scappoose is twenty miles north of Portland on the Columbia River Highway. We were seven miles off of there. The road was graveled for three or four miles. The rest of it was dirt, ruts, and mud holes. There was a logging camp three-quarters of a mile from where we lived. The workers there—buckers, whistle punks, donkey operators—all stayed in these bunkhouses.[2] They had cookhouses there and they fed you good. When the workers would get their cars stuck in a mud hole, my dad would take a horse and charge 'em a little money to pull the cars out and haul them down to the gravel road.

I went to grammar school, then to a little over a year of high school. I left home when I was fourteen and went to work on a farm milking cows at night. I was still going to high school. I wanted to get away from life back there in the sticks, but then I worked in the woods. I was what they used to call a whistle punk. They used to give signals to the donkey operator with a wire that's hooked up to the steam whistle on the donkey. They'd give signals like go ahead, back up, tight lines, and all these other words that you use in the logging industry. The whistle punk had to string wire out there in the woods maybe a thousand feet to where the logs were down and already cut and ready to be pulled in to a landing for loading onto the train. Then they'd haul the logs down to the Columbia River and dump 'em. There were no radios or logging trucks then like they have now.

In 1929 and early 1930, it cost us a $1.50 a day for board, meal, and insurance. It was just the beginning of insurance compensation, and it didn't amount to nothing. This was just a forerunner to what we have now. But for a boy then, working in the woods was pretty good. You'd have two or three kinds of meat on the table, and vegetables and fruit. You'd be out there with that fresh air and a lot of oxygen and I couldn't believe how much I could eat. I got out, though, when the Depression set in and jobs weren't so plentiful. I also always wanted to go to California and I didn't like the lousy weather in Oregon. I was headed for Los Angeles, but I got to San Francisco and went to work in a restaurant.

I come down to the city in May of 1930 with a fellow that had been there before. He'd worked for Compton's restaurant and knew the people there. The first time they needed a dishwasher, I went to work dishwashing. I moved up to busboy, then counterman.[3] When I was working in the restaurant, the Cooks' and Waiters' Union was already in there. We went on strike for better conditions and a forty-hour week. I did picket duty. The owner, Gene Compton, accepted President Franklin Roosevelt's whole NRA program. He signed up for it. We got a raise and we was working five days a week instead of six. Compton's was the first restaurant in San Francisco to get the NRA emblem.[4]

Our Compton's settlement came shortly before the 1934 West Coast maritime strike. We helped out on the '34 strike, too. We aided the longshoremen as much as we could. All the unions backed them when they paraded up Market Street just before the San Francisco general strike. I was there that day. I was working in a restaurant right down by the Ferry Building. The longshoremen were just out there walking. They didn't cause any ruckus or problem. They deserved what they won. That Harry Bridges, their leader, couldn't be bought off. That's what the ship owners didn't like.[5]

During the San Francisco general strike, pretty near everything closed down. It looked just like it did on the Golden Gate Bridge when the people came walking across when it opened in 1937. The people were walking right down the middle of the street in '34 because there was no streetcars running. The sidewalks couldn't hold 'em all. And there wasn't very many cars like there is now.

I voted for Franklin Roosevelt for president in 1932 and 1936. He did the workingman a lot of good. I used to vote every time. I was not involved in politics, but I had bumper stickers or something like that. After a while, it got so hard to get 'em off the bumpers I didn't put 'em on. I voted Democratic pretty near all the time.

At Compton's we ended up making pretty good money. In those days, the people that worked in City Hall were getting a hundred dollars a month, and I was getting twenty-eight dollars a week and my meals. You could get rooms in a livable hotel down in the Tenderloin then that were a lot better than they are now [1987]. I lived there and in different places in apartments.[6]

After Compton's I went to work driving a truck for a nursery at Colma, California, just south of San Francisco. I only got thirty-five cents an hour driving a dump truck, but I'd just got tired of Compton's. I was trying to figure out some way I could become a carpenter or a sheet-metal worker or something like that. Where I was living is how I got a break to get into the ironworkers' union. The business agent for the union lived in the back apartment of the building where I had the front apartment. I'd recently quit the job down at the nursery. I was out of work. The business agent's wife says to him, "Everybody else is getting apprentices into the ironworkers. Why don't you get John work?" So he sent me out from the Ironworkers' hall to the Golden Gate Bridge to work on the rigging of the two main cables.

It helped that I belonged to the Cooks' and Waiters' Union. That's the evidence I had to prove that I lived in this area.[7] But that didn't mean nothing. I knew a lot of guys that come from New York and where have you, and all they did is have their landlords swear that they'd been living here for a year or whatever was the requirement. That's the way it was, and nobody said nothing. As an apprentice I got two-thirds of a journeyman ironworker's scale, which was $1.25 an hour. We worked from eight to four-thirty with a half-hour for lunch.

This was in 1935. It was November 11 when I went out there on the bridge. I never will forget that because it was Armistice Day. They didn't

John Urban, cable spinner, near the top of one of the Golden Gate Bridge's towers, probably early 1936. Once leery of heights, Urban overcame his fear while working on the bridge. Courtesy of Labor Archives and Research Center, San Francisco State University.

celebrate it then. Later they called it Veterans Day.[8] That was also the first place I ever had to take a physical. After they gave us a talk, got us all signed up and checked with the doctor, they handed me the end of this galvanized wire to take to this tower top. The wire was just a little bit smaller than the lead in a lead pencil. That's the way that cable is built.[9]

Before, I was always kind of leery of heights. When I worked in the woods, I would of never been a high climber. Twenty or thirty feet didn't bother me, but it seemed like when I got up higher, I'd even hate to look over the edge of a building. I belonged to the YMCA in downtown San Francisco, and I even hated to look over the side of that. Then I got out there to the bridge. But you'd be surprised. After a while, sometimes, you get used to it. Some of those bridge guys were just like a monkey on that iron.

That first day, I looked at the catwalk and up to the top of the tower and I says, "Am I going up there or not?" I gritted my teeth and said, "Here goes," and I took off. I went up to the tower top.[10] Then another crew of guys come over from the Marin side. They took the end of the wire and we just stood there and pulled slack. Then the rest of us that were spotted alongside 'em went clear down to the Marin anchor block and back to the San Francisco anchor block, and they were then able to put the wire on the spinning wheel. Then they did the spinning mechanically. But they had to get that first wire over there by hand. It seemed to me like they could have pulled the wire over with a wheel going slow. But they didn't want to take any chance of scraping the wire because anytime they scraped the wire they'd [have to] cut that section out. Then they'd put a ferrule in to splice the wire.

I worked most of the time up on the top of the tower for the John A. Roebling's Sons Company. In making the strands for the cables, we had to keep the wire under control when the wheel spinning the wire come over the bridge tower. They had what they called a spinning sheave. It was a round pulley with a groove in it so the wire would fit down in there and not jump out. There was two wires because there was a live wire and a dead wire, as we called it. One wire kept going and the other one set down. We had to drop the live wire in the sheave, being sure it went down in the pulley and didn't lay down on the iron and start tearing the galvanize [zinc coating to prevent rust] off. Then we'd drop the dead wire down in the tower's saddle where we were making the strands of the cable.

They had to do that all the way down along the catwalk, clear to midspan of the bridge and back up over the tower and down the other side. When the sheave came back, then we'd have the wire that was live going that way and the dead wire coming back. We had to keep those wires straight. They couldn't be crossed. They had to be right in perfect line so that one sat inside the groove of the next one. If you had wires crossed, any movement would wear that galvanize off and wear the wire out. That was a no-no.

Working on the bridge, I don't know how some of those guys even moved, they had so many clothes on. But you had to dress pretty warm. The men mostly wore long-handled underwear.[11] This was before the days of thermal underwear. They're not that hot unless you wear a T-shirt under 'em. A lot of 'em wore coveralls with jackets. You didn't know what weather you was going to get out there.

Sometimes when we was working for Roebling on the tower top, it would be nice and warm. We'd be in shirtsleeves. This fellow Pinky who was working the first quarter point, as they called it—although it wasn't a quarter of the way down—wouldn't be over a hundred feet below the tower. But he was freezing and he had all the clothes on that he had. The wind was blowing there, and there wasn't a breath of wind blowing on the tower top. When the spinning wheel would shut down or something, he'd come up and get warm. He'd say, "Boy, it's cold down there." I believed him. I remember that he did that more than once.

We had all kinds of gloves. These canvas ones come up to here [taps the middle of his forearm] because, working around iron, you get your wrists all scratched up. They was all right for certain things. Other things, they weren't so good. This was a heavier canvas. It wasn't like these cotton white gloves. This was a kind of imitation leather or maybe part cloth and part leather. It was fuzzy on the outside and smoother on the inside so it wouldn't hurt your hand. Other fellows wore leather gloves. I wore leather gloves for a lot of different jobs.

Roebling and Bethlehem Steel, which I worked for on the bridge later, furnished us with hard hats. They were kind of like plastic, but they had little fibers in 'em. We had the first ones of that kind that come out. They had these other brownish-looking ones that were rounded with a brim. You had to buy your own. Foremen had those if they wanted to be fancy-looking. But the brim stuck out too far and got knocked off too easy and if a rivet or something would hit those, they could shatter. These we had would only dent a little bit. They were also better if you come up under something and banged your head. These hats were black with a little protrusion to protect your ears. I seen 'em demonstrated by dropping rivets and bolts through pipes from way up and I was convinced. I didn't want one of those brown ones. The black ones saved a lot of hard knocks.

When we was working for Roebling, they had portable toilets on the tower top, although down along the catwalk, guys usually went just over the side. What else could you do? If you had to urinate, that was all. If you had to do the other business, well then, you had to find a place. Some of the guys who were just below would come up to the

Cable spinners like Urban at work on the bridge, 1936. Urban described the careful attention to detail that cable spinning required. Photo by Ted Huggins. Courtesy of California Historical Society, Huggins Collection, CHS.Huggins.012.

top of the tower. Other guys would go down. For the toilets on top, they had a cable so they could hook up about four of 'em at a time. They had a crane on top of the tower that you could use to hoist about anything you wanted up there. To clean them, they'd just drop 'em down. They cleaned 'em right there, right over into the bay. In those days, they weren't particular. When the toilets was cleaned up, they'd send 'em back up again.

When we was working on the cables, the only thing that stopped us was the wind. We worked rain or shine. When it was raining working for Roebling, we wore raincoats. But if the wind come up it would catch the wheel, which was about four feet in diameter, and turn it and the wire would jump off. Then we went home. You were paid for only the time you worked, too. Later, when I worked for Bethlehem, we didn't go to work on a job when it was storming. But like I said, just the wind is all that stopped us with Roebling. They wanted that cable in. They got it under their time limit, too.[12]

Roebling give us a big compliment after that. They told us we were the best bunch of ironworkers, and that they put more wire in every day than on any other jobs they'd ever worked. So we had a feather in our cap there. They give us a party up at Paradise Cove, too, that was a doozer. They took us up there by boat. There was all you could eat and all you could drink. They had barbecued steaks. Everything was really good. All the big shots were there, but there was very little speeches. There was no hanky-panky, either; it was just a party. When it was all over, they brought us back on the boat. There was no bonus. Instead, they give us that party and everybody was happy. I guess a lot of 'em had never seen anything like that. It was the first party I'd ever seen like that, so I was quite impressed with it.[13]

After my Roebling cable job is when I went to work for Bethlehem. First I worked down on the pier, on the bottom of the bridge where they had a dock built right there where the caisson was. Bethlehem used to bring the steel for the bridge roadway over from Alameda on a barge. It had come by ship for Bethlehem from Pennsylvania. It was all fabricated there and off-loaded in Alameda at the yard there. However rotation this iron

Workers using a cable squeezing machine, Golden Gate Bridge, 1936. After spinning was finished, the main cables were compressed into their final shape. Photo by Ted Huggins. Courtesy of California Historical Society, Huggins Collection, CHS. Huggins.041.

ROEBLING PARTY
GOLDEN GATE BRIDGE EMPLOYEES
MAY 23, 1936
PARADISE COVE, MARIN COUNTY

This is your invitation and pass for transportation from Pier 14 at 10:30 a. m. to Paradise Cove. Returning at 3:30 p. m. from Paradise Cove.

CELEBRATING COMPLETION OF
CABLE SPINNING

(Please bring this card with you)

Urban's invitation to the party thrown by the John A. Roebling's Sons Company for the Golden Gate Bridge's cable spinners on May 23, 1936. Fifty years later Urban still treasured his invitation to Roebling's Marin County event celebrating the completion of the company's cable spinning work. Courtesy of Labor Archives and Research Center, San Francisco State University.

went up [or order in which it was installed], they'd bring it out on those barges and then we'd off-load it. They had a crane set up. They'd take this iron up onto the bridge deck and they'd start erecting the roadway out from there. There would be five hundred ton of steel on that barge when it come in. We'd unload a lot of it on the dock. They had a ten-part line and with all that cable going through all the blocks they needed, it would take quite a while to get the steel up onto the deck.[14]

I did get hurt down there. They needed a big block of steel. It probably weighed a thousand pounds or more. They unloaded it off the barge and set it down on the dock. They had a four-inch pin on the end of the block where they put on the eye of the cable. There was a handle on there to pull the pin out with. I was doing the tag lining of all the steel that was going up so it wouldn't spin in the wind and get the cable tangled up.[15] I had to keep tension on it so that the piece of iron would go straight.

I was on top of one of those floor beams, which are about twelve feet high. I was standing there so I could see what was going on. This fellow didn't notice that the handle on the pin was rusted out where the threads were. He put the tag line in this handle. When the iron started to turn, I give the line a pull. The handle broke. When I fell, I gave myself a flip with my foot. The dock was planked over, but steel beams were sticking up two or three inches above the plank. I hit the beams right on my face and on my feet. I mashed my nose and broke it. My wrists were so sore from where I had protected myself. One toe got about four times bigger than normal. They put me in the hospital for I don't know how many weeks.

When I come back to work they put me up on top on the deck. Now I started punkin'—that's what they called it—rivets and bolts out to the riveting crews. We had carts that run on the beams that run longways with the bridge. The carts were four-wheelers just like on a regular railroad. We'd load 'em with bolts and rivets and push 'em out there as far as we could go. Then we'd off-load 'em and distribute 'em to the construction points. Sometimes there was a thousand rivets or more at one point.

We'd also get coal for the rivet forges, help the crew with moving the scaffold, and so on. They had the net in there then and we went out in it. The apprentices and the riveting crews would get careless and drop four-by-fours down there and boards and what have you. So they'd tell us to go down in the net and get those things cleaned out. Some of 'em would go sliding down a beam. Most of us just jumped off and into the net. It was just like walking on a trampoline. You was bouncing up and down. We'd pick up all the stuff and have a guy with a rope pull us up and get us back on top.

There was a lot of things going on. There were make-up bolts that were used to put the iron together and hold it in place. We'd pick up those bolts and they'd use them again unless the threads were all messed up. Once in a while we'd drop a few on the Japanese merchant ships when they'd come through because the longshoremen said, "All the scrap iron we're selling to Japan is going to come back in bullets."[16] We give 'em some they wouldn't have to take to their dock. Those bolts and burnt rivets and so on would hit that boat down there like a machine gun. Pretty soon the Coast Guard would be out and they'd say, "Don't drop things anymore on those Japanese ships."

I was working the day Kermit Moore was killed, October 21, 1936. We weren't too far apart when this happened. I was on the San Francisco side and Kermit was working on the Marin side. I looked up and here this boom, instead of being up, was laying on the deck. A bunch of guys were ganged up there. You knew something had happened. When the boom come down it hit Kermit, sheared his face off, and killed him instantly.

We called it a day and took off. That seemed to be the habit of the ironworkers. In the woods, it was different. They never stopped there. They killed too many. Kermit was about my age. He was a nice, easygoing, well-mannered fellow. I used to see him at the union hall and talk to him. I especially liked him and I was shook up when it happened. That was the first one as an ironworker that it happened to.

In February 1937 I was looking for new work. They were pouring concrete on the bridge roadway out toward midspan. I was out there just a day before a platform collapsed and tore the safety net from midspan clear back to the San Francisco tower. Fred Dummatzen said, "Why don't you come down here? There's no work for the apprentices, but you might as well come out here and work as a laborer." I says, "No, Al Maillioux don't like the scaffold you've got there and I don't trust it either." Then the next day, that's when it happened. There was ten men killed in that deal.[17]

When we got through on the Golden Gate Bridge there was about thirty apprentices. Maybe six or eight months after the bridge was completed, I was the only apprentice out of the whole bunch that had a paid-up union card. I managed to get work on the painters' little walkways that are around the bridge's tower. We put that railing in up around the top and around the light that's up on that beacon light up there. We worked out there for several months on that. That's the last of the jobs that I worked on the Golden Gate Bridge.

When I was working on the bridge, I used to go to union meetings quite a bit, but I mostly listened. That way, you find out what people are thinking. One time, though, we had a guy come from the Ironworkers International. He was talking about unionism and sticking together. Then the next damn thing he says is, "We got to fight this CIO with all of our might. We got to get 'em beat." And I got up and said, "Well, you just said the opposite a minute ago. I think you're wrong. Labor shouldn't be fighting labor." They asked him a bunch of questions, but he went on the same. I thought that they should of got together like they did later and go that way.[18]

We didn't socialize much, but we did get in the Labor Day parades. We marched up Market Street in San Francisco and acted liked respectable people. We didn't cause any trouble or anything. I did ride in a carpool with one guy, George Buttner. We called him Chew Tobacco George because he always had a pouch out to here. He was from Texas and he used to be a boxer. I knew his family and his kids and I used to go over to his house. When George got hurt, I helped his wife out. I split wood for her and did different things that she had to have done that George was in the middle of when he got hurt. He was in the hospital for quite a while.[19]

When it came to the paint color for the bridge, most of the guys didn't care. With the Bay Bridge, they had it silvery color. I guess it still is. I didn't pay any attention to it. Is it still the same color?

After my main Golden Gate Bridge work, I went down to the hall and waited for some job to come along. Finally I was sent down to the Federal Building in San Francisco to work as a finisher doing ornamental work. I was there for about six months from the latter part of 1937 on. I liked that type of work, too. They had a federal inspector there. One day he told us, "I want this molding put around these windows." Here I was still an apprentice and we were cutting miters. The federal inspector looked at some of the miters where these moldings fit in there and he says to the ironworkers, "Come here. See how this apprentice cuts 'em and how he fits 'em. That's the way I want 'em done." Well, boy, that was a big feather in my cap. I learned a lot from that federal inspector. I admired the man. He wanted stuff done right and he got it done right before he got through with it.

I put up rolling doors for one company for four years until World War II started. I used to go to Fresno, Bakersfield, Stockton, and Sacramento for them. I went over to the Alameda Air Station, too. Those weren't rolling doors. They had metal roll-up doors at the naval supply base. I was there about six or eight months. During the war I worked in the shipyards as a sheet-metal man doing the shelving on destroyer escorts. I had to join the sheet-metal workers' union then.[20] I kept that card for a long time, but I never did go back to sheet-metal work.

Later there was more money in ironwork, where the wages kept going up. So I went back to that. At the tail end of the war I quit the shipyards and moved up to Redding, California. I did quite a bit of work on ventilation for air-conditioning there. I worked on gas stations and utility buildings. I've also worked on railroad bridges and high-rise buildings and done a lot of rod work, or reinforcing bar work, too, in my time. There is some of 'em stick to one thing. A lot of 'em won't even do any rod work. But I wasn't afraid of it. Once when I was in San Francisco they were looking for rod men. We were sitting there playing cards. I said, "What's this rod work?" They called it rat trapping. "Oh," they said, "you don't want to do that. Stick to the structural and ornamental work." I says, "I tell you what. You know what I'm going to do? I'm going to try it. It's the same union. You're paying dues anyway. I might as well get some benefit out of it." I went out and run into a man I knew who I'd worked for doing structural. He said, "I'll give you a chance. You can try it for a day or two." I worked for him for six or eight months.

I did rod work for two generators on the Shasta Dam and for the tunnels on a Trinity County job. But after twenty-one years there was no more work in Redding. So I came back to San Francisco to work at Bay Salt. I worked for them my last seven, eight, maybe nine years steady. For forty-two years I kept my dues paid in the ironworkers' union. Since I became a fifty-year member in 1985, I don't have to pay any more dues. I retired in 1977 when I was sixty-seven.

One time when I was working for Bay Salt, this young guy named Bill comes out, whiskers and hair hanging way down to here. His first day he says, "This is my first day as a journeyman." I looked at him and I says, "Well, I'll tell you, Bill, why don't you go home and get a haircut and a shave and look like a journeyman?" Now, I voted Democratic pretty near all the time, but I voted for Hayakawa in 1976. Then he slept in office for six years. He was the first Republican I voted for. I don't know why I voted for him. I just knew of him and what he did and what he stood for, so I voted for him.[21]

In May 1937, when the Golden Gate Bridge opened and they celebrated, I was there. I felt proud that I'd got to work on that bridge. It's beautifully built and beautifully designed. I thought it was an honor to be able to work on something like that.

Fred Brusati

ELECTRICIAN

We called the Coast Guard right away. They came out in a matter of minutes. We could see these men out there trying to stay up in the water. . . . But heck, they had spud wrenches and everything else on 'em. They tried to stay up, but they just couldn't do it.　　　　**FRED BRUSATI**

Fred Brusati was born in 1911, the son of Italian immigrants who settled north of San Francisco in San Rafael, Marin County. He became an electrician in nearby Kentfield, California, during the early years of the Great Depression. In late 1934 Brusati took a job working at his trade on the Golden Gate Bridge. He served there during the cable spinning process, completed between 1935 and 1936, and remained employed on the bridge into early 1937. Brusati remained a working electrician for many years. I interviewed him in San Rafael on April 28, 1987.

■　■　■

Angelo Brusati was my father's name. His brother came to Butte, Montana, from Italy and sent money back home so my father could come to America. In 1911 and 1912, my dad worked in the Butte copper mines. They'd be drilling holes and there'd be lots of dust. Half the people he knew back there died from miner's consumption. But my dad's other brother went to San Rafael in Marin County. He said, "You better come here because Montana's very cold and those copper mines aren't the healthiest place to work."

So my dad came to San Rafael in the beginning of 1912. He had gone back to Italy briefly in 1910; met my mother, Irene; and they'd married and come back to America. She was from Turin. My father was born near Milano. He went into the drayage business in Marin County and stayed until he retired. He had a team of horses and a big wagon. They'd haul stuff like furniture around the town.[1]

I was born in Butte in 1911, but I was raised in the Woodland Avenue part of San Rafael. There were a lot of Italians and they congregated in the same area. They all used to make their own wine in the fall. You'd almost get drunk from the fumes of the fermenting wine just walking through the area.

The roads then were all rock and gravel, and there were big ditches. Sometimes in the evening we would build a bonfire in the ditch and throw some potatoes in there, right in the street. We always spoke Italian at home. When we'd get among our friends, who were the younger people, we'd speak English. We learned it at school.

My mother passed away when I was fifteen and a half. After my sister got married, my father, my brother, and I bached together. By then my father was a cook. He made minestrone soup and cooked tripe and pig's feet. We belonged to Saint Raphael Church uptown. I made my first communion and my confirmation there.

I used to have a paper route where I sold a pictorial review magazine to make some money. And I cut grass for different people. I went to E Street Grammar School up on Fourth Street. In 1927 I came to San Rafael High School. I went a year. It didn't seem like I was learning anything, so I quit.

Then I painted cars for six months. Those were the days that paint and varnish were going out and lacquer was coming in. We used to use flaxseed and lye and put it on the car. Then you'd sandpaper with gasoline all day long to get down almost to bare metal. A lot of cars and trucks came in. We were painting army trucks and we had to use lead oil. We didn't know it at the time, but that's not supposed to be very safe for you. I lost fifteen pounds on that job, I guess just from the hard work.

When I quit there, I asked Gus Hines, an electrical contractor uptown, if he had a job or knew anybody that needed a boy. One day a man called me up from Tamalpais Electric and says, "Would you like to go to work for me boring holes?" I said, "For how long?" He says, "Two weeks." So I went there and stayed for four years and learned the electrician's trade with 'em. That was in Kentfield in Marin County near San Rafael.

I decided to go to Heald engineering school in San Francisco at night. I didn't have a car, so I would take my bicycle to work and get the twenty-six-minutes-to-six train out of San Rafael to go to Heald's. There used to be a train that would go to Sausalito more or less where Highway 101 is located now. Then I'd take a boat to get to school in San Francisco around seven.

We got out of school about nine o'clock and I'd go like anything to get a streetcar to make the nine-fifteen boat back to Sausalito. I would get home a little after ten o'clock. The next night I would study and the night after that I would go back to school. I done that for two and a half years.

What I took up at Heald's was motor winding and electrical theory, but I found out that winding motors wasn't paying as good as being an inside electrician, so I stayed an inside electrician. I remained with Tamalpais Electric until 1930, when work was really getting scarce because of the Depression. I decided to go contracting. I got a contractor's license and did that for about a year and a half. Then in 1932 Hamilton Air Force Base started up near Novato, which is also in Marin County. I went up there looking for a job because even at contracting it wasn't easy to get any work.

I used to go out to Hamilton every day. I kept pestering the same company there—Ben and Taylor, an electrical contractor from Los Angeles—for a job. One day a guy says, "You know, I'm getting tired of seeing you here. How about coming to work tomorrow?" I says, "Okay." So I went to work at Hamilton. I was there for about a year and a half working on underground distribution, landing lights for airplanes, and the beacon on top of the water tower.

When that job ended it was 1934. I'd heard that they were going to start work on the Golden Gate Bridge. The John A. Roebling's Sons Company was hired to install the bridge's two main cables, which it made out of spun wire. The company was putting up a building at California City a little north of Sausalito. The engineer that was at Hamilton happened also to be the electrical engineer for Roebling. He says, "Yeah, come to work tomorrow."

At the California City plant, we were wiring the building, putting on the motors, and then the lighting on the inside. California City was a twenty-four-hours-a-day operation. They had to work three shifts to keep the wire going for the bridge cable.[2] I was there about three or four weeks and the electrical engineer said, "Would you like to go to work on the bridge?" This was around the end of 1934. I says, "I'll try it. I've never been up 746 feet, but I'll try it anyhow."

My first day I got on the Marin-side tower.[3] I was a little scared because I had never been up there. You had to go up a ladder on the outside. Then you crawled across these I-beams. I figured, "Boy, if anything happens, I'm a goner." But everything was all right. I was a little scared for a couple of weeks there, but then I got used to it. So it never really bothered me after that.

That first day there was myself and maybe three or four other electricians. The boss picked me out. He says, "Take these wires up inside the tower." That was at the Marin tower on the side towards the ocean. So me and a few other electricians scattered all up and down inside the tower with flashlights. We got to the top and there was no way to get out. I relayed the message down to the boss. He says, "Tie 'em off and come on down." It was almost two o'clock in the afternoon by the time I got down.

The boss says, "Tomorrow you and Chapman"—Chapman was my apprentice—"go up on the side towards the bay, get over on the other side, and see if there's any way to get out from the top on the side towards the ocean." The next morning we climbed up inside the tower, got about twenty or thirty feet from the top, stepped across the elevator, and saw a door to get out. So we got out there on a little landing. Then we climbed up on this straight iron ladder with rungs up to the top.

Next Chapman and I crawled across the top of the tower to get over to the side toward the ocean. We looked around and there was no hole to get out. So we crawled all the way back, got all the way back downstairs, and told the boss there was no hole. He says, "Well, tomorrow morning go up, get those wires down on the side towards the ocean, and take 'em over and put 'em on the side towards the bay." It took us three or four days to get those wires up there.

We were putting in the control wires for the Chicago boom up on top. A Chicago boom is like a big whirley boom.[4] There was a hundred-horsepower motor down at the base of the tower. We had to make sure that there was control wires so this guy running the engine would know what to do. We also put up the wires for the lights for airplanes. These were red lights up on top of the tower.

Later there was eleven or twelve electricians on the Marin side and twelve or thirteen in San Francisco. We put temporary lighting up through the tower to light the way so you could climb up and down. Then they decided to put up an outside elevator. We had to wire the motor for that and for all the signals up and down on the outside.

Another job that I done there once was on this five hundred pounds of circular mill wire that went from the bottom of the tower up to the top to run equipment. San Francisco had pulled some of the wires up. Whoever made the splices didn't make them good. All the cables fell down inside the tower. So Charlie Hackenberg, our foreman, says, "Fred, make the splices on these wires." It bothered me because I knew they had dropped 'em in San Francisco and if I made a bum splice, then I might get my walking papers.

The day in August 1935 when they laid the first wire across the Gate to make the bridge's cables I was watching 'em. They put this great big reel of wire on a barge and towed it across to the San Francisco side. They had shortwave radio and flags to signal with in case anything was happening. They pulled the wire up and anchored it off the top of the towers. When they were doing that, they had to stop all the ships. Nobody could cross there, see.[5]

After that was when they started to build a catwalk up on top of the Marin and the San Francisco towers because there was no other way to get out to the middle.[6] Of course, there was no handrails or nothing else to protect you.

For the spinning of the cable, Roebling started with just one spinning wheel on each side of the bridge. In other words, each catwalk had one wheel and, of course, the Marin wire was anchored at the Marin anchor block.[7] From there it would go to midspan. At midspan, they took the wire that came from San Francisco. Marin would take the San Francisco wire back to Marin. And San Francisco would take the Marin wire and go back to the San Francisco block. The wire was just going back and forth all the time until the cables got made.

I was an electrician when they were spinning the cable. The spinning was controlled by one man at midspan. There was a little shack there at midspan where the control room was. After the catwalk got built, we had to run control wires. We had 440-volt power wires on one side of each catwalk. Then as the spinning wheel was coming and you saw that something was going to happen that would cause injury or breakdown, you'd just push a button and stop all the operation of the spinning.

We had telephones all along the catwalks. You'd call up to midspan and tell 'em what was the matter. When it got repaired, you'd call 'em back and the guy there would start the operation. Nowadays [1987] they have a lot of different controls to tell where the spinning wheel is. But not in those days.

One day after they got the catwalk built on the backspan, the boss says come on down and see if you can get some temporary wires down there.[8] The catwalk wasn't latched down or anything. The wind came up and started to bounce the catwalk all over. I had a safety belt on and I just tied it on to the steel cables that were coming down to hold the catwalk. I said, "Well, if the thing flips over, I might be hanging up there, but I'll still be there." Nothing happened, so I was glad.[9]

But the day in February 1937 that the safety net broke, the scaffold went down, and ten men died, I was working on the catwalk right there about midspan. This was near where the net broke. Somebody said, "The catwalk is falling." So I jumped up on the big cable. The cable is down real low there. Then somebody says, "No, the net broke." So I jumped back down on the catwalk, walked out on the road, and looked down. You could see the net down below you. It was gone all right.

We called the Coast Guard right away. They came out in a matter of minutes. We could see these men out there trying to stay up in the water. The reason they didn't get crushed falling is that the net coming down broke the water. If they just jumped down, the water would be hard, but when something else was ahead of 'em and broke the water, it saved 'em. But heck, they had spud wrenches and everything else on 'em. They tried to stay up, but they just couldn't do it.

In a matter of minutes, too, some men were way out by the lighthouse that's out there in the ocean on the San Francisco side. The Coast Guard, though, did come out in nothing flat. I think they saved two men.[10]

There was a space on the bridge where the road hadn't been poured yet with concrete. There was some man hanging on to the steel. Me and three or four other men lowered a rope down and pulled him up. The

Catwalks under construction, 1935. One windy day Fred Brusati feared that the catwalk he was on might flip over, but he was wearing a safety belt and thought he would survive. Photo by Ted Huggins. Courtesy of California Historical Society, Huggins Collection, CHS.Huggins.033.

man had a pipe in his mouth! He didn't drop the pipe or nothing. He just started walking towards San Francisco. I never did see him back there again. His name was Tom Casey. I guess I would have done the same thing if I were that close to getting killed.[11]

The next day they came out there with a big floating crane and pulled up the net. A lot of men who died had been caught in it.

A different morning when we came to work we were up on top of the Marin tower and we could see an ambulance. We'd seen 'em throw a white sheet over something. There was a man that went there after hours to grease his bulldozer. It was his own rig. A blade had come down and killed him. But they didn't consider that as an accident on the bridge because this incident occurred at night and off of the bridge. But we knew that it happened.

Another day I was working on the Marin backspan. There was an engine with five or six gondola cars loaded with concrete. They was coming down to pour the bridge roadway.[12] Pretty soon I seen the engineer jump out. The engine and the gondolas landed into the anchor block [the concrete block into which the cable eyebars are embedded]. All the gondolas got smashed. The day before there was fifteen or twenty carpenters working near there. That day, though, there was nobody working, so nobody got hurt. All that went down was the engine and the gondolas.

See, there's quite an incline there. You can't tell it when you're driving on it, but from midspan to Marin it's a little hill-like. It was really foggy and wet that morning and the cars were all loaded with cement. There was a lot of weight and the engineer couldn't hold it with the brakes. They were pouring sand on the rails, but the wheels just slipped and wouldn't stop. So the engineer saved himself by jumping out.[13]

When I was working on the bridge, we worked five days a week for eight hours a day. There were no work breaks. You went to work at eight o'clock and you'd work until twelve and stop a half hour for lunch. When I first started there, I used to take five lunch sandwiches. It got so I couldn't eat 'em in a half hour, so I had to cut down to eating three.

Sometimes at lunchtime we would get a thousand-watt lamp and bring a little wire out there. A switch could go on and then we'd cook hot dogs. You put the wires in each end. I think the electricians figured that out on the bridge.

About four-fifteen in the afternoon everybody would start coming down. It would take better than a half-hour to climb up in the morning, but climbing down you could do in fifteen minutes.

We got nine dollars a day. At least that's what the electricians got. They tell me the steelworkers got around eleven dollars a day. At nine dollars a day you got along all right.

I used to get up around six or six-fifteen in the morning, have breakfast, and then walk uptown around where Lincoln Avenue in San Rafael is now. A carpenter named George Solovini used to pick me up there and we'd ride down toward the bridge in a little Model A Ford. We'd check in with the timekeeper, get on the bridge, and go to work.

One thing that Roebling was very strict on was if you were caught on the catwalks without a hard hat on or without your safety belt on, they'd fire you. And if they caught you smoking on the catwalk, they'd fire you. They tell me this was because one time they had a fire on one of these catwalks back in New York someplace and they had to take some of the cable down that they had formed. The heat had knocked the temper off the steel.

The partially completed Golden Gate Bridge in the fog, October 10, 1936. Brusati described working in cold, foggy conditions on the bridge. Photo by Clyde Sunderland. Courtesy of Labor Archives and Research Center, San Francisco State University. Copyright Quantum Spatial, Inc., KY.

What bothered me the most about the job was that in San Rafael it would be seventy or eighty degrees and sometimes on the bridge it was real cold. What I used to wear on the bridge was 76 percent woolen underwear. I couldn't come home and change for fear that I would catch a cold. So I used to have to wear the woolen underwear in summer around San Rafael because some of the coldest weather on the bridge is in June, July, and August when the fog is there.

Some days when you were working up on top you were above the fog. You could see all over and it looked real pretty like there was a blanket of snow up there. Of course, some days it wasn't pretty. Then sometimes when it was clear it was hotter than blazes up on top. You'd get down to the bottom and you'd be almost freezing.

One day a friend who worked with me had a box camera. His name was Leonard Muller. He brought the camera up and took a picture of me on the cable. We also took pictures of the surrounding area. Of course, they were all black and white.[14] I don't think they had any rules about cameras, but you couldn't have a camera and flip pictures all day long, either, because you had a job to do.

On a real windy day you could put a few pieces of newspaper under your coat and on your chest so you wouldn't catch a cold. I done that a couple of times.

A few times when it was really windy you could feel the motion of the bridge swaying. I'd get home and I felt like I had been on a boat all day. Even the catwalks swayed. Another thing that you used to see was the expansion and contraction of the bridge. In the morning after part of the groups of cable were built, the ones towards the bay were low down. In the afternoon, the ones towards the ocean were low down and the ones towards the bay would be higher up.

One extra-cold morning we went to work and heck, all the water lines were frozen. They sent everybody home but the electricians because we were more or less the firemen on the bridge in case of a fire. So we stayed all day, but we didn't actually do any work since there was icicles that were dropping that were up to four or five feet.

Roebling issued us rubber raincoat, pants, jackets, and hard hats. We used to tie a string around our arms and on the bottoms of our legs, whether it was raining or not. If it was real cold, that was one way to keep warm. I used to wear tan pants and tan shirts. I'd wear a jacket that was like a windbreaker of some kind. I also wore heavy dark brown overalls. They called 'em iron pants. The steelworkers all wore 'em. The rain gear would be on top of all that. On warm days you'd take stuff off, but I always wore overalls to store my tools because if you dropped 'em, it's good-bye.

I had ordinary seven-inch work shoes. I guess they would be considered like a short boot. They had composition rubber

Brusati sitting on one of the bridge's main cables, Marin County to the north behind him, circa 1936. Brusati's friend and coworker Leonard Muller took this photo with a box camera. Courtesy of Labor Archives and Research Center, San Francisco State University.

Workers examining ice on the bridge. Brusati remembered icicles four to five feet long. Courtesy of San Francisco History Center, San Francisco Public Library.

and cord soles almost like a tire cord. That way you didn't slip as easy as with other kinds of soles.

Our hard hats were black. Bullard Company from Sausalito was the original one that made those hard hats. I still have mine from the bridge down in the basement. It has Bullard's name in it. Bullard still makes a lot of safety equipment.[15]

Around the same time I went to work on the bridge I joined Local 614 of the International Brotherhood of Electrical Workers [IBEW] in Marin County. Local 614 wanted to get four or five men onto the bridge project because we were out of work over in Marin County, where it was just as bad as in San Francisco.

Of course, once we got on the bridge, we would sometimes go over and help the San Francisco people. If Marin County needed extra help, they'd come over and help us. In other words, we all got along, but still the union locals had to try to get as many men on the bridge as possible or the business agent would hear about it.

When I joined Local 614 up in San Rafael at the end of 1934, there was only about seven or eight members. They had a drive to get more members in, so they lowered the initiation fee from fifty dollars down to twenty-five. In those days fifty dollars was a lot of money. When they dropped it down to twenty-five, seven or eight of us electricians went in at the same time. Sometimes at meetings if we wouldn't have enough men for a quorum, we couldn't hold meetings. This was because there was a lot of unemployment and there wasn't that many members.

One time IBEW Local 302 from Contra Costa County wanted us to go in with them. They wanted to get more members over in their local. We discussed it and voted for merging. Then we looked at our watches. It was after eleven o'clock at night and in the electricians' union anything that took place after eleven o'clock was illegal. So we didn't go over to Local 302.

During World War II, our local was at Marinship in Sausalito.[16] IBEW Local 6 of San Francisco wanted us to go with them then. That way, you'd have more power in negotiations. If you're just a small local, it isn't easy. So we went to Local 6 for a couple of years. After the war, IBEW Local 551 up in Santa Rosa wanted us to join with them. They were bigger than us. So we transferred from Local 6 to Local 551. I'm still a member of that local.[17]

In late 1934, though, I was happy to get into Local 614. When I was at Hamilton Air Force Base around 1932, '33, the unions weren't very strong. Work was very scarce then, too. But when we got on the bridge, you'd almost have to belong. You heard through the grapevine that a project like that was bound to be union. That's when I decided, *Well, I better join.*[18]

In those days, you were allowed to go out and look for your job. Where you'd see a job, you'd go in and ask if they needed anybody. Now it's different. Today [1987] in our union, IBEW Local 551, you have to go on the book, and whenever your turn comes up, they hire you. That was done so older members would get a chance to go to work. Otherwise the contractors would always want younger men. Being on the book gives everybody a chance.

In the 1930s, I went to union meetings, but I was not active in politics. I used to vote all the time, though. I always voted for Franklin Roosevelt, who I think was one of the best presidents we've ever had. Anytime he spoke, I would listen. It was just radio in those days. I don't think we even had television in '35.[19] Roosevelt done a lot for the workers. When Social Security came in as part of his New Deal in 1935, I was working on the bridge. I remember we had to sign papers that was supposed to help us when we got older.

I got married to my wife, Elvira, in 1935. We rented a little duplex. We tried to haggle the owner down to twenty dollars a month. He said, "Nothing doing." It was twenty-five dollars and we had to take it. We rented for two years. Then we bought the lot in San Rafael where we're still at and had a house built. I think I paid a thousand dollars for the lot.

When we got finished with the bridge, I went back over to California City. We overhauled all the electrical equipment there for John A. Roebling's Sons because the company was going up to Washington to build the Tacoma Narrows Bridge that later went down.[20] From there I went to work for Tamalpais Electric again doing residential or commercial buildings. I was working one time in 1937 and was up about seventeen feet when I got a shock. I fell and broke a heel. So I was laid up and couldn't get on the Golden Gate Bridge when they opened it that May.

When the war came along, there wasn't too much residential building going on. So when Marinship opened up in 1942 and started to build ships, the boss asked me if I would like to go there as general foreman of the electrical maintenance crew. I said yes. First Marinship built Liberty ships to carry cargo. From there they built tankers. We put up the power and the lighting for the welders and kept the gantry cranes going. As foreman I walked from ship to ship and paid 'em all a visit.

There was quite a few colored people at Marinship. One Chinese man and a couple of colored people worked for us in the electrical gang.[21] I don't remember seeing any minority members on the Golden Gate Bridge job, though. At Marinship we only hired one woman electrician in maintenance. Now, for wiring the ships they had quite a few women, but we only had the one. She was young and they said the only reason they had her there was to charge up the men.[22]

After the war ended they dismantled Marinship. Then I went to work for Cimino Electric Company in San Rafael and stayed with them for thirty-three years. We wired the library building at the San Francisco Theological Seminary, put in automatic switching for these radar balloons on Mount Tamalpais, and wired the library at the Dominican Convent in San Rafael. My last job before I retired at sixty-five was running the wiring for Radio Corporation of America up at Point Reyes for the big dishes where they get the stuff off of satellites. That was an interesting job because it was different.

But back in 1937, to me the Golden Gate Bridge was just another job. I didn't think of people ever having a celebration like they're having this year [1987]. When the Golden Gate Bridge District had some other celebrations, like for the starting and a few other times, I've always went there. But in the 1930s I didn't realize that there'd be so much going on over the bridge.

Today whenever I drive across the bridge I'm sure happy to have been one of the workers on it. I'm also happy that I had a job at that time because a lot of men weren't working. Younger people nowadays can't realize what a real depression is like. You didn't have welfare or anything. It was really tough.

One thing I'll say is that the bridge was special because earlier nearly everybody said that it couldn't be built. So after it got all built I said, "I guess everybody who figured this couldn't be built must have been wrong. It's all finished now and it's going to stay up." And it's been up there a couple of years now, you know!

Martin Adams

LABORER

I didn't learn how to do this; I just experienced it.   **MARTIN ADAMS**

Born in rural Arkansas in 1912 and raised in Ozark Mountains farm coun-
try, Martin Adams came to the Bay Area of Northern California in Novem-
ber 1934. He went to work on the San Francisco–Oakland Bay Bridge in
1935, where he was a laborer and a deep-sea diver's tender. Adams found
employment on the Golden Gate Bridge in fall 1936. He stayed on the job
there through the bridge's opening the following spring. Shortly after that,
he became a pile driver, a trade he plied until his retirement. I interviewed
Adams in Oakland on May 21, 1987.

■   ■   ■

Our family lived out in the country, right in the heart of the Ozarks. This
was twenty miles north of Fayetteville, Arkansas. It was beautiful country,
mostly all hardwood timber. We had different kinds of oaks, dogwood,
and redbud. The spring of the year it was beautiful with all kinds of wild
berries. I don't know where they have any better fruit for taste.

I was born on October 12, 1912, at Pea Ridge, Arkansas. That's where I
went to high school and lived until I was around twenty-one or twenty-
two years old. My parents were pretty much all American. My mother's

name was Lee, my father's Adams. There's some English and German in there. About Adams I know they were in the starting of Indiana when that was settled. So they've been in this country for a long time. One of my great-grandfathers was an Irishman. That's about as far back as I know.

My dad was a farmer. We raised hogs, corn, wheat, oats, berries, and apples. I had four brothers and four sisters. With that big family, we had to cover about everything that come along. We didn't have anything extra. We grew our own vegetables, had our own cattle and chickens, and canned our own fruit. There was very little that we bought, just salt and sugar. Overalls we bought, but mother and the girls all sewed their cotton dresses.

Dried apples was one of the big crops. We had a commercial apple dryer. Every year in season we put a lot of time into it. I grew up with that. I run automatic peelers when I had to stand on a box to reach 'em, I was that small. We had two power peelers. You could put fifty bushels of apples through a peeler and it would peel and core 'em. We had an automatic slicer that sliced 'em into rings. From there they were bleached with sodium. Then they went onto the floor of the dryer where we had wood furnaces. It would take twenty-four hours to dry them. We'd put 'em in burlap bags anywhere from fifty to a hundred pounds and sell 'em for shipment east. Usually we worked six days a week. We didn't peel on Sunday. The other six days we put in long shifts of ten or twelve hours. But this didn't last but a couple of months.

Our house set up on kind of a knoll. There was two streams run through the farm, so we had plenty of water. We was raised on water, swimming, fishing, and trapping. We would catch bass, suckers, and sun perch. I've done a lot of fur trapping. That's the way we made our pin money. I trapped skunks, opossums, muskrats, and raccoons. They was quite a few fox around, too. But deer had been killed out before that. We'd run our trap lines in the morning before school. Whenever we set traps, we tended them all the time. We didn't leave animals in 'em because that's the hard way [for animals to die].

The first school I went to was in a little country schoolhouse. You had the first eight grades there. I went to that for two and a half, maybe three years and found out we was going into the wrong school district. We had to go to a larger school, which was the high school in Pea Ridge. They had all twelve grades there and probably 100 to 150 students. That's where I finished high school. Up until the last two or three years we always walked to school. Then they started buses and we got to ride. Oh, we was doing good then.

When the Depression came in 1929 it did affect us quite a bit. There was just no money. It was really tough. But we done all of our work with mules and horses and we made 'most everything we had. We managed to live. We didn't have money to go anywhere else, but we got a high school education.

I got very little work off the farm except in apple harvest time. If I didn't work on the dryer at home I worked hauling apples. Just before I came out to California in November 1934 and got a chance to go to work on the Bay Bridge, I was hauling apples for a big orchard. I had a pair of mules and a flatbed wagon. I'd haul sixty-five bushels per load and I was taking around eleven loads in ten hours. That was for a dollar a day, ten cents an hour. And there was a lot of people who wanted your job. If you didn't make it, why, they were there to do it. That's a dollar a day, six dollars a week, for sixty hours of work.[1]

About this time a young fellow who married my oldest sister got a job working for Bates & Rogers, a construction company out of Chicago. They traveled through the country on different jobs—bridges, tunnels, railroad work. That company got the contract for the deck job on the Bay Bridge. He and my sister were coming out to California and they asked me if I wanted to come. Well, I was twenty-two years old. I was adventurous. I'd get a chance to work on the bridge with better money. Sure I wanted to come! They started at 68¾ cents an hour. That was the cheapest wage the state would let 'em pay, and I was pretty well assured of a job if I could hold out long enough for my brother-in-law to get me hired.

I was out in the Bay Area three or four months before a job opened. Before that happened I worked a few days here and there unloading coal in the West Oakland yards or anything I could do. It didn't amount to much. My brother-in-law and my sister had to pretty well finance me until I went to work on the bridge. I put in applications over at American Can, Judson Steel, and all those places. But the bridge job opened up before I got a call on any of the others. This was a good working climate, too. When the company left, I stayed right here.

My first day on the Bay Bridge we got in some carloads of lumber. I'd say it was February or March in '35. They were getting ready for concrete form work. I did just labor work, unloading lumber and cleaning out cars. Then we got cement for the bridge. I got the job of unloading cement. A whole boxcar would be loaded with about six hundred barrels of it. I got to where I could unload a car in half a day.

A little later the engineer that was operating the batching plant moved up into the office.[2] I moved into his job. There I had a good job that was all push-button. It was all automatic—the conveyor belt, setting the scales, the whole works. You opened these hoppers and added so much dry cement, fine sand, rough sand, and small gravel. It all went in by weight. My brother-in-law showed me how to operate the system. Operating that batching plant for the deck on the Bay Bridge was one of the main jobs I done. I did that just about to the finish of the bridge.[3]

There were times, two or three months at a stretch, when we would get caught up [i.e., the decking crew would catch up with other operations and have to stop work]. Then we'd slip over and go to work for American Bridge Company. Those times I worked out in Alameda loading the steel for the Bay Bridge. The steel was shipped to Alameda and stored. We had to take it out and load it on flatcars. Then we'd wheel the cars onto barges using a steam locomotive. They'd send the steel to the bridge, where cranes picked it off. Each piece as needed was right there in place. We set it out that way.

We loaded the steel with cables and a crane. You put two slings around each end of the steel. We loaded the big hydraulic jacks used on the cantilever span of the Bay Bridge when that was put together. I didn't learn how to do this; I just experienced it. You done about everything on the farm, and I was mechanical.

Actually, I was working as an ironworker in Alameda when we were loading this steel, going out in the yard and finding the right piece. When you had a bargeload you knew exactly how many pieces were going to go. The last piece they wanted you put in first on the barge.

I also went to work under the cantilever span of the Bay Bridge. We drove pilings in the water and capped those pilings off. We had to put falsework in there and build it up so they could erect the bridge on it.[4] When they got it all built we had to go back in there and tear all that falsework out. We pulled all those pilings out of the water, too. I loved that work. Since I'd been raised around water, I liked working near it.

They used a derrick barge in pulling the piles out.[5] Then we had to raft the piles in to shore because we couldn't let 'em get out in the ship lanes. They were sixty to eighty feet long. You'd throw a cable across each one and you'd pull 'em together and staple 'em. But you had to stay on those wet, slick pilings because if you went down between 'em and they come together, they'd crush your foot off. You only made two or three slips and they'd fire you. They made you safe. We had a general foreman they called the Mad Bull. He was usually up on the bridge. But if you made a slip, someway or another he always saw it. I slipped through once and he hollered, "Get that damn foot out of there." You could hear him holler from here to the bridge. He wanted the work kept going because an injury would hold the job up. But he was a pretty nice guy at that.

Another thing I liked around water was to work tending divers. I wanted to go down as a diver, but our job wasn't quite long enough or I'd have had it made. You could make five dollars an hour as a diver, but you'd only work a couple or three hours a day. You couldn't stay down too long.[6] In tending you had ropes and you sent down anything the diver needed, like these wrenches, those bolts, or this drill. You was hooked up to him with a telephone and he'd tell you what he wanted.

For the first little while on the Bay Bridge our day was six hours because they was putting as many men as they could to work. Then we went to the eight-hour day, which was from eight to four-thirty. You had thirty minutes for lunch. Sometimes they double-shifted if they needed work to get done faster. When we were working out on that pile work, we were double-shifting. We'd go to work at six in the morning and work until twelve. Another crew would come on and work from twelve until six. Then that same crew would come back the next morning at six and work until twelve. They'd work two shifts together that way. When we came on at twelve and worked until six, we'd come right back the next morning, doing the same thing. We worked the six hours and that was it. There was no lunch break then, no coffee breaks, nothing like that. We'd work right straight through.

When I started out I wasn't in any union. They organized one in 1936 while I was on the Bay Bridge. This was the Laborers in San Francisco, Local 261.[7] Bates & Rogers was an organized company back in Chicago. When the union come after 'em out here, San Francisco was going union pretty strong. The longshoremen on all the docks were well organized. That's when they were spreading unionization in all the construction industry and everything like that. Actually, they organized more through the company than they did with the workers because the firm was already a union company. They blanketed us all into the union. We just went down and paid ten dollars and we were in the union.[8]

Getting a union was good because a lot of the time we'd go out to work at eight and work for an hour and they'd say, "We don't have a thing to do. Go." With the union they had to pay you for at least two hours if they sent you home. And they couldn't work you and then leave you stopped and then go back to work again. Either you got a half day's or a day's pay that way.

When the union first came in, our wages didn't change. General labor was seventy-five cents an hour. But the union also seen that you got the amount of pay and the hours that were right and you weren't abused. You got an honest day's pay for an honest day's work. And if personalities got into things and they fired a man without cause, the union would stand up to that, which was very good.

Before I went into the union, I worked all these different jobs. You could work at any of 'em. The union was not strong at that time. Then when we went into the union you stayed within your jurisdiction. I took that because I could make more money than I could at the other jobs. Like with the ironworkers, you'd work for a while and your job finished. It could take you a long time to get another job. It was the same under the pile drivers and the carpenters. And it was awfully hard to get those jobs. With the Laborers' union, you could get them very easy. We'd work steady. After a year or two, I went on to labor foreman and then I could follow from job to job. That way I never had any problems getting work.

With the construction companies going union, they got something, too. They could call the union for men 'cause the unions always had a good apprentice program. They'd get qualified workers that way. Before a fellow would come out and say, "I'm a carpenter," but I seen 'em come out and they couldn't even drive a nail. But this way, if a worker wasn't knowing enough, the union put him through the apprentice program and trained him. The companies liked that because they was getting qualified workers. They could get the job done right and, that way, for a cheaper price.

When we finished the Bay Bridge job, and I was right down to the very last, I done night-watching on the San Francisco waterfront. That's when they had that waterfront strike in '36. This was just as the bridge was finished.[9] The company had its plant and lumber yard set up on Beale Street near the piers. The longshoremen was coming around there and I never saw a bunch of nicer fellows. They wanted this lumber. Everything we had that we wanted to get rid of they'd take. They figured they was going to be tied up for the winter and they wanted firewood. They had barrels they'd build a fire in to keep warm at night because they picketed round the clock. But I had no trouble with 'em.

Sometimes it'd raise your hair. You would go into those shacks and you'd hear somebody come in on you in the night. All you had was a flashlight. It would make you wonder because they would be kind of in a gang and you was by yourself. One time I heard a noise at the other end of the yard. I looked to see what it was and it was about ten of 'em. They had a whole big roof section off of one of the houses and they were carrying it off. I got up my nerve and says, "Fellows, I can't let you do that." They said, "We thought maybe you was going to throw it away," and they carried it right back and put it where it was. They were nice and we sat and talked. They were just a bunch of working people going for a little more when the company's taken advantage of them. I told 'em, "Anything I can get for you, I'll get."

In November the bridge opened and we was gone. The company sold the finishing machines we used to finish the deck on the Bay Bridge to Pacific Bridge Company on the Gate.[10] A bunch of us guys moved right over with the machines. Pacific Bridge gave us a job. We'd been on this bridge, why not on that one? So we went right over there, signed up, and went back to work doing the same things.

There was seven or eight of us that went over there. I knew the two finishing-machine operators. The whole crew of us helped them tear the machines down and put 'em together again on the Gate Bridge. We had small-gauge railroads on the bridge and we'd haul out the parts and then put everything together. The machines vibrated and leveled the deck. A machine covered two lanes of traffic. They were quite an intricate deal and they were heavy. I had a thumb split wide open by one. We was changing something around one time, and it was more weight than I could handle. It took my hand down in with it 'cause I wasn't going to drop it. We bound my thumb up and I went right on back to work. It was just part of the job.

I got a lot of different experience with the finishing-machine crew.

I was still a laborer, but I could do any of that work. And then we done about everything on the Gate Bridge, from moving lumber to moving track to the stripping of forms. When they were putting forms in, we'd get 'em all ready and lay 'em out. We done all of that. That was labor to keep the construction crews going.

I was working with the ironworkers moving these hanging scaffolds used for stripping forms when the February 1937 accident occurred and ten people were killed. They designed these big scissors hooks to hold the movable scaffolds. The hooks were hung to the bottom flange of the bridge's beams. They had wheels on the bottom of these big hooks and they just rolled the scaffolds right through them.[11] To put weight in there, you'd draw the hooks tight and bolt 'em up. That was one of the main causes of accidents. We didn't have enough bolts for all of the hooks. When that scaffold fell, the hooks had opened up. There was nothing to hold the scaffold.[12]

We'd worked there for two days, starting on Monday morning. Our crew would move one scaffold while the stripping crew would use another scaffold to strip and get the lumber out. Any extra time we had, we helped strip. But they wanted to really get going. So Wednesday, the day of the accident, they sent a second crew out to move scaffolds. That crew was brand new.

At nine o'clock my crew was working on our scaffold. I crawled a beam over to the new crew and talked to those guys for a few minutes. We were all friends. I was over talking to all of 'em for three, four, or five minutes. Slim Lambert had worked for a long time before in our crew. We were buddies. He'd been made their foreman. I'd left my coat hanging on their scaffold. We'd worked that one from six until about eight, just before they came, and then moved. I got my coat and crawled back across the beam and went onto our scaffold. Ten minutes later it happened. The new crew started to move their scaffold. That's when it went down. It was nine-twenty in the morning.

I was on the back corner of our scaffold. There was so much noise you couldn't tell what was going on. I looked down over the edge of our scaffold. Their scaffold was going down to the water. The safety net was coming down on up the line. The net was good and solid. I know because I went down in there. You'd walk around in it and it was safe. But the scaffold tore it loose at the center.

I raised my head and looked around. There was two fellows hanging there by their fingers on the flange of the beams underneath the bridge. One of 'em hollered, "For God's sake, get a rope!" Our foreman, T-Bone, and I hit for this ladder right quick where you could go up onto the deck. I don't know what the foreman's name was, but we called him T-Bone. I got there a little before he did. I went up the ladder, he followed, and then here come the whole crew up.

There was some other fellows on the deck, too. I heard one of the electricians talking about how they grabbed an electrical cord in order to slip down and put it around the guys' legs. But there was a big rope, oh, about inch and a half rope, laying there. We grabbed that and everybody pulled it. We put enough slack in it that it made a loop. We run it down between the guys' legs and pulled 'em right up. We got both of 'em within just about a minute or so.

We could hear the fellows in the water hollering. They picked two of them alive out of the water. One was Lambert. The other one that came out was a carpenter. I don't know what his name was. He was badly broken up. He had a broken pelvis and several things. He never did come back, I don't think. But Lambert was right back out there in a few days.[13]

Afterwards I crawled back down and took a look at what remained. There was one of those big hooks that had bolts in it, and it was sheared off right straight. Another one that was hanging had no bolts in it. The other four hooks of the original six were gone. There was only the two hooks that were left. We never went back on those hooks anymore. They brought in different ones with a lot more rollers. They had no more problems after that.[14]

When that scaffold went, if we'd been close enough to the water, half of our crew would have jumped in. There was a lot of 'em hurt by falling lumber and we could have got to 'em. But there was no chance of going down from there [where we were].[15] We headed back to the office and everybody went home. It was on the radio that they'd had an accident and several men were killed. So we headed for home quick because we didn't have a telephone. It was get home and let our folks know that we were safe. But the next morning at eight o'clock we were back out there again, right back to work. We knew that this wouldn't stop the job. It was an accident and it happened and there's nothing we could do about it.

I talked to Lambert later. He said that when it all started there was a

Fred Dummatzen (*left*) and coworkers banding cable strands on the bridge, 1936.
Martin Adams sadly recalled the terrible accident on February 17, 1937, that killed
Dummatzen and nine other men. Photo by Charles Hiller. Courtesy of Labor Archives
and Research Center, San Francisco State University. Copyright Golden Gate Bridge,
Highway, and Transportation District.

lot of lumber on the scaffold. The carpenter foreman and a carpenter had
just come down there to fix some railing on it. So they were on it, too.
Lambert said that when it started to go, he run and jumped. He got clear
of the scaffold itself. That way he wasn't falling in the lumber. He was in
the net. Maybe this saved his life because the net going down would be
a little slower. That might have cushioned his fall a bit when he went in.
He said he was in the net to his knees and he come back out of it and got
his feet under him so he could go into the water feetfirst.

The state held hearings on all of this and what was the cause. My
testimony's in there with all of the ones who worked and knew the scaf-

folds. The union backed us all the way. They weren't as strong at that time in their safety efforts, but they were driving for it. The state had a safety deal, too. They had a law.[16] The president of Pacific Bridge said that he designed those scaffolds himself. It was kind of bad structure, but I think it would have held but for the bolts. We didn't have enough, and somebody didn't think.

Earlier, we'd worked with Lambert when we were pouring. We were up on the deck of the bridge pouring for a while before it come to the stripping. We was putting the concrete in. Lambert was the dump man on these narrow-gauge railroads. Charlie Spoon, one of my friends, drove the dinkey. It had a heavy railway wheel box and everything. So Spoon was hauling concrete one morning with Lambert as the dump man. We were pouring down close to the Marin tower. It was raining.

They loaded these cars on the flat on the San Francisco side, but the bridge had quite a good arch in it. Spoon had six yards of concrete behind him and these two extra cars they put in. He only had a six-ton dinkey and they had nine tons of concrete behind him, plus the cars. He had to give it everything he had to get that thing really rolling or he couldn't get it up over the slope. Well, he made it over the slope. He was really laying into it.

Spoon came over the slope probably about ten miles an hour. He started down the other way and he reached over and set his brakes. The track was wet and he went faster. That dinkey was sliding and it had no brakes on the cars. It went right on by us, clear over to the Marin side past the Marin tower, came to the end of the track, and dumped the whole thing—the six yards of concrete, the dinkey, and the cars. The engine went over first. But before it went off, Charlie Spoon and Lambert jumped out on the deck. Spoon slipped down and I never saw a guy limp as bad in my life. He wasn't hurt, but he was scared to death.

We were all a little scared, but it was just one of those things. Nobody got hurt, although the day before there'd been a crew of about fifteen carpenters working on falsework in there where everything crashed.[17] The load went down through a bunch of falsework and right into the ground. It stripped everything out of its way, but there wasn't a soul working in there. They put Spoon on the finishing machine the next day. He didn't get fired because he was doing his job. He just didn't have enough power to stop the dinkey with the track wet.

A lot of days it would be rainy and windy like that on the bridge. You couldn't pour concrete in heavy rain, but after it got where we could work underneath, why, we didn't hardly stop. We could tell what the weather was going to be by the crab boats. They'd come right along the shore. You'd think they were going to hit the rocks because the water was so rough and the wind was blowing so hard. They'd work right around the coast and stay out there until nine, ten o'clock. If the weather stayed that way, they'd work their way back in and we knew we had a bad day because the wind was hitting you, too. I also found out that you didn't take a leak on the ocean side of the bridge. The first time I tried, about when it got running good, the wind hit. I got a shower right in the face. I never went back to that, 'cause on the bay side the wind blew it away from you.

And cold! The Gate was the coldest place I've ever worked. You put all the clothes you could get on and worked hard or you'd freeze. They didn't have to push you to get you to work. You worked to keep warm. I'd been used to snow and ice. This wasn't snow and ice, but it was just about as cold. There was a little bit of ice a few times. It was a cold, rainy winter and you were just careful.

I wore a sweatshirt underneath a shirt. I seldom ever wore long johns, but then I had a pair of overalls on and a coat. You'd put all them on and button 'em up. Then you had the steel man's six-inch high-top shoes with fiber cord soles so you had as good a footing as you could get. Those shoes were a must. All the steel workers wore 'em. You couldn't wear leather soles out there. That just wouldn't work when you get that steel and it's wet and cold.

Usually I wore cotton socks, and maybe two pair at times when it was real cold. But I never noticed that my feet were cold 'cause we were moving all the time and that kept us warm. We'd wear gloves to protect ourselves against the concrete. They had a calf leather basing and canvas. The ironworkers used an all-leather glove for riveting because of the hot sparks. But we didn't get into that too much, so we wore just enough to protect our hands.

I've got the hard hat I wore on both bridges setting down in the basement now. It's kind of a brown fiber with a flat rim all the way around it. The ironworkers, most of 'em, was the ones that wore those other smaller black ones on the Golden Gate. They didn't have much rim on their hats, which were like a miner's hat. The brown fiber one had enough rim on it so if anything hit you, it'd only knock you back. It made a good rain hat, too. I split the front rim of mine. It's got a nice split in it where a cable hit it. But it saved my face. The cable come right across and it would have mashed my nose. It knocked my head back, but I didn't get hurt.

You always had to wear a safety belt, too. It was a two-inch leather belt around the center with a rope on one side so you could tie it off. I never did like that very well. We had to move too much. If you were working in one place, you could tie off close. But if you had a twenty-foot rope and you tied that off and you fell twenty feet, that'd catch you around the middle. I'd rather fall all the way than have that catch you and break you in two! This was an ironworker's belt. I still have mine. It's pretty old now.

I lived on Post Street in San Francisco when I was working on the Gate Bridge. I didn't have a car. I'd ride the streetcar down to the guardhouse in the San Francisco Presidio. Then you'd walk on up to the bridge and walk across it. This was after they got the cables up and the bridge up itself. That stopped any boats [for transporting workers] right quick. I never took a boat. You just walked. A lot of times we were working on the Marin side. You still wanted to be out on your work spot at eight o'clock.[18]

There was one more incident that scared the life out of me. We were back over Fort Point near San Francisco working around the walkways. We were working on some two-by-fours that were five feet long. I'd get down there and was holding 'em. This other fellow was hitting 'em with a sledgehammer. He reared back and hit one hard. I couldn't hold it. There was a crew down under on Fort Point, 100 to 150 feet below. We started hollering and they moved out of the way, but that thing hit on end and splintered into half a dozen pieces. If it had hit somebody, it would have killed 'em for sure.

Those guys talked back to us, and they didn't talk back real easy. When you drop something on somebody down below, why, he's been depending on you to take care of him and you've got to do it. I hated that incident. I could see myself in the same position they were in. If people weren't safe, some of those guys wouldn't work with 'em. You pretty near had to be that way out there.

They was always pushing, though, to get as much done as you could. You didn't take time out to smoke, you smoked as you worked. You'd hang a cigarette in your mouth and just keep going. If you didn't work too fast, they'd just lay you off. There was always men setting there waiting to go to work. Most of the men were anywhere from twenty to forty. They weren't the older ones, they were young guys. You had to be pretty agile. Your reflexes had to be good, and you had to be alert.

I didn't take any pictures of the Golden Gate Bridge. I didn't have money enough for that. When I was on the Bay Bridge I married a girl from back home. At the time I was on the Golden Gate Bridge we had a six-months-old boy. We didn't have anything when we started, so I was just trying to pick up enough money to get a car.

About May 1937, when I finished with the Gate Bridge, I came back to the East Bay. My wife liked it out here in California, and I did too, so this is where we stayed. I transferred from Local 261 of San Francisco into Local 304, the Laborers' union in Oakland. I was on the executive board of Local 304 for quite a while, probably from 1938 to 1940. About 1938 I got a concrete foreman's job. This was for work on tracks, sheds, and buildings so they could store the trains going to the Bay Bridge. I had a good crew. Most of 'em were black. That's the guys I wanted because they'd get out there and work. But I don't remember one black worker from the Golden Gate Bridge.

I was not active in politics in the 1930s, but I thought everybody should vote. In 1932 and 1936 I voted for Franklin Roosevelt for president. I thought he done a lot of good. I thought he was just as good as we could have got, and I still do. When the Depression hit in 1929, President Herbert Hoover was kicked an awful lot. But he was the man that started these bridges when he was in office. Hoover was from the South Bay and he gave the bridges a lot of good strong backing when they raised the money and had the plans worked up. Roosevelt was in on the finish.[19]

After that Bay Bridge work in '38, I got a foreman's job with Healy-Tibbitts Construction Company when they were putting in the foundation for the first building at the Alameda Naval Air Station. Then I moved over to dockwork and done a lot of that. In 1940 I went into Local 34 of the Pile Drivers, Bridge, Wharf and Dock Builders Union.[20] On one job I was doing some concrete work as foreman. When they didn't need a labor foreman for a little while, one of the guys says, "Why don't you join the riggers?" A couple of fellows from Local 34 was there, and they signed the card for me to join. I took the examination and passed. One day I was a laborer there and the next day I come back I was a rigger. Been one ever since. I still carry my card.

As a Local 34 member I done carpenter work and jobs with concrete pilings and forms around the docks. That's all Local 34's work. Local 34 is in the Brotherhood of Carpenters, too, so I could go to the carpenters' union hall and get a job building a house or anything else. I could work as a carpenter or as a rigger. Our Local 34 scale was a little higher, though. Pile driving was rougher and tougher. You had to dig all your manholes and move all those timbers. A lot of it was manpower. And you was in the water and mud and everything.

I'm telling you, a lot of pile driving was hard work. I did it all, but when World War II came, I was turned down for the war. I was a heavy smoker. They said my lungs was scarred. I never had any trouble with my lungs that I knew of, but they wouldn't take me. So I just worked straight through doing construction.

In the early 1960s we did a twenty-eight-story concrete high-rise job by Lake Merritt in Oakland. As the layout man I had to carry the building up plumb. I enjoyed that job and I remember it well, but the Gate's just about as good a memory of work as I have. That's where I cut my teeth. It was cold, it was windy, but it was refreshing. You was up in clean, fresh air. And I liked the structure. You like to see something that's going to stand that you can look back at.

I quit construction in 1974 after thirty-four years in Local 34. Now I can go back through all the jobs I worked over about a forty-year period in the whole area from Sacramento to San Jose down to San Francisco. I can pretty near go to 'em and point 'em out. They're still standing. But I think there's more special to the Golden Gate Bridge. A lot of people said it couldn't be done. It went in just like it was planned. It's something that was badly needed and it's been a boon to the country.

Evan C. "Slim" Lambert

SURVIVOR

When I was picked up, I had a dead man by the feet. That was Fred Dummatzen. Well, he wasn't dead, he was alive then. He was alive until we were coming in on the crab fisherman's boat. On the way in he died. He had been moving up until that time and finally he stopped. **EVAN C. "SLIM" LAMBERT**

Born in 1910 and raised in Washington state, Evan C. "Slim" Lambert worked in an Alaskan cannery and as a cowboy in Arizona before coming to San Francisco, where he found a job as a laborer on the San Francisco–Oakland Bay Bridge. In 1935 he became a labor foreman on the Golden Gate project, where he worked building the span's supply railroad and pouring concrete. He was badly injured in the Golden Gate Bridge accident of February 17, 1937, but returned to work just a month later. Lambert stayed on the Golden Gate project as a labor supervisor through the bridge's opening in May. After World War II he built a prosperous tourist-boat business in Hawaii. I interviewed Lambert in San Francisco on May 25, 1987.

■ ■ ■

My father took off from home when he was fourteen. He'd been sent to live with an uncle because his parents were quite poor. His uncle mistreated him, so he ran away. He became a cowboy at first, then gradually wound up on the West Coast up in Puget Sound in Washington. There he took to the water and became a boatman. I followed the same pattern as my father. I have been a cowboy and a boatman all my life.

My mother and father originated in the Dakotas. Maybe it was Wisconsin and later the Dakotas. Then both of them came west. They were married in Bellingham, Washington, where I was born in 1910. My mother's family was Scotch-Irish and French. My father's family was primarily Welsh, but there was a great mixture there. One of my ancestors on my dad's side was Spanish. One was American Indian. At the time they were married, my father was the superintendent of the biggest salmon cannery in the world, which was in Puget Sound, and my mother was a schoolteacher.

When I was fourteen my father died. When the Depression hit, things were hard. That was part of the reason I took off. My mother was having a hard time supporting us. There was a stretch when she was selling stuff like women's hosiery door-to-door. We were in bad shape.

I finished up at Fairhaven High School in Bellingham and went to Western Washington College in town for one semester. But I was terribly antsy. So I went to Alaska in my late teens. I worked in the fishing industry up there, where they called me Spike. In my cowboy days I was called Whitey. I got the name Slim on the Golden Gate Bridge job in San Francisco, where they started calling me that. I was a fisherman before I became a cowboy. After my teens I just worked in Alaska during the summers. In the fall I went to Arizona and got ranch jobs working as a cowboy.

In my younger days when I wanted to go somewhere, I hoboed because I didn't have any money for transportation. Always rode the trains. I did hitchhike a little, but there weren't too many cars in those days and people didn't like to pick you up if you got dirty. And it was hard to keep clean when you're doing that sort of thing. But with the train it didn't matter how filthy you got; the trains went just the same. I'd wind up under a bridge somewhere, swim in the river, clean up as best I could, and then grab another train and go off.

In Alaska you worked long hours. You worked as long as you had to. I didn't actually fish in Alaska, although I fished sardines one season in Monterey Bay, California. In Alaska I worked on a canning line in a cannery. We canned all the fish that came in that day, no matter how long it took. If it took twenty-four hours, that's how long you worked. Usually we got a couple of hours' sleep. Then when there was a lull, you slept as long as you could. A lot of jobs used to be like that. I remember working in a fruit cannery in Bellingham where the standard shift was fourteen hours. In Alaska I got sixty dollars a month. But I was fed and housed, so I'd come down in the fall with two or three hundred bucks.[1]

They used to put on a dandy rodeo at Sumas, Washington, right on the Canadian line. I started going to that when I was about twelve and got hooked on the cowboy bit. Later I walked to a ranch and pestered them so they'd give me a job. Cowboy wages were nothing, twenty-five bucks a month or something. But when you went to town you were rich because you had no way to spend money on the ranch. So I never lacked for anything.

Cowboy work was all horseback in those days. Nowadays, they often expect cowboys to work on fences and stuff or possibly haying. But in those days, in a big outfit, you worked on horseback totally. I liked the excitement, I liked to ride, and I liked those horses. That was a great life. I loved it.

I picked up the name Whitey when I was a cowboy down in Arizona in the Southwest. There were very few blond men in that country. The men were almost all dark for some reason, and I stuck out like a sore thumb with blond hair. In Alaska they called me Spike because I was slender, that's all. Tall and slender.

When I was an Arizona cowpuncher a horse fell on me and I got hurt.[2] So the foreman sent me to Los Angeles with a shipment of steers. From there I went back to my hometown to visit my mother, then came back south to San Francisco. I was walking down the Embarcadero with my friend, Bob Halley, and a man came out of a shed underneath the Bay Bridge.[3] He said, "Do you fellas want to go to work on the bridge?" We'd been walking along looking up at this thing, never having any idea we'd wind up there. The man's offer came right out of the blue. We didn't even live in San Francisco. But we told him, "You just hired a couple of men." I didn't get back to Arizona until I went back for a visit after the big Golden Gate Bridge accident in 1937.

On the Bay Bridge we were roustabouts. We did all the carrying, moving materials around. When the Bay Bridge was finished, we went to the Gate. Anybody that had experience on the Bay was hired immediately on the Gate if they needed men.[4] At first, we went off to work on the Gate Bridge by launch and climbed the towers. I was living in a boardinghouse on Eighth Street in San Francisco then. Later on, when the steel deck was in, we traveled on the deck. When we got on the Gate Bridge, we did more technical things. We built the railroad across the Gate Bridge that carried supplies, and then we poured the concrete.[5] Nowadays it would be the concrete union that would do that. In those days, the roustabouts did it. Then we stripped the forms afterwards, and that's when the big accident happened.

I hear all the time that you had to be a resident for a year to work on the Gate Bridge. No, when they needed anybody, they hired 'em. Same everywhere. You go to any company anywhere and they've got a stack of applications that high. But if you're there and qualified when they need anybody, you get the job. I don't have any recollection of a black person working on the bridge, though. There were immigrant fellows whose parents were immigrants, and a few older men who were immigrants themselves.

Building the Gate Bridge railroad, you had ties just like on land that span two beams. You lay the ties out and unload the rails off on each side on a stack of ties. Then you would carry the rails. No lifting equipment. Men carried all the rails. The whole gang of men would pick up a rail, walk out on the steel deck, and set 'em on the ties. Others would spike them in place, and then the next trainload of rails that came out would come out that much farther, and it just kept going.

We had some close calls in connection with that railroad. We were unloading rails off of a flatcar at the end of the track once and another train came out with more rails. It started to sprinkle, and that's dangerous as can be on steel and on railroad tracks. The engineer couldn't stop the train in time and he ran into the car we were unloading. The steel rails were flying around. We were all working there on bare steel. The bridge wasn't decked yet. How wide were those spans? Three feet, six inches or something? And we were running around trying to avoid those rails that were flying by us. The rails fell in the drink. It was a wonder that nothing fell on a ferryboat. That was a close one.

After we built the railroad, the concrete came out on the track in gondola cars. It would stop wherever the pour was progressing. We'd have a plywood walk laid out to the far corner. We had big two-wheeled dump carts. We'd go to the spot of that gondola and fill a cart, back off, take it out, and dump it. Some men were working out there with vibrators to be sure that the concrete got spread into every corner to get rid of all the air pockets. Others were wheeling the carts or working the door on the gondolas. I remember my job. Most of the time I was up on top of the gondola with a long pole keeping the chute clear so the concrete would flow when they opened the door. That was up where I could watch everything.

When the railroad was built and they were pouring concrete, the train was going clear to the Marin tower. One time I had to go back in to the office for some reason. I would always ride the train once they were running the trains back and forth. When I came out of the office, I got on the train. There were three of us aboard—a brakeman, an engineer, and a passenger, me. It started to rain. Again the engineer couldn't stop the train. You'd have thought they'd figured out some way to make that foolproof, but they hadn't. They relied on sand on the tracks, and I think he ran out of sand.

We went over the high center and started down the slope. People don't realize that, but there's quite a slope there from the center both ways. The train started to gather momentum and he couldn't stop it. Just beyond the Marin tower they had a huge wooden scaffolding being built. There were a lot of men working on that wood. We were gathering speed, and I knew there'd be plenty of people killed if that train ever went to the end and went off. So I stayed on the train and hollered my head off instead of bailing off, and so did the brakeman.

Finally the men working on that wood staging realized there was something wrong. They looked up and saw this train bearing down on 'em, and they scattered like flies. They all got off of that staging and the engineer, brakeman, and I bailed off the train. We made it successfully, too, even though there was no deck there. We just went off of bare steel, but panels had been set here and there, and I remember going off on them. We slid all over, but nobody went through.[6]

When I survived the big accident of February 1937, I was fortunate in one way. I was a foreman of the stripping gang, so I wasn't engaged in anything when the accident happened. I was watching everything as we moved along. The rest of the men were busy doing things with their hands. That first hanger [hook] let go and then the second hanger went.

The southern (ocean) corner stage started to go down first. That's right where I was standing, so I just went off like a frog into the net headfirst.

When the staging tore loose and one corner went first, I think the men slid off the staging and it fell on 'em in the net. The net stopped 'em until the staging hit it. So I think some of 'em were probably badly hurt before they ever hit the water. But I was not hit by the staging. I just took a free fall. I knew that to have a prayer to survive I had to hit the water feetfirst.

People ask me what went through my mind. The only thing that went through my mind was survival. One thing that never occurred to me is anything of a religious nature. After my father died, I had to go to Sunday school, and then I had to go with my mother to church. I got all I could take of that. I stayed with my grandparents quite a bit, too. My grandfather was a real Bible-pounding minister. At his house, I had to attend prayer meetings several times a day. He would get drunk on religion and just holler, "Amen, amen, praise the Lord!" I got so full of that stuff I got turned off on religion as a kid.

Well, when I fell off the bridge, I did manage to hit the water feetfirst. I was hanging on to a piece of net that was hanging on to the staging. I was hanging on it headfirst. Before we hit the water I straightened up, let go of the net, and hit feetfirst. The only problem with that was that I jammed down into the piece of net with both feet. I went way down into that net because it stopped temporarily when it hit the water, and I was still moving. That's the only time I panicked during the whole thing. I was caught in the net and it was headed for the bottom. It was dragged down by that six-ton staging.[7] At first I couldn't get loose at all. I was fighting it. Then I finally calmed down and began to wiggle. I slid right out of it. But I was down a long ways, because I was bleeding at the nose and ears when I came up.

When I got up, I looked around, and an interesting thing happened. I was trying to take my gloves off. It was a matter of habit. I used to take 'em off and stuff 'em in my hip pocket. I threw 'em away when I realized what I was doing. Then I tried to get out of my coat, but I couldn't because of my broken shoulder. So I knew I had to have something to keep afloat. I couldn't swim well with all those clothes on, including a heavy coat. There was a lot of debris floating in the water. There was the wooden deck of the staging and the wood that the workmen on the bridge were throwing over the side because they felt that if anyone was alive, they'd have to have something to keep 'em afloat. I got a couple of planks together, at first for myself.

Then I saw Fred Dummatzen thrashing about. There were two or three people floating around. I had a choice. I went to Fred because he was still thrashing around and I knew he was alive. The others appeared to be done for. So I got ahold of him and got him up on a couple of boards. Then I was going to see what I could do for the others. But the minute I'd let go of Fred and there was big wave action, the boards would separate and he'd start to go down. I decided, *Better stick with what you got,* because I knew he was alive. So I stayed with him. The others disappeared.

The Coast Guard came out and circled several times. But they never came far enough. They would always get out near me and then turn around and head back. There was so much debris in the water, it would be awful hard to see a person floating with just their head sticking up. It would be a real difficult job to spot us. But they actually didn't come far enough.

After a while I heard this power boat coming in, *putt, putt, putt.* It was coming in from out at sea. I looked around and here was this crab fishing boat with one man at the helm.[8] He was looking at all this stuff in the water up ahead of him, trying to figure out what in the world had happened. He kept looking from side to side and he almost went by us. The fisherman was some little distance off, maybe fifty yards. He was almost by and took another look around. His eyes hit me, and what a relief. I figured, *My gosh, we're going to make it.*

Slim Lambert, Golden Gate Bridge labor foreman, circa 1936. Among the twelve men who fell two hundred feet into the sea in February 1937 when a huge staging board tore through the safety net, Lambert was one of only two who survived. Courtesy of San Francisco History Center, San Francisco Public Library.

But when I was picked up, I had a dead man by the feet. That was Fred Dummatzen. Well, he wasn't dead, he was alive then. He was alive until we were coming in on the crab fisherman's boat. On the way in he died. He had been moving up until that time and finally he stopped.

The fisherman had an awful time getting Fred aboard, and then he had a hard time getting me aboard, because I had a broken shoulder, broken ribs, and a broken neck.[9] Very few boats are rigged so you can pull anybody or anything over the side, and the fisherman wasn't a big man. Fred was big. I wasn't very big, but Fred was a pretty big man, and I was a wreck. But the fisherman managed to get us into that boat and bring us ashore. We couldn't help Fred any, or very little. It was too bad Fred died, but that's how it happened. Nobody ever reported it that way, and I was in the hospital for a while and in no position to refute anything.[10]

Coming in it was terribly cold. The fisherman put Fred alongside of the engine. I stood on the other side. The fisherman tried to get me to lie down by the engine, too. But I was going to be tough. I knew if I laid down I'd never get up. Instead I stood on the way in, crouched over that engine, trying to get a little heat. The fisherman took us in to the Coast Guard Pier, which is out near the bridge. Then, when it came time to try and get off the boat, I couldn't walk. So I didn't walk off after all.

They put me in an ambulance. I think it was the third hospital before they accepted me because mine was an industrial accident. Unless you went to the right hospital, they wouldn't touch you. I think I went to St. Mary's, I'm not sure.[11] I was in the hospital for maybe ten days. When I came out, I was wearing an airplane splint, the kind they stick up over your head. I had that on for a month while my shoulder was healing.

A close friend I grew up with and went to school with came to see me in the hospital. This was my friend Bob Halley. He was the foreman of the other staging. There were two stagings that started at the center of the bridge, going in opposite directions. I had a whole lot of people who visited me in the hospital. But Halley was my close friend. My other close friend, Jack Norman, was on my staging. He died in the fall.

Fred Dummatzen, who died in the tragic February 1937 accident, standing under Golden Gate Bridge cable strands. Lambert struggled valiantly to save Dummatzen that day but was ultimately unable to do so. Courtesy of Labor Archives and Research Center, San Francisco State University.

I had worked with Dummatzen for months. We didn't buddy together, and I never saw him other than work, although he was a friend. He had a happy disposition and was well liked by everybody. But we never sat around shooting the breeze on that crew. I never got well acquainted with any of them.

Things were a lot different in those days. There was no coffee break where people could talk. You hardly ever slowed down to a trot. There was men waiting right there for a job if anybody slowed down a little. Everybody felt pressure. To keep your job, you had to move fast. No sitting around. Lunch was only half an hour, and you had to hurry right along to get your lunch eaten comfortably and get back to work. We started at seven-thirty, had lunch at eleven-thirty, and then worked till we were through at four.

If you went to the restroom and stayed more that thirty seconds, the boss would come and see if you were sick or what was wrong with you. Lots of men were fired right on the spot if the boss thought they were malingering a little bit. Jobs were very scarce and valuable, so you didn't spend any time chit-chatting. Anytime you weren't working you were trying to rest. You weren't chit-chatting.

After the 1937 accident I went back to work on the bridge.[12] I was in charge of cleanup on the main deck. I don't think I ever went down on staging, though. So I never really had to work with my hands after that. I was just supervising. I was still there the day the bridge opened. We were doing the final bit of cleanup. They tried to get it all done before the opening day, but you know how those things are. We were still there with trucks, taking lumber and all kinds of stuff off the bridge and getting it cleaned up when it opened.

The May 1937 opening celebration was something on the order of the one they had in 1987. The people walked across the bridge, but very few compared to the mob that hit the bridge yesterday.[13] Automobiles crossed with dignitaries and there was a lot of hoopla. It was much the same, only not near as big.[14]

After the bridge job I went over to a job on Treasure Island in San Francisco Bay. Anybody that stayed through the work on the bridges would be hired immediately on any construction job because you had to be a pretty good man or you wouldn't have lasted on the bridges. On Treasure Island they were putting up lots of structures for the 1939 San

Francisco World's Fair. I worked there until the spring of '39. Then I grabbed a ship and went to Hawaii.

I was actually on my way to Tahiti, but I went to Hawaii first. I'd dreamed about the tropics all my life as a kid. Going to the tropics was something I had to do. I've always been a warm-weather guy. I don't care much for this San Francisco weather. Of course, I was young then. It didn't much matter. From the Gate Bridge job I used to watch those ships going off to Hawaii. I knew I had to be on one. So when the work wound up over on Treasure Island, I jumped on a ship and went.

I had gained some notoriety from the big bridge accident. A reporter on a newspaper in Honolulu got the word somehow that I was on that ship. So I made the front page when I hit town. The superintendent of a steel work gang hunted me down because they were short of construction workers. He offered me a job I couldn't refuse. I went right into the steel gang, and we built everything connected with buildings and steel structures, including huge steel storage tanks and all the structural parts of power plants.

When the Japanese bombed Pearl Harbor on December 7, 1941, I was living in a little cottage in Waikiki across the street from the Royal Hawaiian Hotel in Honolulu. I was married then to Elinor "Cotton" Jenkins and we were living there. She had come over in the fall of that same year. We met on the beach in Waikiki. Isn't that romantic? She was fresh out of school and looking for a job, had visited Hawaii from Pasadena with her folks, and decided Hawaii was where she wanted to go. Well, a bomb fell right in the middle of the street, about a half a block from us, so we knew they weren't fooling. It was an accident, the Japanese weren't trying to bomb Waikiki, but stuff was flying around everywhere.

I was deferred from military service all during World War II as key personnel. That's what they called us. I got bored with my job in the steel industry and tried to get out of the deferment, but I couldn't get out. After the war, another fellow and I started a little construction company. Mostly we did destruction. We bought surplus metal of all kinds. He was a welder by trade, and I learned to weld during the war when I was in steel construction. We bought all manner of military equipment. It was for sale cheap after the war.

This fellow and I were great boaters in our spare time. We wanted to get into the boat business. It turned out that he was color-blind and couldn't get a license. Instead of joining me on an idea I had, he went back to work at his trade. I got another partner. He and I bought thirty LCMs—landing craft mediums [LCM actually stands for "landing craft, mechanized"]—from the military. We scrapped them out and sold the engines. We made ten thousand bucks in sixty or ninety days. That was the first real money either of us had ever seen. With that I got another partner, and in 1949 we got into the sightseeing boat business. I've been at it ever since.[15]

I was a staunch Democrat in the 1930s, and I was strong for Truman in the 1940s. I voted for the Democratic candidate, Adlai Stevenson, for president instead of Eisenhower in 1952 and 1956. I thought Stevenson was a good man, and I'm suspicious of military people running a government. They're used to giving orders and that's how it is. Civilians are used to being elected. But when you become more affluent you usually become a Republican, which has happened to us. This was quite a few years ago now.

When I was young after high school it was otherwise, and I did many different jobs. I had itchy feet and I couldn't stand one thing for very long. I even worked in the sawmills around Tacoma for a short time. When you had to belong to a union, I joined, although I never had much to do with them. I've belonged to the ironworkers', the boilermakers', the carpenters', and the laborers' unions in my life. On the Golden Gate Bridge job we had to join the union somewhere along the line. But I never went to union meetings if I could avoid it. They are the most boring things in the world.[16]

Regardless, looking back, everybody that worked on the Gate Bridge in the 1930s absolutely knew it was special. I'm sure any man that ever had anything to do with that bridge thought of it as his bridge. I've heard that said so many times when I worked there. Of course, none of us ever dreamed we'd be around when they celebrated the fiftieth anniversary. That wouldn't even have occurred to us.

Al Zampa

LEGEND

Before I got out of the hospital, all my buddies would come to visit me. They told me, "Al, you are all through. You lost your nerve. You'll never be an ironworker anymore." Now, this was 1936, and I worked all the way until 1970 before I retired. Well anyway, I said, "I don't know," and I kept thinking about it. Then I said, "Hah, I know I can make it."   **AL ZAMPA**

The son of Italian immigrant parents, Al Zampa was born in 1905 in the town of Crockett in Northern California. He was already an experienced ironworker when he found a job on the San Francisco–Oakland Bay Bridge project in 1934. He worked there for two and a half years before moving on to the Golden Gate Bridge in mid-1936. Zampa broke his back in four places in a fall that October, but he recovered fully and returned to his career as a high-steel "ace" a few years later. A veteran of many construction projects, including the Carquinez Strait bridges built in the 1920s and the 1950s as well as the Golden Gate, Zampa became an ironworker of legendary reputation. In 2003, when a third Carquinez bridge opened, it was named the Al Zampa Memorial Bridge in his honor. Isabelle Maynard interviewed Zampa in Crockett during sessions held over the winter and spring of 1986.

■ ■ ■

I went to work on the Bay Bridge in 1934 and joined Pile Drivers Union Local 34. The Bay Bridge job was non-union then. It did not follow craft lines. You just worked at the best thing you were good at. I was working in the raising gang, putting up steel on the Bay Bridge, at the time the Golden Gate job was going. By 1935 to 1936, we could see them spinning the cables on the Golden Gate. I knew then I wanted to work on the Golden Gate Bridge, which was an all-union job. So I went to San Francisco and joined the International Association of Bridge, Structural, and Ornamental Iron Workers Local 377. I think I got in for five dollars. The business agent said when this job stops, it's going to cost you a hundred dollars. At the time, the union was just getting started.[1]

When I joined the Pile Drivers Union I had first worked on the foundation on the Bay Bridge. It had the deepest pier in the world.[2] We got through there, and we went up on the bridge driving rivets and everything. Then we got done there. This was for American Bridge Company. I'd worked previously for them on the Carquinez Bridge.[3] Then we got just about done with most of the steel work that we wanted to do on the Bay Bridge, including work for American on the San Francisco side of the span. I had worked earlier on the camelback spans on the Bay Bridge for Bethlehem Steel.[4] Now Bethlehem said, "Well, we are all ready for the steel on the Golden Gate Bridge. Come on, Al, we will all go there."[5] That's how I went on with the Golden Gate Bridge. I was already hired, but I just went in and signed my name like the rest.

My first job on the Golden Gate Bridge was putting up steel for the roadway. That was on the Marin-shore towers. We were going from there toward Sausalito in Marin County. Another gang was going from that tower area toward San Francisco. So I was working on the Marin side, and we got quite a bit towards there, I guess about two-thirds across. The steel would come up to the towers. They put it on a flatcar and rolled it to us. We would get it and put it in one or two days at a time. Then we would move the rig ahead and start all over again doing the same thing, putting in top chord, bottom chord, floor beams, and stringers.[6] The floor beams go across and the string around the length a ways.

One Monday morning I just started work. It was wet, cold, and slippery from the fog. We were getting ready to move the traveler construction rig ahead. In order to do that, we would go out so far, then have one of the floor beams ready to be put into place so we could move the rig. I'd

Al Zampa (*second from right*) on the Bay Bridge, 1935. Expert high-steel men like Zampa were known as aces. Courtesy of Richard L. Zampa and John Robinson. Copyright Alfred Zampa Memorial Bridge Foundation.

come over to help jack the stuff up to get it ready to move, or slide along down the stringers. The stringers are twenty-four to twenty-six inches high. When you get down, it is quite a deep step. As you go down, you put your foot down straight, which I did. Evidently I stepped out too far. I hit my heel in the wet steel and I flipped.

As I was going down, I remember that I flipped three times.[7] I was just rolling around. I didn't have any fear because I figured the safety net would catch me and I would bounce up and land on my feet, like I seen on the trampoline in the circus. Well, I hit the net and the rocks below at the same time. I bounced, but I bounced off the net. The net went down and hit the rocks, and I came up. The first drop when I first hit didn't seem to hurt as much as when I bounced and I came down.

That's when I had the pain. I was taken to the hospital right away. They slung me to the tower, picked me up in a basket, flipped me up in the air over the top of the tower, and lowered me down to the ambulance. They took me to St. Luke's Hospital in San Francisco. There they jacked me up and put a body cast on me right away. I was in the hospital about twelve weeks. We figured it was about forty-three feet I had fallen.[8]

That fall was when I got to be a member of the Half Way to Hell Club. There was about eight of us that fell in the net.[9] The first three got hurt and I was one of them. I was the first one who fell in. Those men came to visit me because I was in the hospital, and we formed a club there at St. Luke's. They took pictures of us. We were all jolly and shaking hands. I was up and around pretty good then.[10]

Before I got out of the hospital, all my buddies would come to visit me. They told me, "Al, you are all through. You lost your nerve. You'll never be an ironworker anymore." Now, this was 1936, and I worked all the way until 1970 before I retired. Well anyway, I said, "I don't know," and I kept thinking about it. Then I said, "Hah, I know I can make it." When I got out of the hospital, instead of coming right home, I went out to the bridge and walked all over. I was a little pale from being there, but everything was okay. It didn't bother me at all when I got ready to work.[11]

I had a steel brace on when I left the hospital. I took it off a little each day and then put it on. It kept you straightened out. I didn't do ironwork for about two years. I had to take time off. But I got compensation, which wasn't much. Twenty-five dollars a week for eight weeks, and I had a wife and a couple of kids.

I couldn't get by on that compensation, so I had to do little odds and ends. In order to get by, I had a couple of rowboats I would rent out for bass fishing. I would get a dollar a day for the boats. Pretty soon I built some more. At one time I had twenty-six boats while I was a convalescent. I'd rent them out.

People would give us credit for groceries, three hundred or four hundred dollars at a time. I owed three hundred dollars for groceries several times, but when I worked, I paid them off. One man would come out to our area every three months. He'd say, "We have one pump full of Oakland Macaroni Company macaroni." They were the best. We'd put in an order for maybe a hundred, one fifty, or two hundred dollars' worth, everything we needed. It would last us for three months. A couple of times we didn't have enough money. We'd say, "Nah, I think we'll get by with what we got." He'd say, "No, don't worry about me and don't worry about the bill. It's just like money in the bank with you. We know you." He duplicated the order we had done three months before. I didn't want to order nothing because I didn't have the money. They just done it anyhow. Ha, them people were good to me and good to my wife. She'd go out and get credit anyplace, just looking at her, even when I couldn't get ten cents' worth of credit.

My wife left it up to me about not quitting bridge building. She knew I was stubborn. When I walked out on that bridge instead of coming home, she knew I was going to go back because I told her it didn't bother me at all. She got used to the danger. Later a couple of times she said, "Well, I don't know, you have been pretty lucky, but how about this job?" I'd say, "Don't worry about it."

I got married at twenty-three years old. I knew her in our high school at Crockett, California. Her folks and my folks came from the same town in Italy. She was born and raised here like I was. We're the only ones that stayed true—an Italian and an Italian. All the rest are mixed. We're the only ones that stayed straight.

Back then they hated Italian people just like they do the blacks and the Mexicans and all now. It was kind of hard for us, but it didn't bother me too much. Later on I understood. I didn't understand what it was all about at the time when I was young. Now I know what my dad had to go through: "Damn dago" and this and that. My dad worked seven days a week at a smelter company near Crockett. He had to. He never got more than four dollars a day and he had five kids. Them days there was no welfare, no nothing. If he didn't work, we'd starve.

Many times when I was a kid we didn't have too much to eat, so mom would make bread that would last for three or four days or a week. It would never mold, but it got hard. For breakfast I had to soak that hard bread in a bowl of wine. The Italians took wine for food then. But we didn't have all the ham and eggs and stuff you have now, like hotcakes and all. We didn't know what that was. We come up the hard way.

I didn't own a car until 1928 or 1929. It was an old Ford. We had to take the bus or the train. There wasn't too many buses, either. Mostly we'd take the train. We'd go way out in the hills and bring a lunch. There used to be all kinds of game around here. You'd see birds, robins, rabbits, and once in a while a coyote or wildcat. Sometimes we'd barbecue out there. Remember, we didn't have no radio, no TV or nothing in them days. We were interested in the fights and the World Series, but we would have to wait for the paper or when the telegraph office nearby would announce it to somebody and we would find out who won.

We used to go to San Francisco on the train. We had a little depot down here in Crockett, but they don't stop here anymore. You'd go to Oakland at Sixtieth Street, get off the train, and walk to get on the ferryboat to go across the bay. In San Francisco we'd take the streetcars where we wanted. For a nickel you used to go all over San Francisco and transfer there. You'd get off one streetcar and transfer to another.

I traveled for work, too. I was married while I was in Stockton, California. My firstborn was in Stockton. We was building a bridge for Santa Fe Railroad then. I built three of them up by the Stockton area: Old River, Middle River, and the San Joaquin River. From there we went to Arizona. My wife went with me. We took the baby with us. He was only about a year old. I worked in Arizona for about seven or eight months. From there they sent us out to Texas. We were forty miles out of Amarillo, way out in the sticks. They built a camp there. They had a camp for the men and then the married men built little houses, for they were going to stay a long time. Me and my wife lived in a tent. I boarded up one floor about this high with a ten-by-twelve. We had a four-lid wood stove. I made a stationary bed in a corner, everything all ten-by-twelve, for me, her, and the baby.

I worked as a sandhog in Texas.[12] You work under compressed air down underneath a pier. It was different from coal mines. They don't have compressed air. This was air pumped in to you. In Texas they had a flood; it washed all our tramway out and there was no work for us outside [because we couldn't get in materials]. So a guy says, "Al, you can go down the hole to sandhog until we get our piles." In Texas they don't have no trees or nothing. We had to wait about six weeks to get piles from Oregon to bring to Texas. I said, "Okay," so I started there.

I guess I was about fifty feet deep already underneath the pier. The pier had a steel cutting edge all around and you had wood planks on the sides. You'd have to work in there, dig underneath the concrete and the pier. The air pressure held the water out. To dig, you'd have to have air spades and cut up hard mud. You're working in a chamber the size of the pier that was underneath the water and underneath the pier.

The air wanted to escape and we had a four-inch blowpipe. You fed it a little water and a little mud and kept digging so much at a time. You'd get all that mud, rocks, gravel, everything, and it went up through the pier. It shot out like a cannon outside. I went down about ninety feet. It was kind of like working underneath a bell. There was air under there all the time you were digging farther and farther. If you got a blowout, you'd be drowned like rats. When you were finally done, that's the base. You come out of that, and that stays down there while you build up from there.

Pretty soon we got done with Texas. My mom was awful sick, so we came back to Crockett and stayed until mom got well. Then I went to different jobs. When my two boys were getting five or six years old, I figured that I didn't want them to go to this school and that school. I wanted them to go to our school in Crockett. So I came back right here where I was born and rented us a house. I wanted them to go to the school where I went. When I graduated from grammar school, there was only five of us in the eighth grade. I wanted the boys to come over here and live like I did. I thought my kids was "it." I just loved my kids.

Later on, in high school, the boys got to play sports. I was working as a rigger for a contractor at Union Oil. Every Friday afternoon the kids would play baseball. I'd take off. The boss would say, "Hey, you don't be taking off every Friday." I'd say, "What do you mean I don't? I've been raising my kids and waiting all these years to watch them do that. They come first. If you want me here, I take off Fridays. Otherwise, write it out, give me my pay, and I'll work someplace else." That's the way you have to be in this kind of world. Otherwise, they will step all over you.

I done that and I never had no trouble. I would get calls all over to go to different jobs. They all knew all about me. I'd get a job anytime. I'd never starve. They'd say, "That guy, he's all right. Hire him, you'll make money with him. He works and he knows what to do and how to do it." Them things were tough and I had a wife and kids, but nobody steps on me. I had confidence and I knew all I had to do is get a job. Once I got the job, I'm there because I'd work. They were paying us top money, so you got to give them a good job. I always did, and I'd preach that to my kids.

I did box a little bit, too. I had fifteen professional fights. I only lost the first one. I had to fight under a different name. If my dad found out, he'd beat the hell out of me. This was when I was sixteen, seventeen, eighteen years old. My dad didn't want me working on the bridge, either. He said, "That job is for desperate men who don't care. They're ready to go down and get killed any minute. You're crazy to do that kind of work." I said, "I know, Dad, but I love it. I'm going to do it anyhow." Afterwards I would see him. He'd get a few shots under his belt and he'd be bragging about me. My mom always told me, "Be careful, honey." I'd say, "I'm always careful." I got tired hearing about it.

I met the best bridge men in the world on the Golden Gate. Different fellows were from all over the country. I would take them home for dinner because they were away. Pretty soon the job would be over and they would go back home. Some of them got killed. I lost quite a few of them that were damn good friends of mine. The good ones we'd call aces. That was a fellow that can do the work, do it good, do it quick, and do it up in the air all the time with no scaffold, no nothing. I was one of the aces. I was pretty good until I seen some of them. Some of them were as good as me or better. Most of them were older than I was. I was thirty.

At the time, most people didn't think that bridge could be built. Nine out of ten would say, "No way, never could be done." The water was too rough, the tide would go out fast, and waves would come in higher. Earlier I was doing the same thing over on the Oakland side. It wasn't very rough there. It was nice in the bay. The Golden Gate was out in the ocean. When we used to go to work from the San Francisco side, they used to ferry us over on a little passenger boat. It could scare me going to the job and coming back. There were big waves coming back that went from one side to the other. That was the only time we were kind of leery. We weren't leery up there.

Building a bridge, you hope that everything will do well. It works on you a little bit. You say, "Well, I wonder if that's going to hold up? I hope those engineers are right." God bless them, they were right on the Golden Gate. The engineers designed the bridge and checked every piece of steel that went in there. They said, "This one got to do this work, this one got to do that work." They were very good. I'm sure glad they were.

I never met Joseph Strauss, the chief engineer, but I saw him around a lot of times. I never shook hands with him or nothing. I was out there working. We were busy. We couldn't leave and go shake hands with him. That was for the upper man. See, all the big shots were the ones that were doing all the hand-shaking. In fact, they should of come out and hand-shaked us. We were the ones doing the work.

While working on the Golden Gate Bridge you didn't have much time for lunch. You would have half an hour. So we would bring a brown bag up there. When we were up in the air, we would just bring lunch in our overalls or something and sit it someplace, eat it up there, and then go back to work.

When you are putting up steel, you can't be tied off. We got to be moving around. The riveters and the bucker-ups, they're tied. They had a float, or scaffold, to work on. We didn't have no float. They had a swinging scaffold tied with four lines with six-by-four panel board. It has four lines in each corner tied up. There's no place to stand or nothing. We would use that to connect and just walk the beams. On the beams, the wind would blow. Once it blows, you got to lean toward the wind. It was so windy on the Golden Gate Bridge moving from one place to another that we had a wire that we tied on the suspenders for a handrail. Once in a while we could grab it. The nearby steel cord was, oh, two and a half feet thick, but still it was slick with nothing to get ahold of.

Rain didn't bother us much. If we got too wet, we would knock off. We'd quit if it was too dangerous. Bethlehem Steel and American Bridge were self-insured. So if I had an accident, they had to pay. That's one of the reasons they worked the safest. Now there is no more Bethlehem Steel and no more American Bridge in the erection department anymore [in 1986]. I did try at one time to sue Bethlehem for negligence on the net. But they kept postponing and all the guys who were my witnesses took off. I never got a dime out of it. If it happened now, I'd be a millionaire.

Sometimes during that Depression I'd look down from the Golden Gate towers when I was up there and there'd be 150 people waiting for a job, waiting for us either to fall off or quit. They'd have these five-gallon tins with big fires where they were cooking bacon butts and beans. We were cold up there looking down at that fire. It would warm us up just looking at it.

Once in a while some guy might have enough. He'd have a close call and he would quit. Or maybe some guy got hurt and there'd be room for someone. Sometimes they'd have a little extra work and they'd hire a few men. They'd ask for their experience and pick them out. They didn't even have to write an application, but somebody always knew them. He'd say, "I know this fellow there. He's okay, he worked with me on this job, he's a good man." A good hand they called them. So that's how a man got hired. If they didn't know you, it was pretty hard. You'd be "best man" [left jobless] if nobody vouched for you. There was no work no place out around the country, and that's one reason they come from all over. But they were also like me: they wanted to work on the Golden Gate Bridge, one of the most famous bridges there is.

The Depression was tough, but not for me because I had a job. Working on the Golden Gate, once in a while we would go to Sausalito by ferry to raise a little hell. When you worked five days a week, Saturdays and Sundays were ours to recuperate. Sausalito was wild in those days. I had a lot of good times there. I would drink mostly. Most bridge men drink like hell anyway. We used to drink and shoot dice and play poker some days. Sometimes we would be there all day. That's another story.

To start with after my back healed, I did safer jobs. I went to work at Mare Island [Naval Shipyard] during World War II. I got to be a first-class shipfitter, so I worked there for about two years. Then a fellow said, "Well, Al, it's time to come on back." I thought, *Might as well.* I was making $9.40 a day at Mare Island, and I went back to bridge and building work and I think we were getting about eighteen dollars a day. I worked mostly railroad bridges, high-rises, and rigging.

We used to go all over for jobs. Then we would come back home. They would either call us or write us to come on up to work: "I got a big job here and there." We'd go chasing rainbows. Wherever they'd pay the most, I went. But then I wanted to stay put. I got tired of going around. So I had to take a lot of heavy rigging and high-rise jobs. You'd work for one company, go to another, and then back to the same company. I remember when there were no buildings out on Market Street in San Francisco. Now you go up there, it's a different city. I practically get lost, but I lived there when I was working on the Golden Gate job.

When my sons wanted to be ironworkers, my wife said, "Why do you want to be an ironworker?" My son said, "Because Dad is home most of the time in between jobs." Both my sons became ironworkers. They had two years at junior college and they were both good football players. Finally they wanted to do the same things I did. I left it up to them. "If you want to do it," I said, "it's good work. If you want to work with your hands, I don't think you can beat it. You don't have no tools, no nothing, just your ability. Bet you could do it."

My boys went through apprenticeship in the early 1950s. They didn't have to because I was on the Local 378 executive board and helped run the local. I could've got them a union book, but I wouldn't go for that. I thought, *They got to go through the same way as the rest of them.* I was honest all the time, even for my own sons. All I had to do is say, "I want a book for them." That's how easy it was for me to do, but I didn't do it. I wanted them to go through apprenticeship to start off.

About the time they built the second Carquinez Bridge, I guess it was 1958 or 1960, we was working up in Fairfield, California, putting up these hangars.[13] When the American Bridge Company first started the Carquinez, they brought in practically all their old followers. They were allowed to bring in some of their key men from the East after they got a transfer into our local. See, you had to be out of Local 378. Little by little, all them hotshots from back east quit. They wasn't making enough money. It had been raining off and on. They would lose two or three days a week. "Hell with it," they'd say, "we're gone."

Pretty soon the company needed a lot of men. But we were getting the same money for a lot easier jobs. My two sons, Gene and Dick, and Giggs Madden, who was just like one of our sons—they were all raised together—and I were sitting there talking in the union hall. We said, "Why should we go on that bridge? That's hard work and it's dangerous." We wouldn't go unless we had to. Then the union business agent came out and talked to us. He said, "Al, they want fifteen men out there and I can't get anybody to go out on the bridge. God darn, I'm worried."

It was warm, so the boys and I went outside, sat on the grass, and talked some old times. The business agent came out. He said, "You have to go. Otherwise they are going to hire non-union guys from the street." "Well," I said, "if they can do it, let them have it." He said, "No, no, we got to keep the jobs over here. I know damn well that if you and the kids go out, I could get these other guys to go out, too." I said, "Dick, Gene, Giggs, how about it? If you guys want to go, I'll go. You guys say no, I won't go either." They said, "Oh, yeah, Dad, let's go. We'll do it. We live near there anyhow." So we went and sure enough, the next week, here they all start coming. They said, "Well, if it is good enough for Al Zampa and the kids, it sure got to be good enough for us." So father and two sons helped bring the men over there. One or two ironworkers had one son, but I'm the only one that had two sons.

In 1970, I was sixty-five years old and I was still connecting steel up in the air. I didn't have to retire, but one of my sons was the president of Local 378, the other was the financial secretary, and I was still on the executive board. There was no other place in the United States where two brothers had every local office locked up and their dad was on the e. board. So I said that's the time for me to quit because I could only hurt them. Naturally they would want to give me all the good jobs. The other ironworkers would say, "You give the old man the best jobs." When the next election came, the members wouldn't elect them.[14]

I was never scared for my sons. I knew they could do the work and were good at it. They were chips off the old block. Of course, you had to be good. Otherwise you'd get laid off. Some guys just starting out—this was before the apprenticeship school—could do it. In three weeks they were pretty good men. Some of them could never make it. They were scared. One time, one man fell in the Gate there. He just froze. It took three of us to break him loose and lower him down. We had him tied up and we let him down. He went on and never did come back. That happens to some of them. They just grab everything. I don't know what comes over them. I never had none of that. I could look down. Some said, "Don't look down." It never bothered me.

I figured if I fell, I'll just double up. This was on the Bay Bridge. "If I roll up and hit on my back," I said, "I'll have a chance." I always thought I'd have a chance. I figured I could grab something. You had that in you. It took confidence and courage. You just have to have it inside and know you can do it. If you didn't have it, you couldn't do it. It's according to guts. You have to have about ninety percent guts and ten percent know-how.

You also have to have strength, good hands, and be quick. Your feet count, too. You have to be the athletic type. You got to have balance and you can't be clumsy or you won't hold. But the Golden Gate spoiled a lot of us because we had the safety net. That was the first time they used one. There was nothing on the Bay Bridge. From the Golden Gate on, they all had nets. We had a net on the second Carquinez. There was no net when we put the steel up, but then we put a little net up for the guys coming behind us, like the bucker-ups and all.

All of the bridges are different. The 1936 Bay Bridge is about six or seven kinds of bridges. You got trusses, you got camelback spans, you got cantilever, you got suspension, and you got all the approaches. It is eight and a half miles long. Its suspension section is longer than the Golden Gate span.[15] The Golden Gate is just one type. It's suspension. See the difference? The Bay Bridges are far more beautiful than the Golden Gate.[16] But the Golden Gate is a great bridge. Both of them are beautiful. I think they're the most wonderful bridges there is in the world. That's not because I worked on them, but just if you looked them over.

For about fifty-two years now [in 1986] I have been a union man. I worked for ten years before I joined the ironworkers' union in 1936. But I'd already joined the Pile Drivers for the foundations on the Bay Bridge in 1934. I paid all my dues. I don't know what I would do without the unions, especially Local 378 in the East Bay. I joined the ironworkers' Local 377 of San Francisco first. To be on the Golden Gate, you had to be out of 377. Then I transferred over to Oakland and been there ever since.

I also still remember President Franklin Roosevelt, who helped the unions a whole lot. He was "it." If it wasn't for Roosevelt, we'd still be fighting for unions.[17] Yeah, he was a great man. Now [1986] Ronnie Reagan's there as president. He's against our union. He was a union man himself and president of his local. He was a Democrat, now he's a Republican. I don't know—I can't understand his job and I know he couldn't understand mine.

I've been up on the Golden Gate towers and I've been ninety feet below the water working as a sandhog in Texas. So I've been close to hell and I've been up near heaven. These younger kids read about it now and they come and meet me. They say, "That's Al Zampa. I see him on TV all the time. He's an ironworker. Hell, he's a legend." I feel a little proud, naturally.[18]

Working on bridges, you just got a wonderful proud feeling that comes up to you. Some of us that done the Golden Gate are still very proud to be one of the boys. It was a big thrill to me. I loved it. Hah, you had to love it. Otherwise you couldn't do the work.

9

Mary Zita Felciano
and Patricia DeWeese

NURSES

No one really realizes what those men went through. In those days, we only
had two or three different kinds of medications. We had morphine, Panafon,
and sleeping tablets. There wasn't much else, but the men seemed to get
along on not too much medication, although they would be sick to their
stomachs and suffering from the shock of having fallen, been injured, and
been brought into a hospital.   **PATRICIA DEWEESE**

*Mary Zita Felciano, Sister of Mercy, was the daughter of a Portuguese
immigrant father and an American-born mother whose parents were from
Italy. She was born in 1909 in Santa Rosa, California, and was raised there.
Sister Mary Zita trained as a nurse in San Francisco during the mid-1920s
and took her religious vows as a Sister of Mercy in 1930. She supervised the
orthopedic floor at St. Mary's Hospital in San Francisco when the Golden
Gate Bridge was under construction and helped care for the workers who
were injured in the tragic Golden Gate Bridge accident of February 17, 1937.
I interviewed her in Burlingame, California, on August 6, 1987.*

*Born circa 1918 and raised in Watsonville, California, Patricia DeWeese
entered nurse's training at St. Mary's Hospital in San Francisco in 1936.
There she helped care for Golden Gate Bridge workers injured on the job,*

including those hurt during the February 1937 accident. She walked across the bridge when it officially opened in 1937 and did so again in 1987, when the iconic structure turned fifty. I interviewed her in Burlingame, California, on August 6, 1987.

■   ■   ■

SISTER MARY ZITA FELCIANO

In 1926 or 1927, I came to San Francisco when I went into nursing. I graduated from St. Mary's Hospital in the city, worked for seven or eight months, and went into the novitiate down in Burlingame.[1] Then I went back to St. Mary's.

I was born and raised in Santa Rosa, California. My father was from the Azores off Portugal. He came to America when he was sixteen and started bottling beer in a lager company in Sonoma County, California. He took night extension courses from the University of California and worked his way up from accountant to secretary of the firm. My mother was a Tuscan. She was born in Santa Rosa, but her parents came here from Italy.

When the Golden Gate Bridge was being built, I was in charge of the orthopedic floor at St. Mary's. The insurance company that dealt with the bridge was bringing the injured men to our hospital. They would come up to the orthopedic floor. That's how I happened to meet the boys that built the bridge. I always called them "the boys." I'm sure they were all men, but they acted like boys.

They were rough-looking men, they were big, and some of them were bearded. They looked so manly and yet they were just like little kids. They loved to have attention. I think that poor men didn't get much attention, you see. But I found them to be just softies. They had big hearts and they were particularly thoughtful of each other. It did your heart good.

I can still see myself going into this six-bed ward and seeing this man who had permission to be up. He was over at another man's bed. He was up in his nightshirt and he's over helping the other man by holding a basin for him. The other poor fellow was sick. The first man got up and went out of his room to go over and help the other man instead of getting a nurse. He thought he could help. They were always helping each other. They were very rough and ready, but they were very thoughtful men.

And they'd tell me such tales. I was sure they were putting elastic in them. One day they told me that when they were pouring concrete one of the men fell into the mixture and so there was a man buried out there in the concrete in the bridge. I kind of believed it at first, but it wasn't true at all. They were just pulling my leg.

But then they couldn't stand shots with this little bitty needle. I gave one fellow an IV in the arm. Oh, he didn't think I could do it. Here were these big burly men building a bridge and going up near the top of these cables and then you want to shoot them with a little needle. They were like children, they were so afraid of it.

I was a fiery little supervisor then. I used to go on the wards to see if the men were misbehaving. One day I went and they were playing cards. All the cards were risqué ones. Oh! You never in your sight! I just put my hand down and collected the whole deck and walked out. They never said a word. Most of the men thought it was very funny when I collected the girlie cards. I'm sure they had another set the next day and saw to it that I wasn't making rounds when they were playing.

Once the patients complained to one of the doctors about my picking up their girlie playing cards. The doctor's response was, "I only wish we had more Sister Zitas around." They never told on me again. Oh, they did have one other thing. They used to have little girlie magazines. They had them underneath the pillows and the sheets. But I didn't go around pulling them out.

One time some women came to see this poor man. That night he was as drunk as he could be. We couldn't manage him. He was a big man and he had a splint on and was in traction. Most of the men had skeletal injuries of their backs, legs, or hips. When a man got wild with traction it was pretty bad business. You had to have a man nurse hold him down in bed. So we had to get special male nurses. Those nurses were never plentiful, but we had some, thank goodness. This man especially had to have a male nurse because he was so strong. I felt like a heel having to call the doctor up and tell him I couldn't manage this man at all.

The next day the man felt terrible and was humiliated. I could understand and wasn't mean to him. I was forgiving. But they made him pay for the special nurses. They took it out of his compensation check. I was so provoked with those women I could have brained them. I wouldn't care if the men had a little drink. But not enough to get completely drunk.

I remember a group of eight men coming in to the hospital at once. It was a trial and tribulation to see that they were all cared for because in those days we didn't have these big emergency rooms. It could very well have been the day the net broke. They were telling me about this net. They explained it to me and told me where it was hung.[2]

Some of the men were so sick at first that they had to have their backs elevated. But the beds didn't crank in those days. You had to do it with pillows. You had to use maybe sixteen or twenty pillows to get them so they'd be high enough.

We used Thomas splints for broken legs. They were terrible things. I don't think they use them anymore. A Thomas splint was a big ring that fit up around the man's hip. It came up on the bed and then it was suspended. It had two heavy wires that went down the ring. The wires gradually got nearer together until they joined at the bottom. They would put this ring up around the man's hip and then put dressings like moleskin along his leg. There were certain padded foot things down by the man's ankle. They would put a rope through the splint. The rope went on a pulley. Then you had weights hanging down off the bed. The splint had to be suspended from a frame above the bed to keep the leg raised. You had to either take on or put off weights according to the instructions of the physician. Think of the poor man with one of those things on.[3]

In the 1930s, you never thought of your nursing duties as being something that would be written up in history. It never occurred to you. But the bridge itself did have a lot of meaning to me because I lived in Northern California. It was marvelous to think that I could get on the bridge and get home to Santa Rosa. In those days the sisters weren't permitted to go out like we do now, so I didn't see the bridge for a while. I saw pictures of it and I heard a lot about it from the men, but it was some little time before I got to see it. Oh, I just think it's a beautiful bridge. It's exquisite from both sides of the bay.

PATRICIA DeWEESE

I was born at St. Mary's Hospital in San Francisco. My mother brought me to San Francisco to be born, but I was raised in Watsonville, California. Nancy O'Brien, a cousin of mine who was a nurse from St. Mary's, always said to me, "You want to be a nurse." And I always wanted to be one. My dad died when I was six years old. My Irish mother said to me, "You'll never leave the ranch." But I did leave it when I was accepted into nurse training at St. Mary's in 1936. Your heart and throat are all tied up until you get that letter, you know?

Nursing care then was bathing the patients, seeing that they had drinking water, and taking care of their casts. You also accompanied the doctors. When the doctor walked in, you stood up, gave him a patient's chart, and walked to the patient's room with him.

The doctors were nice to the injured workers who constructed that bridge and were very understanding, but no one really realizes what those men went through. In those days, we only had two or three different kinds of medications. We had morphine, Panafon, and sleeping tablets. There wasn't much else, but the men seemed to get along on not too much medication, although they would be sick to their stomachs and suffering from the shock of having fallen, been injured, and been brought into a hospital. I don't remember that we ever had an infection, though. And all we had was mercurochrome, methylate, and soap and water.

The men also didn't have the convenience of having the lovely beds like they have now. If they were in a cast, and there were lots of them in body casts, they were in a cast bed. That meant they just laid out flat. There was no way of getting them up and walking them around. We didn't have the type of care that you have now where you recuperate quickly. They would be allowed to be up and to walk around after a period of time, but there was no such thing as a day in the hospital if you were injured in 1936. They didn't come in for a week or a few days. They were always there for a month or longer.

Yet those injured workers were very patient, wonderful men. Some of 'em were so sick, but they never complained. One man was there for a year. There was so much fuss about the bridge at that time, it's just a shame that there wasn't more done about the men that constructed it. They were the ones that did it or we wouldn't have the bridge. I cared for the hurt ones before there was a net under the bridge, when they would drop and be injured. When they put the net in, we didn't have quite as many injuries. We still had injuries, but some men would fall into the net instead of getting hurt.

Those injured young fellows who were our patients were also very nice men. They protected the nurses from the sisters. They made sure there wouldn't be dust around when the sisters came in. That way we wouldn't get scolded or punished. Dusting was most important in the hospital in those days.

Sometimes the men would say, "Miss Boen, wear your cape tomorrow because my wife is coming." My name then was Madeline Patricia Boen. So we'd wear our capes. Their families would bring along bread, a long thing of salami, and a bottle of red wine. We'd put it underneath our capes and go back to our rooms across the street at ten o'clock when lights were out and the sisters could no longer see into our room. We'd take our spreads off our beds, put them up on the windows, and have a feast. The families brought food to us frequently, like twice a week. And they never stopped bringing food to us. That was the highlight in our life. I guess we looked emaciated.

They didn't have television in the 1930s. That's why the men would play cards to entertain themselves. They would have a radio, though. I remember taking my radio over to one man that didn't bring a radio in. You know, when you are caring for someone, you really don't realize the historic importance of it. In those days we just did our job.

My roommate and I went out in our white shoes on May 27, 1937, the first day that the bridge opened and so many people walked it. We walked right down the middle of the bridge before the cars came across. There were no cars or anything. It was such fun. I can remember my hair was blowing, and it was a lovely day. We wore our white shoes, a gray skirt, a sweater, and a jacket. We took a picture at the beginning of the bridge down by the Palace of Fine Arts and another around the turn where you would go onto the bridge. The sisters had given us five cents to get over there. They always gave you five cents for the streetcar and five cents to be sure to get home.

The day that they closed the bridge for people to walk on it in 1987 was not on the exact birthday of the bridge, which was May 27. On the actual birthday of the bridge, I put on my white shoes and wore my gray skirt, blue sweater, and jacket, had my picture taken that day, and walked the bridge again. People thought that it was so funny that I would be wearing the same skirt fifty years later. I've walked the bridge several times. Of course, we were much younger in 1937. This time I huffed and puffed a little bit, but I love to walk.

Sister Mary Zita Felciano (*left*) and Patricia DeWeese at their 1987 interview for the Labor Archives and Research Center's Golden Gate Bridge Fiftieth Anniversary Celebration. Photo by Harvey Schwartz. Courtesy of Labor Archives and Research Center, San Francisco State University.

That bridge is a wonderful thing. You can go back east and there's no thrill about walking on any of the bridges back there. No matter where you go, it's not as much of a thrill as there is walking on this bridge and looking down when there is a ship coming through underneath. It is a beautiful bridge and from my home now, which is in Berkeley, I can look directly west, right into the middle of it.

Walter Vestnys and Joyce "Big J" Harris

MAINTENANCE IRONWORKERS

Short of them building a new Golden Gate, they will always be fixing that one. I went out there to help set up some stuff. They were gonna do some rebracing. I was privileged to go all the way to the top and stand there. I was just amazed at the structure. . . . I thought about my brothers before me who put this thing together. It's a structure that people know all over the world.

JOYCE "BIG J" HARRIS

Born in San Francisco in 1928, Walter Vestnys went to sea toward the end of World War II, when he was sixteen, and sailed for seven years. In 1953 he became an apprentice ironworker. During 1965–66 Vestnys performed maintenance on the Golden Gate Bridge, where he replaced many of the structure's original rivets from the 1930s with more modern fasteners. After leaving the bridge, Vestnys became coordinator for the ironworkers' union apprenticeship program for Northern California. He held this job in San Francisco for many years. I interviewed him in Saratoga, California, on April 4, 1987, and in San Francisco two days later.

Walter Vestnys's father, Bert Vestnys, adds brief but valuable comments to his son's testimony. Born in Seattle, Washington, in 1906, Bert Vestnys spent most of his working life in the San Francisco Bay Area. He labored as a truck driver hauling cement to the Golden Gate Bridge construction site in San Francisco when building began there. A few years later, in 1936, he delivered machinery and cable materials to the bridge as well. Vestnys retired as a truck driver in 1968. I interviewed him in Saratoga, California, on April 4, 1987.

Joyce "Big J" Harris was born in Fresno, California, in 1957 and raised in Oakland. She is a veteran of the Job Corps and the U.S. Army. Harris labored as a shipyard worker in San Francisco before she became an ironworker. As an African American woman, she overcame numerous challenges in the construction trades. Two generations younger than the workers who built the Golden Gate Bridge, she worked briefly doing maintenance on the bridge in the late 1990s or early 2000s. A few years later, Harris took a job with the California Building and Construction Trades Council, promoting apprenticeship programs to young people. Still later, she became a job developer. Since 2010 she has gone by her maiden name, Joyce Guy. I interviewed her in Alameda, California, on February 8, 2008.

■ ■ ■

WALTER VESTNYS

When I got out of the service in 1953 I became a lineman in San Francisco for the Pacific Gas and Electric Company. We used to go to the same bar in town as the ironworkers. This was a Norwegian bar at Nineteenth and Folsom Streets called Old Homesteaders. That's where I found out that an apprentice ironworker made more money than I did as a PG&E lineman. PG&E didn't pay enough, had a terrible accident rate, and didn't cover their people who got injured. So after six months at PG&E I transferred over to the ironworkers.

I'd worked in the woods and I was seven years going to sea. I started sailing with the Sailors' Union of the Pacific in 1944 during World War II. I sailed until 1950, when I got drafted for the Korean War. In the service I was in the Signal Corps. By 1953 I had a lot of rigging experience. I went down to G. W. Thomas Drayage and Rigging Company in San Francisco, and they sent me to the ironworkers' union to get a membership. A Scandinavian guy who was the president of Local 377 at the time suggested that I'd be better off coming into the union as an apprentice ironworker instead of as a journeyman. He was certainly right. I learned my trade through serving my apprenticeship. Now I've been in the ironworkers for thirty-five years [as of 1987].

I was born in 1928 at San Francisco. I started to work when I was twelve years old and out of school. In the summer of 1941 I went into the sawmills and joined the Lumber and Sawmill Workers Union. We were making eighty-seven cents an hour. Once I got a taste of that man's wages, I didn't want to go back to school. So I just kept working. I've belonged to unions ever since. I grew up around union people, and I guess my father, Bert Vestnys, probably had a lot to do with it.

BERT VESTNYS

In 1928 I transferred from chauffeurs' Local 265 into Local 85 of the Teamsters union.[1] This was in San Francisco where I'd driven a cab for about four years. I've been in Local 85 ever since, except for some years around World War II when I worked in Seattle. I was born in 1906 and retired in 1968, but I still have a membership in Local 85. During the big 1934 maritime strike, I had a patrol on the San Francisco waterfront. We rode up and down on the front to see if any of our members got in trouble. I was really close to the Battle of Rincon Hill on Bloody Thursday in '34 when the longshoremen and the cops got into a fight. I also saw the cops chasing workers away from the docks.

My father was born at Rock Diamond, California, in 1873. That used to be a coal mine in Contra Costa County. His father was a Norwegian. My father was a plasterer. They called 'em masons then. He done that for about forty-five years. He belonged to several different locals of his union. There was one in San Francisco and one in San Jose. But I can't recall the name of the union now.

When they were building the Golden Gate Bridge, I got dispatched to different employers who had contracts for hauling bridge material. There was no highway out like there is now. We used to go through the Presidio of San Francisco to the delivering spot at Fort Point. I hauled some cement there when they first started to build, but I worked on the bridge mostly for W. R. Ballinger and Son for about six months in 1936 hauling machinery to Fort Point as well as some of the cable that was used for the cable splicing.

There were a lot of skeptics back then that didn't think the bridge would ever be built. They thought it was a big pipe dream. The few Local 85 drivers I talked to occasionally about the bridge just considered it another job. They didn't see anything special about it. Most of those guys didn't even think it would ever be finished.

WALTER VESTNYS

In early 1965, the Local 377 business agent asked another ironworker, Benny Muvillo, and myself to go to work on the Golden Gate Bridge and change the gratings. They already had a regular crew of five ironworkers out there working all the time. We went out as two extra guys. While we were there, they decided to start knocking the old rivets out to see if it was a good idea to replace 'em. I stayed for more than a year and a half doing that. I quit that job in December 1966 to come on to the apprenticeship coordinator's job I've had up to now.

To replace the old rivets, we busted out the old ones and replaced 'em with high-tensile bolts.[2] They used rivet busters, hell dogs they called 'em. That's a pneumatic tool that busted the head off the old rivet. To bust the head off, you sheared it off at a right angle with the buster, which had tremendous power through its air drive. Then you used a B & O to drive the rivet back out of its hole.[3] Next you stuffed the hole with a high-tensile bolt of the proper length and torqued it up to so many pounds per square inch as required by the engineers. We'd test the bolts with a torque wrench to see that they were tight. They were far stronger than a rivet.

But it was a lousy job. You were working in awkward positions. Either that or you were inside the iron, and as soon as you made that machine noise you'd go deaf. You couldn't hear. That's why everybody shouted. Over the years you'd get where you couldn't hear at all.

Besides that, most of the time the weather is terrible on the bridge. It can change in just a couple of minutes, so you had to dress for the worst. The first day I worked out on the bridge I froze 'cause I didn't have thermal underwear on. It was just terrible. That night I stopped at the Sears and Roebuck store and bought my first pair of thermal underwear. Everyone wore thermal underwear every day, tops and bottoms, a heavy pair of pants like Frisco jeans, a good heavy work shirt like a hickory shirt or a blue Levi's one, and an insulated or even a rain-repellent jacket.[4]

When you got to work in the morning, you'd put on your overalls. The three layers kept you pretty warm. I wore two pairs of socks, very much like in the army. One would be like a pair of dress socks. The outer pair would be made of heavy wool. My boots would be a little big to accommodate the two pairs of socks. I wore boots with some kind of fabric sole. They didn't have waffle-type soles yet. You wore anything other than leather soles.

The hard hats the bridge required were called boiled glass. This was a plastic hat with a liner inside. There was a strap on the hat that would go under your chin so when the wind was blowing you didn't lose your hat. White hats was for the pusher [supervisor] and blue hats was for the guys in the work gang.

The ironworkers on the Golden Gate Bridge performed all kinds of different tasks. They did new construction. They hung all the rigging for the painters, which got to be very intricate. It's a big bridge with big areas, and we had fifty or sixty painters out there. It required a lot of rigging for 'em to get around. You did whatever else was necessary. We replaced the fog horns a couple of times 'cause they were blasting over to the mayor's house and he got mad.[5] Then we walked the cables once a month to check them for abrasions, erosion, or breakage. We also tested the airplane lights.

The ironworkers even went after all the jumpers, the people that were suicidal. People jumped off there all the time. We'd fish out all the bodies and turn 'em over to the Coast Guard so they could haul 'em to the coroner. They'd blow the horn in the ironworkers' shop and you'd know there was a jumper. You'd go out to wherever you'd find 'em. We chased one woman around a better part of an afternoon to try to find her. She was pretty fleet-footed. We never caught her, and we never found a body. I don't know what happened to her.[6]

We put up television cameras when I was out there, too, so the policemen there in the shack could see everything going on in the roadway, like wrecks and jumpers and stuff. After the years I was out there, the ironworkers took on jobs for the ferry system. They do all the dockwork for the ferries. They also fix the bus park for the Golden Gate Bridge, Highway, and Transportation District.[7]

From growing up in San Francisco, I imagine that building the Golden Gate Bridge was a means of support for a good percentage of the town.

We was right in the middle of the Depression, and folks were starving. The bridge was a godsend that paid the rent and paid to raise a lot of families. The two years that I worked there was a learning process that was extremely educational. It was so good that when I got this job as apprenticeship coordinator twenty years ago, the first thing I did was talk to the bridge manager and make a deal that we'd have two rotating apprentices working there all the time. We rotate 'em every six months, so during one year we'll have four apprentices out there. Many of the apprentices that started there went back again as journeymen and are now steady ironworkers for the Bridge District. They all profited from their bridge experience.[8]

JOYCE "BIG J" HARRIS

My dad was a laborer. I was his oldest child. They always teased me that my father wanted his oldest child to be a boy. So, his oldest child being a girl, I learned how to be tough and aggressive. We lived in Oakland, where I grew up, although I was born in 1957 at Fresno, California. I remember me and my dad going to build a fence for somebody. I loved doing that. But back in the day, people assumed that if you were a girl you were going to be a nurse or a schoolteacher.

Mom really had a hard time with how attentive I was to working around my father as opposed to working around her. She did everything she could to change me. She put me in typing classes in high school. But then I actually got kicked out of typing class!

For that my mother put me on punishment. They put me in an automotive class. But I loved it. I'd come home from school and me and my dad would fix the car. We'd change the carburetor and do everything else. It was psychologically hard because I was torn between what I really liked and my mom. She even took me to a psychologist. Now, though, she realizes that's just who I was and that was my gift.

When I was sixteen I went into the Job Corps. A teacher at Tongue Point started a welding class.[9] That's when I really became fascinated with construction. We built things and I got to go to Seattle and work. I loved every

Maintenance workers on the Golden Gate Bridge, 1958. Walter Vestnys performed maintenance jobs on the bridge in the mid-1960s. Courtesy of San Francisco History Center, San Francisco Public Library.

minute of it. I even graduated from high school while in the Job Corps. When I came out of the Job Corps in 1976, I went back to my parents' household. Now I was an adult, but I was stuck in a house with a mom who still said, "No." The reality check there, too, was that as far as construction was concerned, there was nowhere for a female to go. People weren't looking at me as employable, even though I now had welding certifications.

I ended up going into the military. I can play sports really good and made an all-Army basketball, volleyball, and softball team. So I got to see other parts of the world. But I kept being drawn to construction. In 1980 I decided not to reenlist and came back to the Bay Area.

By going through a program called Women in Apprenticeship I got hired in the San Francisco shipyards. I did anything from ventilation to reflooring work. It was heaven. I was working with my hands. The guys I worked with were nice, but the shipyard industry was dying and they knew I was there temporarily. Besides, I was never really part of the clique. I was in the Sheet Metal Workers International Association, which had an apprenticeship program, but no one told me how to get in. When the ships no longer came to the Bay Area, I didn't have connections to know how to get work on the local naval base or any other avenue to keep me busy.

For a short period I got work with PG&E. I dug ditches, whatever it took. The problem was that again I come in on the back end. Everybody was downsizing and PG&E cut a division. I had no seniority and I was out of the loop.

Next I decided to go to the College of Alameda. By now I was a single mom with no job. I'd met a guy and got married, but soon he was gone. I finally got an AA degree in social science. It took me forever to get it. What could I do with it? Nothing. I still wanted to work construction. There were women in apprenticeships now, but information about this was not out there. People were not talking about it. We still had that Stone Age image where if a woman worked construction, she must be some kind of a man. If you weren't a good old boy and your uncle or your dad's not telling you, ain't nobody talking.

I don't know how I figured out how, but finally I got a company to sponsor me and I applied to be an ironworker. I brought my paperwork to Walt Vestnys, the Local 377 apprenticeship coordinator in San Francisco. He said I couldn't have the job I'd hustled myself since he had apprentices out of work. I got on BART and I was crying. I met a guy there who said he'd take me to his union hall in Oakland. I don't know why I went, but I did. He introduced me to Dick Zampa at Local 378. Zampa drove me to meet his apprenticeship coordinator. The next day I went to work as a decker.

I had no idea what ironworkers did. I only knew they welded. Nobody told me I was going to have to walk a beam in the air. That first day, this guy Jim McDaniels says to me, "Come with me. We're going up on the building and screw." Everybody in the room couldn't believe it. But I said, "Sure, I don't mind if you think you can handle it." From then on there was great rapport. That day I used a screw gun to screw down an existing deck. They were willing to teach me right up until the day they told me to walk out on that iron. I thought, *You gotta be kidding me, right?* But then they even taught me how to do that. It wasn't a bad situation at all.

Some guys were resistant. Several had never worked side by side with an Afro-American woman. One Hispanic guy decided to urinate in my lunch box. That was one of the most humiliating things you could do to a person. I thought of giving up being an ironworker. But in the morning I opened up the door to my son's room and realized, *It ain't about me. I have a kid to take care of.*[10] I cleaned and bleached the lunch pail and went back to work. That day the union business agent, Jerry Balmer, came out to the job site. He said, "Don't tolerate that." He let me know that that's unacceptable to him and to the union.

A guy named Keith also told me, "Joyce, you never know when you're going to be that Hispanic guy's boss." I thought, *I'm a black woman. There's no way in this trade they'll ever let me be anybody's boss.* But over the years I established positive rapport with people. They found I could work just as hard as I could talk. I'm six feet tall, and after a while they didn't call me Joyce, they called me Big J. When they said Big J, they were not thinking of a girl. Over time I got to run quite a few jobs. Guess who, about six years later, got me as his boss? He walked up there and said, "Who's the boss?" He only knew it was this Big J. When he found out it was me, I says, "You're only going to stay here one day. Don't ever try to humiliate anybody again like you did me." I just used my power at work that one day. Then I let that issue go.

When I was still an apprentice I fell twenty-seven feet through a building. I didn't get hurt, but I got out of the trade. But about 1990 I went back to complete my apprenticeship. When I see Dick Zampa, he gives me a big old hug. He realized I'd been in apprenticeship before. He says, "We're going to give you credit for the classes you took." I thought, *How great can that be?*

We still had good old boys in our apprenticeship class. One guy, Dan, had a huge swastika tattoo on his arm. For two years every other word was the *N* word. Finally I said, "Dan, I've had it with you." He walked in front of my desk and said, "You n——s need to row that boat back." So I came across the desk on him. After that he changed his attitude and me and Dan became friends.

In all, I've still had way more great experiences than bad ones. Once I was working with a grinder and a guy from the pipe fitters started yelling at me about grinding sparks. Instead of tapping my shoulder first, he snatched the cord out, which made the grinder jump. If I'd been holding this huge grinder with one hand, there's no telling what could have happened. I looked up and saw this white mob of ironworkers coming. I'm thinking, *Oh, my God.* But they surround this dude and are getting ready to beat him. I'll never forget what Donnie Chilton told me. He said, "Joyce, you were inducted into a sorority. You're family. We can pick on you, but can't nobody else."

I don't work iron no more right now. The State Building and Construction Trades Council hired me to go all over Northern California giving out information about construction apprenticeship programs. So I give presentations at prisons, churches, high schools, whatever. I have passion for recruiting people into the trades 'cause it changes lives economically and culturally.[11] But I miss the iron, because there's no finished product now in what I do.

While I was still working iron, the San Mateo Bridge was the biggest project I was ever foreman on.[12] I was out there fifteen or sixteen months. I loved bridge work because I was working on history. When I retrofitted the Bay Bridge, I was dealing with that.

I got to work on the Golden Gate Bridge for a few days, too. Short of them building a new Golden Gate, they will always be fixing that one. I went out there to help set up some stuff. They were gonna do some rebracing. I was privileged to go all the way to the top and stand there. I

Joyce Guy (earlier known as Joyce Harris) at work in the field, Oakland, California, 2014. Breaking into the male-dominated ironworker world was challenging for an African American woman, but Guy persevered to carry on the work of the Golden Gate Bridge builders who preceded her. Photo by Victoria Hamlin, board member of Tradeswomen, Inc. Courtesy of Joyce Guy and Victoria Hamlin.

was just amazed at the structure. The average person doesn't get to go and see how every brace is there for a reason. I thought about my brothers before me who put this thing together. It's a structure that people know all over the world, and that day we got to get some steel ready to put in there. A lot of people don't get injected into history that way, but we will always be a part of it. It's not always about the money.

EPILOGUE

An army cannot consist of officers alone, however talented; and a great bridge—while it owes so much to its designers and construction supervisors—owes an equal, if not superior, debt of gratitude to the workers who built it.

KEVIN STARR

Kevin Starr is a native San Franciscan and the author of an acclaimed eight-volume series called *Americans and the California Dream.* In 2010 he published a brief history of the Golden Gate Bridge (*Golden Gate: The Life and Times of America's Greatest Bridge*) that was uniquely enriched by his admiration for the iconic structure and for those who constructed it. His comment provides a fitting epilogue to this book.

ACKNOWLEDGMENTS

Writers of history books generally get a great deal of help from colleagues, friends, and relatives along the way to publication. I am no exception. I wish to acknowledge the aid I have been given over time by many people, although a sentence or two cannot begin to repay the debts incurred.

First, I deeply appreciate the invaluable long-term support I have received from Lynn A. Bonfield, founding director of the Labor Archives and Research Center at San Francisco State University, who commissioned me to conduct the 1987 interviews of bridge workers that form the core of this book. In later years, I have benefited tremendously from the backing of Bonfield's successors at LARC, initially Susan Sherwood and later Catherine Powell. Recently, Powell provided much understanding and patience while I worked to complete this project. I must also mention the grant to LARC from the California Council for the Humanities, won by Bonfield in the mid-1980s, that funded LARC's 1987 Golden Gate Bridge Project and most of the oral histories recounted here.

Three retired construction workers with long experience in their trades and as union officers read chapter drafts when this book was in manuscript form. I asked them to vet the technical passages dealing with construction and especially with bridge building. All three responded with insightful comments and suggestions. I have tried to make suitable adjustments wherever they pointed out errors or unclear descriptions; any remaining mistakes or oversights are undoubtedly due to my own shortcomings. For their aid I am deeply grateful.

Dick Zampa, Al Zampa's son, read all of the chapter drafts. He retired in 2006 as national first vice-president of the International Association of Bridge, Structural, Ornamental, and Reinforcing Iron Workers. He served, too, as president of the Iron Workers California District Council and secretary-treasurer of the California Building and Construction Trades Council. As a young man in the mid-1950s, he worked with his father, Al, and his brother, Gene, on the building of the second Carquinez Bridge between Crockett and Vallejo, California. Early in his career he was also business manager, secretary-treasurer, and president of Ironworkers Local 378, based in Oakland, California.

Bob Mettacola, who worked as a union carpenter for thirty-six years, reviewed all of the chapter drafts as well. He spent most of his union career, spanning 1977 to 2013, as a member of San Francisco Local 22 of the United Brotherhood of Carpenters and Joiners of America. Mettacola has been a delegate to the UBCJA regional council, to a national convention, and to the San Francisco Building and Construction Trades Council. He has served as Local 22 recording secretary for the past decade.

Derek Green, who retired after many years as business manager for San Francisco Local 6 of the International Brotherhood of Electrical Workers, carefully read the chapter draft containing the recollections of Golden Gate Bridge electrician Fred Brusati. Green is secretary-treasurer of the San Francisco–based Archie Green Fund for Labor Culture and History, named for his father, the renowned labor folklorist.

I owe a special debt to veteran ironworker, author, and photographer John V. Robinson, who has written extensively about Al Zampa. He graciously shared the research field he has long cultivated so I could utilize Isabelle Maynard's 1986 interview with Zampa, without which this book would not feel complete. Robinson also obliged when I needed a technically sharp image of Al Zampa at work—valuable assistance in the demanding task of collecting suitable historical photographs for book publication.

Many other people likewise helped me meet this challenge. Catherine Powell at LARC was especially generous as I refined my photo search. At the California Historical Society, staff members Debra Kaufman, Alison Moore, Marie Silva, and Wendy Welker aided me greatly when I ordered pictures. So did their counterparts in the San Francisco History Room of the San Francisco Public Library: Thomas Carey, Susan Goldstein, Christina Moretta, and Jeff Thomas. At the Bancroft Library of the University of California, Berkeley, Lark Ashford, Lori Hines, Susan Snyder, and Balba Strads helped as well.

Members of the Sisters of Mercy also lent a hand while I was searching for photos. These individuals included Sister Marilyn Gouailhardou, historian at the order's Burlingame, California, facility, and Grant Gerlick and Emily Reed, archivists at the Mercy Heritage Center in Belmont, North Carolina. Jake Bragonier at St. Mary's Hospital in San Francisco looked for historical pictures too.

Alice Fredericks and Dana Fehler of the Golden Gate Bridge, Highway, and Transportation District aided me when I sought permission to use district photographs. Dave Ruiz of Pacific Aerial Surveys, an associate of Quantum Spatial, Inc., helped me obtain permission to use a photo in his group's collection.

I also benefited in my picture search from the advice and generosity of Joseph A. Blum, Joseph A. Blum Photography; Robert E. David, retired Bridge District architectural photographer; Marjorie Dobkin, Bay Area architectural historian; Joyce Guy; Victoria Hamlin, board member of Tradeswomen, Inc.; Richard A. Kandel, docent at the Angel Island California State Park; Susan Morris, historian and bridge archivist; Carl Nolte of the *San Francisco Chronicle;* Dan Prince, president of Ironworkers Local 377 of San Francisco; and Ron Zampa.

For more than four decades I have studied and often worked for the International Longshore and Warehouse Union. Many officers, staff people, and rank-and-file members at the union's international headquarters in San Francisco as well as in its many locals along the West Coast and in Hawaii and Canada have helped me in my historical research in a variety of ways. I remain appreciative of this support.

In recent years, Ronald E. Magden, the prominent historian of the ILWU in the Pacific Northwest, along with his wife, Beth, have patiently encouraged and aided me with my Golden Gate Bridge project.

Numerous other good friends and colleagues have sustained me as well while I have been preparing this history. These include George Beavin, Oscar Berland, Kiley Brokow, Paulette Burnard, Peter Cole, Lauren Coodley, Howard A. DeWitt, Louis M. Isaacs, Margaret Jonas, T. Nyan, John Rieber, Sheena Schwartz, and James B. Snyder.

I have been helped as well by many staff members at the University of Washington Press. In particular, I am appreciative of the guidance I received for this book from senior acquisitions editor Ranjit Arab and editing, design, and production manager Jacqueline Volin.

Rachael Levay, the UW Press marketing and sales director, and Thomas Eykemans, the press's talented designer, worked hard to enhance this volume's appeal. Proofreader Judy Loeven and indexer Kevin Millham did the same to enhance its utility.

I have benefited tremendously from the ongoing love of my family. My son, David Schwartz, who brings a serious historian's perspective to every discussion, has been an inspiration. To my wife, Marilyn M. Schwartz, who retired at the end of 2011 as managing editor at the University of California Press, I owe a very special debt for many things, including her great forbearance and her extraordinary editorial aid while I was working on this manuscript.

NOTES

INTRODUCTION

1   Studs Terkel, opening day comments, StoryCorps facility, Grand Central Terminal, New York, October 23, 2003. For similar sentiments in a pioneering book about bridge workers, see Gary Talese, *The Bridge: The Building of the Verrazano-Narrows Bridge* (New York: Harper & Row, 1964).

2   The writings of Charles F. Adams, John van der Zee, and Stephen Cassady come immediately to mind. Adams and van der Zee describe notable workers, and Cassady quotes some to good effect. Cassady's book includes numerous photos of the construction process, as does a volume issued a few years earlier by Richard Dillon, Donald DeNevi, and Thomas Moulin. See Charles F. Adams, *Heroes of the Golden Gate* (Palo Alto, CA: Pacific Books, 1987); John van der Zee, *The Gate: The True Story of the Design and Construction of the Golden Gate Bridge* (New York: Simon and Schuster, 1986); Stephen Cassady, *Spanning the Gate: The Golden Gate Bridge*, rev. ed. (Santa Rosa, CA: Squarebooks, 1986); Richard Dillon, Donald DeNevi, and Thomas Moulin, *High Steel: Building the Bridges across San Francisco Bay* (Berkeley, CA: Celestial Arts, 1979). Tom Horton, *Superspan: The Golden Gate Bridge* (San Francisco: Chronicle Books, 1983) also contains brief quotes from workers.

3   Adams does describe individual workers' backgrounds at some length. In his final chapter he also summarizes their later careers. See Adams, *Heroes*, 339–351.

4   Richard B. Morris, ed., *Encyclopedia of American History* (New York: Harper, 1953), 446–450.

5   The Golden Gate Bridge job was 100 percent union over most of its construction, whereas the unionization record on the concurrent Bay Bridge project was more spotty. See Cassady, *Spanning the Gate*, 40; John V. Robinson, *Spanning the Strait: Building the Alfred Zampa Memorial Bridge* (Crockett, CA: Carquinez Press, 2004), 19–20; van der Zee, *The Gate*, 231.

6   Lynn A. Bonfield and Karen R. Lewis, *Building the Golden Gate Bridge: An Exhibition at the Labor Archives and Research Center of San Francisco State University and the Sutro Library Branch of the California State Library, May 17–August 31, 1987* (San Francisco: Labor Archives and Research Center, San Francisco State University, 1987).

7   However, Adams, *Heroes*, 103–113, 319–324, profiles engineer Joseph Strauss's

secretary and a model who reigned as Fiesta Queen for the bridge's opening ceremonies.

8 Lynn Bonfield identified the two nurses as potential interview subjects in 1987.

9 Adams, *Heroes*, 182–186, discusses one male African American worker, William D. Smith Jr., a truck driver who made deliveries to the bridge during its construction.

10 As Kevin Starr observed about the Golden Gate Bridge during a 2009 radio interview, "It dawned on everybody that the minute you finish building it, you have to continue to build it for the next fifty to sixty years. We know that about complex works of engineering. It's the same thing [as] in your home." Kevin Starr, interview by Scott Shafer, *Forum*, KQED radio, San Francisco, July 1, 2009.

11 Sherna Berger Gluck, *Rosie the Riveter Revisited: Women, the War, and Social Change* (New York: Meridian, 1988), 227.

12 Donald A. Ritchie, *Doing Oral History* (New York: Twayne Publishers, 1995), 102. In 2010, in a book cowritten with Molly Beer, the prominent oral historian David Dunaway commented, "The procedure of oral history is well documented, notably in Donald Ritchie's *Doing Oral History*." See David King Dunaway and Molly Beer, *Singing Out: An Oral History of America's Folk Music Revivals* (New York: Oxford University Press, 2010), 200. Another helpful classic focusing on methodology is Valerie Yow, *Recording Oral History: A Guide for the Humanities and Social Sciences*, 2nd ed. (Walnut Creek, CA: Altamira Press, 2005). See also Robert Perks and Alistair Thomson, eds., *The Oral History Reader*, 2nd ed. (London: Routledge, 2006), a collection of seminal articles on the theory, method, and practice of oral history, including many written from an international perspective. Over the years, a suprising number of additional books have been published that offer especially outstanding insights into the utility and craftsmanship of oral history. Paul Thompson's *The Voice of the Past: Oral History* (Oxford: Oxford University Press, 1978) and Alessandro Portelli's *The Death of Luigi Transtulli and Other Stories: Form and Meaning in Oral History* (Albany: State University of New York Press, 1991), *The Order Has Been Carried Out: Memory and Meaning of a Nazi Masssacre in Rome* (New York: Palgrave Macmillan, 2003), and *They Say in Harlan County: An Oral History* (New York: Oxford University Press, 2011) are prime examples.

13 A cantilever bridge consists of two strong structures built out horizontally toward each other and then joined in the center. Many large twentieth-century cantilever bridges have cantilevers made of structural steel trusses. In a suspension bridge, the roadway is supported by vertical suspenders attached to sturdy cables.

14 The contractors engaged to build the Golden Gate Bridge included Barrett and Hilp, the two anchorages and the approach span piers; Pacific Bridge Company, sea-based San Francisco pier and fender and land-based Marin County pier; J. H. Pomeroy Company and Raymond Concrete Pile Company, San Francisco and Marin County approaches; Eaton and Smith Construction Company, Presidio of San Francisco approach road; Alta Electric and Mechanical Company, electrical work; McClintic-Marshall Corporation, a Bethlehem Steel Corporation subsidiary, building steel superstructure; Bethlehem Steel, fabricated steel, a little produced locally in South San Francisco, most built and shipped from Bethlehem's heavy steel manufacturing facilities in the eastern United States; John A. Roebling's Sons Company of New Jersey, main cable spinning and vertical suspension cable system. Mary C. Currie, *Highlights, Facts, and Figures of the Golden Gate Bridge, Highway, and Transportation District* (San Francisco: Golden Gate Bridge, Highway, and Transportation District, 2009), 16; Kevin Starr, *Golden Gate: The Life and*

Times of America's Greatest Bridge (New York: Bloomsbury Press, 2010), 115–118; Adams, *Heroes*, 151.

15　The Ellis story was broached and explored in depth by van der Zee in *The Gate*. See also Cassady, *Spanning the Gate,* 134, and John van der Zee, "Bridging the Gate," *Image* magazine, *San Francisco Examiner*, February 8, 1987, p. 24.

16　A cofferdam is a container that is sunk in water and pumped dry to allow construction on the bottom of the body of water in question. See Adams, *Heroes,* 163; Cassady, *Spanning the Gate,* 50.

17　The caisson designed to serve as a footing for the bridge's south tower was a massive, custom-built, watertight steel structure. Cassady, *Spanning the Gate,* 51–54, 60.

18　This brief overview of the bridge's political background, planning, and construction is based on several of the books listed in the Further Reading section of this volume. Among these, Cassady, *Spanning the Gate;* Adams, *Heroes;* Dillon, DeNevi, and Moulin, *High Steel;* van der Zee, *The Gate;* Starr, *Golden Gate;* Donald MacDonald and Ira Nadel, *Golden Gate Bridge: History and Design of an Icon* (San Francisco: Chronicle Books, 2008); and Currie, *Highlights, Facts, and Figures* were especially helpful.

1. FRED DIVITA: FIELD ENGINEER

1　The Golden Gate Bridge and the San Francisco–Oakland Bay Bridge were both under construction when Divita was attending "Cal," as the University of California, Berkeley, has been nicknamed regionally for decades.

2　The Golden Gate Bridge roadway is suspended from two huge towers. Divita is talking about the north, or Marin County, tower, erected between August 1933 and May 1934. Workers completed the south, or San Francisco, tower between January and June 1935. Cassady, *Spanning the Gate,* 70, 74, 79; Dillon, DeNevi, and Moulin, *High Steel,* 100–101.

3　Fairfax is in Marin County, twenty-five miles northwest of San Francisco across the Golden Gate strait. The Golden Gate Bridge was built to connect Marin and other northern counties to the city.

4　Between 1901 and 1910, more than two million Italians relocated to the United States as part of the "new immigration" from eastern and southern Europe. Most came to escape economic or other difficulties at home. Many ended up working in American industry. Morris, *Encyclopedia of American History,* 447–448; U.S. Bureau of the Census, *Historical Statistics of the United States, Colonial Times to 1957* (Washington, D.C.: U.S. Government Printing Office, 1960), 56. For classic works on the nationwide implications of immigration, see Oscar Handlin, *The Uprooted: The Epic Story of the Great Migrations That Made the American People* (Boston: Little, Brown, 1951; 2nd ed., Philadelphia: University of Pennsylvania Press, 2002); David Brody, *Steelworkers in America: The Nonunion Era* (Cambridge, MA: Harvard University Press, 1960; rev. ed., Urbana: University of Illinois Press, 1998). A helpful, wide-ranging overview of immigration throughout American history is provided in Roger Daniels, *Coming to America: A History of Immigration and Ethnicity in American Life,* 2nd ed. (New York: HarperCollins, 2002). See also Alan M. Kraut and David G. Gerber, eds., *Ethnic Historians and the Mainstream: Shaping America's Story* (New Brunswick, NJ: Rutgers University Press, 2013).

5   On Italian immigration to San Francisco, see William Issel and Robert W. Cherny, *San Francisco, 1865–1932: Politics, Power, and Urban Development* (Berkeley: University of California Press, 1986), 73–74; Robert W. Cherny and William Issel, *San Francisco: Presidio, Port and Pacific Metropolis* (San Francisco: Boyd and Fraser, 1981), 42. For the long-term influence of immigration and the Catholic Church on San Francisco politics, see William Issel, *Church and State in the City: Catholics and Politics in Twentieth-Century San Francisco* (Philadelphia: Temple University Press, 2013).

6   Fairfax was a small, rural community in the 1920s. In addition to there being no bridge connecting Marin to San Francisco in the south, the nearby Richmond–San Rafael Bridge from Marin to the East Bay did not exist until the mid-1950s.

7   Simi Winery was headquartered north of Fairfax in Healdsburg, California, for many years. It can trace its origins back to the late nineteenth century. During the 1970s and 1980s it became a major, high-profile California wine producer.

8   Bethlehem Steel, based in Pennsylvania, served as contractor for the fabrication of the steel for the bridge's towers and superstructure. Bethlehem Steel shipped tons of parts to California in railcars while the bridge was under construction. Adams, *Heroes*, 188; Janet Fireman and Shelly Kale, "Bridging the Golden Gate: A Photo Essay," *California History* 89, no. 4 (2012): 28–29; Starr, *Golden Gate*, 117.

9   It was necessary to scrape damaged, rusty paint and repaint after red lead paint inside the Marin (north) tower failed. Adams, *Heroes*, 269.

10 *Stifflegs* refers to the stiffleg derricks that helped equip the north tower traveler. In raising the north tower steel, the traveler sat between shafts. A stiffleg derrick and a ninety-foot boom serviced each shaft. Cassady, *Spanning the Gate*, 68, 72.

11 The construction cells consisted of plates of carbon seven-eighths of an inch thick and even stronger silicon steel. Dillon, DeNevi, and Moulin, *High Steel*, 83–84. These authors note that the towers were composed of 3.5-foot square cells. See also Starr, *Golden Gate*, 121.

12 A diaphragm in steel bridge engineering is a deck designed to mitigate the potentially dangerous impact of lateral motion caused by wind, earthquakes, or other pressures. Such a deck can provide something for a worker to stand on.

13 Made of groups of hollow cells, the towers had two legs, each with ninety-seven cells at the bottom. The number of cells tapered off to twenty-one at the top. Horton, *Superspan*, 83.

14 A Golden Gate Bridge steel rivet had a cylindrical shaft with a rounded head at one end. The opposite, narrow end was called a buck-tail. A heated rivet was quickly fitted into a hole in large steel pieces scheduled for final attachment and the tail "bucked," or jammed with an air jack, so that it flattened out, making the rivet a strong fastener when it cooled. A rivet catcher would secure a hot rivet thrown his way by a rivet heater or, inside tower cells, sent his way by a tube and immediately make it available to a bucker-up. The bucker-up would steady the rivet in place using a steel backing, while the rivet driver secured the piece using an air jack. This method of joining bridge steel was superseded by the employment of high-tensile bolts shortly after World War II.

15 The ten-thousand-ton floating caisson in question was scheduled to be sunk in place as a foundation base, but was damaged during a storm in October 1934. It was towed fifty miles out to sea and sunk. Dillon, Moulin, and DeNevi, *High Steel*, 81–83.

16 Workers built one of the anchorages for the San Francisco–Oakland Bay Bridge on Yerba Buena Island east of San Francisco.

17 The original Bay Bridge consisted of a suspension section on its San Francisco side and a cantilever span anchored on its East Bay side. Dillon, DeNevi, and Moulin, *High Steel*, 15. The East Bay section was replaced by a suspension span in 2013. For background, see "The Bay Bridge at 75—Looking Forward to 2013," *Panorama: Newsletter of the San Francisco Museum and Historical Society* 23, no. 4 (October–December 2011): 4–5.

18 Chief Engineer Strauss's safety net, which ultimately saved nineteen lives, was installed under the truss work as it advanced from the bridge's towers. Dillon, DeNevi, and Moulin, *High Steel*, 125; Adams, *Heroes*, 265–267; Cassady, *Spanning the Gate*, 104–105; Starr, *Golden Gate*, 133–134.

19 A construction rigger specializes in the lifting, moving, and placing of large and heavy loads. Riggers carefully calculate how to proceed and then typically use cranes, pulleys, and jacks to complete their work.

20 "In the Joe" could mean having extra money for coffee during the Depression, when many went without necessities, much less luxuries. The boxing historian Louis M. Isaacs suggested that it could mean making good money like heavyweight champion Joe Louis earned during the 1930s and 1940s. In later years, New Yorkers used the expression to refer to the Joe Louis Arena in Manhattan. Louis M. Isaacs, telephone interview with author, February 3, 2013.

21 In bridge building, there are top and bottom chords, which are the top and bottom horizontal steel members of a truss. See MacDonald and Nadel, *Golden Gate Bridge*, 106.

22 A stringer is a longitudinal beam installed to help support a bridge deck.

23 Tragically, a pin in the traveling crane had pulled loose. The boom of the crane fell into the water, missing the net. Moore's death was the first fatality during the bridge's construction. Traditionally, bridge builders ceased work when a major accident or a death occurred. Adams, *Heroes*, 273, 278; Cassady, *Spanning the Gate*, 107–108; van der Zee, *The Gate*, 267.

24 Turnipseed was a construction foreman on the bridge. He was also Kermit Moore's brother-in-law. Moore was working on Turnipseed's crew when he was killed. Adams, *Heroes*, 278; van der Zee, *The Gate*, 267.

25 Mohawk tribesmen from Quebec started working on bridges in the late nineteenth century. They became legendary as high-steel men while erecting New York City skyscrapers during the 1920s. See Edmund Wilson, *Apologies to the Iroquois, with a Study of the Mohawks in High Steel by Joseph Mitchell* (Syracuse, NY: Syracuse University Press, 1959), 3–38.

26 Corte Madera is about fifteen miles north of San Francisco.

27 The reference is to the highly publicized April 28, 1937, ceremonial driving of a gold rivet to commemorate the completion of the bridge. Adams, *Heroes*, 313–314; Cassady, *Spanning the Gate*, 122–123; van der Zee, *The Gate*, 293.

28 This was the large, rounded head side of the rivet.

29 In construction, falsework is temporary work that is often made of wood. It is generally removed when building has been completed.

30 The full name of the union is the International Association of Bridge, Structural, Ornamental, and Reinforcing Iron Workers.

31 Originally called the Lake Washington Floating Bridge, this Seattle-area structure was heavily used until 1990, when it sank in a storm.

32 During World War II, the U.S. Army Corps of Engineers built the Alcan Highway connecting the contiguous United States to Alaska via Canada as a military exigency.

33 Shortly after his inauguration in early 1933, President Franklin D. Roosevelt declared a four-day "bank holiday." Dating from the same year, the Works Progress Administration (WPA) provided jobs for millions of unemployed Americans and became one of the long-term mainstays of FDR's New Deal.

2. JOHN NOREN: ELEVATOR MAN

1 Between 1896 and 1921, San Francisco was widely known as "a union town," largely thanks to the power of the city's Building and Construction Trades Council, which controlled jobs through a strict union card check system. San Francisco's construction employers and other business leaders broke this power when they mounted a successful open-shop campaign between 1916 and the early 1920s. Michael Kazin, *Barons of Labor: The San Francisco Building Trades and Union Power in the Progressive Era* (Urbana: University of Illinois Press, 1987), chaps. 2–4, 8–9; Issel and Cherny, *San Francisco, 1865–1932*, chap. 4; Cherny and Issel, *San Francisco*, 33, 47–48; Harvey Schwartz, *Labor's Stronghold: 120 Years of Local 22, United Brotherhood of Carpenters and Joiners of America, in San Francisco, California, 1882–2002* (San Francisco: Local 22, UBCJA, 2002), 16–27; Stanley M. Smith, "History of the San Francisco Building and Construction Trades Council," in San Francisco Building and Construction Trades Council, *Commemorating 100 Years of Excellence in Craftsmanship, 1896–1996* (Oakland, CA: Union Publications, 1996), 6–8.

2 Local 8 can trace its origins in San Francisco back to 1902. Hector E. Rueda, "Excerpts from the Story of the International Union of Elevator Constructors No. 8," in San Francisco Building Trades Council, *Commemorating 100 Years of Excellence*, 62.

3 Thousands of "earthquake carpenters" and other craftsmen came to San Francisco to work during the city's 1906–7 rebuilding boom. Kazin, *Barons of Labor*, 124; Schwartz, *Labor's Stronghold*, 20.

4 The great Pacific Coast maritime strike of 1934 began that May. Ultimately, the National Guard did deploy on the San Francisco waterfront during the strike. David F. Selvin, *A Terrible Anger: The 1934 Waterfront and General Strikes in San Francisco* (Detroit, MI: Wayne State University Press, 1996), 152–153; Charles P. Larrowe, *Harry Bridges: The Rise and Fall of Radical Labor in the U.S.* (New York: Lawrence Hill, 1972), 70–71; Irving Bernstein, *Turbulent Years: A History of the American Worker, 1933–1941* (Boston: Houghton Mifflin, 1970), 279.

5 When Noren met Rickey, the latter was the general manager of the Saint Louis Cardinals. As president and general manager of the Brooklyn Dodgers in 1947, Rickey made baseball and U.S. history by sponsoring Jackie Robinson's successful effort to break the color barrier in Major League Baseball. See Jules Tygiel, *Baseball's Great Experiment: Jackie Robinson and His Legacy* (New York: Oxford University Press, 1983).

6 By the late twentieth century, the Mission District of San Francisco was a heavily Latino neighborhood. In the 1930s it was largely Irish and Italian.

7 Like Fred Divita, Noren was fortunate to get a job on the bridge in the way that he did. Many workers during the Great Depression waited in large groups outside bridge construction sites for days in the hope of landing a job. Adams, *Heroes*, 186.

8 These facilities consisted of open-air buckets with seats affixed. See Fireman and Kale, "Bridging the Golden Gate," 34.

9   The Occupational Safety and Health Act created OSHA in 1970. Nelson Lichtenstein, Susan Strasser, and Roy Rosenzweig, *Who Built America? Working People and the Nation's Economy, Politics, Culture, and Society*, vol. 2: *Since 1877* (New York: Worth Publishers, 2000), 659.

10 The Bank of America was a vibrant, relatively new organization in the mid-1930s. San Franciscan Amadero Pietro Giannini founded it in 1930 when he merged his older Bank of Italy with his newer banking interests. Issel and Cherny, *San Francisco 1865–1932*, 74–75; Cherny and Issel, *San Francisco*, 42–43.

11 Local 8 struck in 1967. The National Elevator Industry, Inc., the elevator employers' association, locked the union out in 1972. Rueda, "Excerpts," 64–67.

3. GLENN MCINTYRE: IRONWORKER

1   *Gandy dancer* is an old expression for a semiskilled railroad worker. In the late nineteenth and early twentieth centuries, most railroaders knew the term. Gandy dancers performed hard physical labor building and maintaining rail tracks. Mechanization eliminated most of their jobs during the late twentieth century.

2   A speeder is a small moving vehicle for traveling quickly along railroad tracks.

3   The Western Clock company's popular "Westclox" Pocket Ben pocket watches were widely sold for many years following their introduction in 1915.

4   Foster's Lunch System was a cafeteria restaurant chain with a number of San Francisco outlets. Foster's, as it was popularly known, was a high-profile institution in that city before the company closed its last San Francisco cafeteria in the early 1970s.

5   "Hustling sheets" meant selling newspapers, in this case for publisher William Randolph Hearst's *San Francisco Examiner*.

6   In the 1930s, Florsheim and Company of Chicago produced and distributed some of America's best-quality men's leather dress shoes.

7   The Embarcadero is a lengthy boulevard that runs for several miles along San Francisco's bayside waterfront. McIntyre would have been looking down two hundred feet in the scene he describes here. Dillon, DeNevi, and Moulin, *High Steel*, 28–29, 37.

8   A dinkey is a small locomotive.

9   A settling tank is a piece of equipment used to separate solids from liquids.

10 The cross-bay section of the Bay Area Rapid Transit system, known as BART, was completed in the late 1960s. BART runs underground where it travels beneath San Francisco Bay.

11 Turnipseed, mentioned in Fred Divita's recollections, was the highly regarded foreman of the crew that built the steel deck on the Marin side of the Golden Gate Bridge in 1936. Adams, *Heroes*, 78.

12 Heaters, or forges, were used to heat rivets for the bridge.

13 Only an extremely small number of African American men managed to secure work during the Golden Gate Bridge's construction. Charles F. Adams describes William D. Smith, who was one, in his volume on the bridge. See Adams, *Heroes*, 182–186.

14 Twenty-four workers lost their lives building the Bay Bridge. Dillon, DeNevi, and Moulin, *High Steel*, 24.

15 Editors Susan P. Sherwood and Catherine Powell included a passage on the Golden Gate Bridge in their 2008 San Francisco labor landmarks guidebook that

describes the sequence of this work: "After a traveling derrick hoisted units of steel into position, 'raising gangs' aligned and hooked up the plates, and 'connecting gangs' pounded the section into place. The 'bolt up crew' then inserted temporary bolts into about half of the holes, followed by the riveting crew. Crews worked from both ends of the bridge and met in the middle." Susan P. Sherwood and Catherine Powell, eds., *The San Francisco Labor Landmarks Guide Book: A Register of Sites and Walking Tours* (San Francisco: Labor Archives and Research Center, San Francisco State University, 2008), 41.

16 A headache ball is the large ball at the end of a crane's lifting cable. McIntyre is here describing the tragic death of Kermit Moore, who died on October 21, 1936. Moore was climbing off a girder the crane had been picking up when he was fatally hit. Miles Green, another worker, was hit by the cable as it whipped around. He fell into the safety net and survived. Cassady, *Spanning the Gate,* 107–108; Adams, *Heroes,* 278; van der Zee, *The Gate,* 267.

17 It was a tradition among bridge workers to quit work for the day following a tragic accident.

18 An impact wrench is a power-driven socket wrench.

19 Ultimately this problem was confronted when respirators were provided for men working inside the bridge's cells. Many of these workers had become sick from toxic fumes emitted when hot rivets touched red-lead-treated steel. Cassady, *Spanning the Gate,* 72; Currie, *Highlights, Facts, and Figures,* 16, 19.

20 The hard hats typically seen in photos of Bay Bridge workers appear to have broader bills than the Golden Gate Bridge hats McIntyre is describing. Dillon, DeNevi, and Moulin, *High Steel,* 37–42, 58, 115–122, 134.

21 While the bridge was in the planning stages, its potential color, which ultimately became its famous international orange, was a major political issue. See, for example, MacDonald and Nadel, *Golden Gate Bridge,* 49–57; Starr, *Golden Gate,* 106–108. For workers like McIntyre and others quoted in this volume, though, employment and job conditions were what mattered. The color of the bridge might preoccupy boosters, government officials, newspaper reporters, radio commentators, and "the public," but was insignificant to many working-class people struggling to survive during the Great Depression.

22 The Depression remained a serious problem in 1937. Unemployment spiked disturbingly that year when President Roosevelt drastically cut federal relief expenditures. The downturn, which lasted into 1938 before the president increased federal spending, was called the Roosevelt Recession. World War II's full employment was still four years away. Nelson Lichtenstein, Susan Strasser, and Roy Rosenzweig, *Who Built America?* 473–474.

23 Engineers and workers built the original Pitt River Bridge in 1942.

24 Construction of the Bay Area Rapid Transit system spanned 1964–72. The tube section that crosses underneath San Francisco Bay is not quite as far down as McIntyre noted, but at 135 feet it is still impressively deep.

4. JOHN URBAN: CABLE SPINNER

1 The Russian Empire controlled Lithuania between 1793 and World War I. Thousands of people left Lithuania for the United States between the mid-1860s and 1914 to escape famine, Russian rule, or military conscription. By 1930 nearly 250,000 children of Lithuanian parents lived in the United States. U.S. Bureau

of the Census, *Historical Statistics of the United States,* 65. For background, see Nicholas V. Riasanovsky, *A History of Russia* (New York: Oxford University Press, 1963), 298–299, 369, 421.

2   A bucker cut up felled trees into logs. A whistle punk worked in the woods sending messages by wire to the steam donkey (small locomotive) driver or as a safety lookout.

3   Compton's was a local cafeteria chain. Its restaurants were typical of the urban cafeteria diners of the mid-twentieth century. The company closed its last Northern California restaurants in the 1970s.

4   The New Deal's National Recovery Administration came into existence under the National Industrial Recovery Act of 1933. The NIRA's section 7A said that workers had the right to join unions of their own choosing, although there was no machinery to enforce compliance with the statute, and many employers fought unionization fiercely by firing activists and sometimes employing less-peaceful tactics. Some installed "company unions" to get around the intent of the law by blocking out worker-controlled organizations. But firms that signed up with the NRA program received certain benefits, including NRA "blue eagle" display emblems. The Supreme Court declared the NIRA unconstitutional in 1935. It was replaced that year by the stronger National Labor Relations Act, popularly known as the Wagner Act. Bernstein, *Turbulent Years,* 30–35, 172–173, 318–330, 639; David Brody, *Labor in Crisis: The Steel Strike of 1919* (Philadelphia: J. B. Lippincott Company, 1965), 181–184, and "The Emergence of Mass Production Unionism," in *Change and Continuity in Twentieth-Century America,* ed. John Braeman, Robert H. Bremner, and Everett Walters (New York: Harper and Row, 1966), 238–253; Robert H. Zieger, *The CIO: 1935–1955* (Chapel Hill: University of North Carolina Press, 1995), 16–17. For background on the Cooks' and Waiters' Union, see Edward Paul Eaves, "A History of the Cooks' and Waiters' Unions of San Francisco," M.A. thesis, University of California, Berkeley, 1931; for a book of wide vision that traces important developments in food-service unionism over time, see Dorothy Sue Cobble, *Dishing It Out: Waitresses and Their Union in the Twentieth Century* (Urbana: University of Illinois Press, 1991).

5   The San Francisco general strike of July 16–19, 1934, followed a massive worker funeral procession up Market Street on July 9 in protest of the police killing of two waterfront pickets four days earlier on "Bloody Thursday." One of the two men killed, Nick Bordoise, was a member of Cooks' Union Local 44. In the aftermath of their victory in 1934, the longshoremen led, sponsored, or inspired the unionization of thousands of men and women along the West Coast. Selvin, *A Terrible Anger,* 11–17, 149–150, 182–222; Harvey Schwartz, *The March Inland: Origins of the ILWU Warehouse Division, 1934–1938* (Los Angeles: Institute of Industrial Relations, University of California, 1978; reprint San Francisco: ILWU, 2000); Schwartz, *Solidarity Stories: An Oral History of the ILWU* (Seattle: University of Washington Press, 2009), 30–31, 168–198.

6   San Francisco's Tenderloin District did not have a very respectable reputation when I interviewed Urban in 1987.

7   To ease local unemployment, applicants were supposed to have resided in the Northern California counties of the Golden Gate Bridge District for one year to qualify for bridge work. James Reed, "Notice to Applicants for Employment, Golden Gate Bridge," Golden Gate Bridge and Highway District, 1932, Labor Archives and Research Center, San Francisco State University.

8 Armistice Day, commemorating the end of World War I on November 11, 1918, became a legal holiday in 1938. Congress changed the name to Veterans Day in 1954.

9 The bridge's two main suspension cables were each made of twenty-seven thousand rows of the thin but extremely strong galvanized steel wire Urban is describing. Themselves made of strands of banded wire, the cables were 36.5 inches in diameter. The strands that made up the cables were anchored on both sides of the bridge in eyebars sunk into huge cement foundations or anchor blocks. The strands for the cables were spun on-site by the contractor, John A. Roebling's Sons Company, between November 1935 and May 1936. Urban was there for the entire process. The technical on-site spinning procedure, which the Roebling Company had pioneered, is described in detail in Cassady, *Spanning the Gate*, 84–101, and Adams, *Heroes*, 250–258.

For the evolution of American bridge building in the nineteenth century and the Roebling Company's historic role in that process, see Daniel Calhoun, "A Case in the Analytic: Bridge-Building," *The Intelligence of a People* (Princeton, NJ: Princeton University Press, 1973), 291–304. On the Roebling Company, which gained lasting fame by constructing the Brooklyn Bridge, see David McCullough, *The Great Bridge: The Epic Story of the Building of the Brooklyn Bridge* (New York: Simon and Schuster, 1982), and Donald Sayenga, ed., *Washington Roebling's Father: A Memoir of John A. Roebling* (Reston, VA: American Society of Engineers, 2009).

10 Urban is here referring to the San Francisco–side tower top, located 746 feet above the water.

11 Long-handled underwear, often called a union suit, was popular between the 1890s and the 1930s. The garment consisted of a long-sleeved shirt and ankle-length drawers combined in one piece.

12 Roebling completed the bridge's main cables in six months. The job ended on May 20, 1936. The company beat its contractual time limit on the cable job by employing extra spinning wheels. This was an innovation at the time. Roebling still had to hang the suspenders to hold the bridge's roadway, but its hardest job was done. Cassady, *Spanning the Gate*, 89–90.

13 Fifty years after that party, Urban still retained his invitation, which he showed to me when I interviewed him. It read, in part, "Roebling Party. Golden Gate Bridge Employees. May 23, 1936, Paradise Cove, Marin County. This is your invitation and pass for transportation. . . . Celebrating completion of cable spinning. Please bring this card with you."

14 Urban is describing a block-and-tackle lift system.

15 Tag lining is managing a rope or cable to control weight being lifted.

16 In the late 1930s, activists associated with the West Coast–based International Longshoremen's and Warehousemen's Union frequently boycotted scrap-iron shipments bound for Imperial Japan. Larrowe, *Harry Bridges*, 131–133; Schwartz, *Solidarity Stories*, 115, 181–182.

17 Urban is referring to the February 17, 1937, tragedy when Strauss's safety net broke and ten workers died. Al Maillioux was the district safety engineer who had recently inspected the platform. Cassady, *Spanning the Gate*, 109–110.

18 The CIO split from the AFL over organizing strategy, which emerged nationally in 1935, reached the West Coast in force during 1937. The new CIO sponsored the unionization of America's semiskilled mass-production workers. Urban, whose union was affiliated with the craft-oriented AFL, was hardly the only worker who

was upset by the threatening prospect of the country's labor organizations battling each other. In 1955, the AFL and the CIO rejoined under the name AFL-CIO.

19 Buttner was injured in April 1937, just weeks before the bridge was finished. He was knocked unconscious and broke ribs and an arm when a metal cable fell on him. Adams, *Heroes*, 306.

20 The reference here is probably to the Sheet Metal Workers International Association.

21 Samuel I. Hayakawa was a semanticist and an English professor who served as president of San Francisco State University during a turbulent, high-profile 1968–69 student and faculty strike, which he vehemently opposed. He became a public symbol of some citizens' negative reaction to unions and to the countercultural movement of the 1960s. In 1976, running as a Republican, he was elected to represent California in the United States Senate. While he was in office, media people frequently reported that he often slept through legislative deliberations. He did not run for a second term.

In the wake of the late twentieth- and early twenty-first-century U.S. political "culture wars," various analysts and writers questioned why numerous workers like Urban sometimes appeared to vote against their own economic self-interests. For one popular example, see Thomas Frank, *What's the Matter with Kansas? How Conservatives Won the Heart of America* (New York: Henry Holt, 2004).

5. FRED BRUSATI: ELECTRICIAN

1 Angelo Brusati's operation, Brusati Brothers Scavenger Service, was the predecessor of Marin Sanitary Service. "Fred A. Brusati worked on the Golden Gate Bridge," *Marin Independent Journal*, San Rafael, CA, July 31, 1989.

2 In 1933, Roebling built a "reeling plant" at California City that used steam cleaning to remove shipping wax from strong steel wire sent from its New Jersey home facility. Workers in the California City plant then spooled the wire for use in spinning the bridge's cables. Adams, *Heroes*, 251–252.

3 Workers erected the north, or Marin, tower between August 1933 and May 1934, although it was not fully ready for cable spinning until that November. The south or San Francisco–side tower was built between January and June 1935. Cassady, *Spanning the Gate*, 70, 74; Adams, *Heroes*, 202, 240–242.

4 The whirley crane got its name not for speed, but because it could rotate 360 degrees in picking up and depositing loads.

5 For more on this episode, see Dillon, DeNevi, and Moulin, *High Steel*, 84; Adams, *Heroes*, 250.

6 The catwalks providing access for cable spinning were completed in late September 1935. Adams, *Heroes*, 251–253.

7 The anchor blocks on the Marin and the San Francisco sides of the bridge were huge concrete edifices with giant eyebars to hold the cables. The spinning process began in earnest in November 1935 and lasted for seven months. Cassady, *Spanning the Gate*, 49; Adams, *Heroes*, 251–258.

8 A bridge's backspan is a section that is located beyond or outside the bridge's middle or main span.

9 A 1936 photo by *San Francisco Chronicle* staff photographer Clem Albers reveals how steep and exposed the catwalk looked during construction. Many good photos were taken showing the catwalk, but this one, which filled a whole page at 22

inches by 16.5 inches, is especially big and dramatic. It also suggests how interested members of the media were in the progress of the bridge's construction. See *San Francisco Chronicle,* Rotogravure Pictorial Section, July 19, 1936, p. 1.

10 One writer argues that there was a slight delay in the arrival of rescue vessels from the Coast Guard station just inside the Golden Gate. A fishing boat skippered by Mario Marybella, not the Coast Guard, picked up Evan C. "Slim" Lambert and Oscar Osberg, the two men who were saved. See van der Zee, *The Gate,* 279–281.

11 News reporters called Casey "the thirteenth man." He told his story, including the part about the pipe, to the press immediately after the accident. See *San Francisco Examiner,* February 18, 1937, pp. 1, 5.

12 Workers completed the last major structural job on the bridge, the paving of the roadway, in April 1937. Cassady, *Spanning the Gate,* 118–120; van der Zee, *The Gate,* 292.

13 This incident occurred before the February 17, 1937, torn net disaster that killed ten workers. Van der Zee, *The Gate,* 268.

14 Inexpensive color photography was not widely available to amateur photographers until the 1950s.

15 In addition to its early patented "hard-boiled" industrial hats, which were made of steamed canvas and came with leather brims, the Bullard Company pioneered sandblasting air respirators for the Golden Gate Bridge project. When I interviewed him in 1987, Brusati still retained his woven canvas safety belt from the bridge job as well as his black Bullard hard hat.

16 In support of the war effort, between 1942 and 1945 Marinship Corporation hastily built ninety-three vessels to transport cargo and fuel overseas. The plant was just three miles north of the Golden Gate Bridge. "Marinship: 1942–1945," U.S. Army Corps of Engineers' Bay Model Visitors Center, Sausalito, CA, no date. For in-depth coverage of the twenty thousand men and women shipyard workers employed at Marinship during World War II, see Charles Wollenberg, *Marinship at War: Shipbuilding and Social Change in Wartime Sausalito* (Berkeley, CA: Western Heritage Press, 1990).

17 When Brusati passed away in 1989 his obituary acknowledged that he had been a member of Local 551 for "more than 50 years." *Marin Independent Journal,* July 31, 1989.

18 After fifteen years of open-shop, or non-union hegemony, unionism in the West expanded dramatically in the wake of the longshoremen's and seamen's victory in the 1934 Pacific Coast maritime strike. Even Local 614 of San Rafael became strong enough to be prominently listed in the *Marin County Directory* for 1939–40, with Harvey E. Smith identified as secretary.

19 There were experiments with television before the 1930s, but no nationwide commercial TV broadcasting until after World War II.

20 The Tacoma Narrows Bridge in Washington State, built between 1938 and 1940, had a suspension system that somewhat resembled the one used on the Golden Gate. In late 1940, a few months after it opened, the Tacoma Narrows Bridge collapsed during a major storm.

21 Use of the dated term *colored people* for African Americans was common before the civil rights and identity politics movements of the 1960s–70s.

22 Although many women worked in industry to support the war effort, old condescending attitudes often persisted. Many African American workers migrated to the Bay Area, too, because of the era's war-induced labor shortage. But scarcely

a decade earlier there were very few African American men and virtually no women in the skilled and semiskilled trades on local jobs like the Golden Gate Bridge project.

6. MARTIN ADAMS: LABORER

1   By way of comparison, in 1934 probably the majority of non-union San Francisco warehouse workers made about forty-eight cents an hour. This was three-quarters of what was then a "living wage" in that city. Even considering the relatively higher cost of living in San Francisco compared to rural Arkansas, forty-eight cents was far better than ten cents an hour. See Schwartz, *The March Inland*, 2, 179.

2   Batching refers to mixing ingredients.

3   Work on the Bay Bridge was finished in October 1936. Officials declared the bridge completed and open for use the following month. Dillon, DeNevi, and Moulin, *High Steel*, 24.

4   Falsework provides temporary support for spanning or arched structures under construction. Between Roman times and about 1900 almost all bridge falsework was made of wood.

5   A derrick barge is a flat floating structure fitted with a crane.

6   Sea diving has always been a demanding and dangerous occupation. The dreaded illness called the bends was only the best-known of the many problems that a 1930s bridge diver could encounter while handicapped by heavy and cumbersome equipment and little or no visibility. The currents under the Golden Gate were especially challenging. Divers performed a variety of underwater tasks in bridge building, including guiding piles into place. Adams, *Heroes*, 224–229.

7   The organization's official name is Laborers' International Union of North America. It has existed in San Francisco since 1916. Bill Talbitzer, "Laborers Local No. 261, Excerpts from *The Laborer in the West*," San Francisco Building Trades Council, *Commemorating 100 Years of Excellence*, 74.

8   Immediately following the union victory in the great 1934 West Coast maritime and San Francisco general strikes, many Bay Area employers accepted organization peacefully instead of risking another major confrontation. See Schwartz, *Solidarity Stories*, 175–176.

9   In late October 1936, the West Coast maritime unions struck for the second time in a little more than two years. Largely because of the growth of union power since 1934, the employers did not try to break this strike by force as they had unsuccessfully attempted to do two years earlier. Consequently, the 1936–37 Pacific Coast maritime strike was peaceful. Larrowe, *Harry Bridges*, 114; Bruce Nelson, *Workers on the Waterfront: Seamen, Longshoremen, and Unions in the 1930s* (Urbana: University of Illinois Press, 1988), 214.

10   In the mid-1930s, bridge construction workers frequently called the Golden Gate Bridge the "Gate" or the "Gate Bridge."

11   Each sliding scaffold or platform was sixty feet long. Adams, *Heroes*, 304.

12   Contemporary news writers reported on this equipment failure extensively in illustrated stories. See, for example, *San Francisco Examiner*, February 17, 1937, p. 12; February 18, p. 36; February 20, p. 36.

13   The other survivor of the twelve who fell was the carpenter Oscar Osberg. Like Osberg, Lambert was badly injured. Adams, *Heroes*, 295–299; van der Zee, *The Gate*, 280–281.

14 The day after the tragedy the State Industrial Accident Commission blamed the contractor for what had happened. See *San Francisco Examiner,* February 18, 1937, p. 1. Official investigations followed shortly. Concerned authorities, including Joseph Strauss, the Golden Gate Bridge District's chief engineer, and Philip Hart, the Pacific Bridge Company's president and the district's contractor, blamed each other. Local 261's attorney, Elmer P. Delany, spoke on behalf of the deceased laborers. Several workers, including Adams, testified about missing bolts, but in the end no one was held legally liable. The last official body to come to this conclusion was the State Industrial Accident Commission. Cassady, *Spanning the Gate,* 110; Adams, *Heroes,* 303–305; van der Zee, *The Gate,* 283–286.

15 The bridge deck's center, where the accident occurred, is 220 feet above the water. MacDonald and Nadel, *Golden Gate Bridge,* 120.

16 T. H. Chambers, the president of the Building Trades Council, spoke on behalf of worker concerns just after the tragedy. *San Francisco Examiner,* February 21, 1937, p. 3. In late April 1937, about two months after the accident, the State of California consolidated older labor statutes into a new California Labor Code.

17 The dinkey and its load smashed into the bridge's Marin-side anchor block. See van der Zee, *The Gate,* 268. Brusati also described this incident in his oral history.

18 Since the bridge proper is 1.7 miles long, this could be quite a lengthy walk. MacDonald and Nadel, *Golden Gate Bridge,* 119.

19 Hoover served as president between 1929 and 1933. Like Joseph Strauss, the Golden Gate Bridge's political crusader who got most of the public credit for that project, Hoover was an engineer with experience in large-scale construction. He did back both bridge projects in various ways while president. In 1932 he supported a $72 million Reconstruction Finance Corporation federal loan for the Bay Bridge's construction. The Golden Gate Bridge, though, was financed by a regional $35 million bond, not through federal funding. Starr, *Golden Gate,* 56–57, 73–78.

20 The members of Pile Drivers, Divers, Bridge, Wharf and Dock Builders Local Union No. 34 are highly skilled in what has historically been specialized, physically demanding work. The local can trace its origins in the Bay Area back to 1877. Since 1920 it has been affiliated with the United Brotherhood of Carpenters and Joiners of America as a local of that organization. Ira B. Cross, *A History of the Labor Movement in California* (Berkeley: University of California Press, 1935), 321; Michael S. Munoz, *"Pilebutt": Stories and Photographs about Pile Driving* (San Leandro, CA: Pilebutt Press, 1986), 20–38, and "Short Early History of Pile Drivers Local No. 34," in San Francisco Building and Construction Trades Council, *Commemorating 100 Years of Excellence,* 278–279; Archie Green, *Wobblies, Pile Butts, and Other Heroes: Laborlore Explorations* (Urbana: University of Illinois Press, 1993), 365–441.

7. EVAN C. "SLIM" LAMBERT: SURVIVOR

1 Ron Chew, *Remembering Silme Domingo and Gene Viernes: The Legacy of Filipino American Labor Activism* (Seattle: University of Washington Press, 2012), contains much useful historical information on conditions in the seasonal Alaska salmon canning industry.

2 Lambert broke his ankle in this early 1932 accident. Adams, *Heroes,* 291.

3 Construction work for the Bay Bridge began in May 1933. This incident would have occurred sometime subsequent to that date, especially considering that the

bridge's towers were apparently already up. Dillon, Moulin, and DeNevi, *High Steel*, 15; Adams, *Heroes*, 291.

4 With its Bay Bridge work nearing completion in 1935, the Pacific Bridge Company sent Lambert to the Golden Gate Bridge job as a labor foreman. Adams, *Heroes*, 292–293.

5 Pacific Bridge paved the Golden Gate Bridge's roadway with concrete between January 19 and April 19, 1937. Cassady, *Spanning the Gate*, 108, 122.

6 These panels would likely have been flat, rectangular pieces of construction material employed to form part of a surface. The train ran off the end of the tracks, fell 150 feet, and smashed on the ground, but no one was badly hurt. Adams, *Heroes*, 293.

7 Estimates of the weight of the staging board vary somewhat, but it probably weighed at least five tons. Van der Zee, *The Gate*, 277; Adams, *Heroes*, 294.

8 This was the crab fisherman Mario Maryella. *San Francisco Examiner*, February 18, 1937, p. 1; van der Zee, *The Gate*, 281.

9 Lambert's neck injury only became known twenty years after the accident, when he went for a physical examination. Adams, *Heroes*, 349–351.

10 Accounts of Lambert's physical condition immediately following the accident and his valiant bid to save Dummatzen's life have varied a good deal over the years. See, for example, *San Francisco Examiner*, February 18, 1937, pp. 1–2; Dillon, Moulin, and DeNevi, *High Steel*, 90–93; Adams, *Heroes*, 295–297; van der Zee, *The Gate*, 277–281; Cassady, *Spanning the Gate*, 109; Horton, *Superspan*, 45; Starr, *Golden Gate*, 135. Amy Standen used brief excerpts from my interview with Lambert to recount his tragic experience of February 17, 1937, on her radio program, "Life on the Gate: Working on the Golden Gate Bridge, 1933–1937," aired on Quest Northern California, station KQED, San Francisco, April 27, 2012. The program text was immediately posted online. It was later printed as Amy Standen, "Life on the Gate," *SF State Magazine* 12, no. 12 (Spring–Summer 2012): 16–17.

11 The ambulance ultimately delivered Lambert to St. Mary's Hospital in San Francisco. *San Francisco Examiner*, February 18, 1937, p. 1; Adams, *Heroes*, 296.

12 Lambert returned to work on the bridge just a month after the accident. Adams, *Heroes*, 349.

13 Lambert's reference here is to the May 24, 1987, Bridge Walk '87 event that celebrated the fiftieth anniversary of the bridge's opening. Bridge Walk '87 attempted to re-create the 1937 opening ceremony walk. It was held on the bridge the day before Lambert's interview with me.

14 Approximately two hundred thousand people walked across the bridge on May 27, 1937. The estimates for the May 1987 event ran to eight hundred thousand. Starr, *Golden Gate*, 143–144; Cassady, *Spanning the Gate*, 122–129; Horton, *Superspan*, 48–53; Currie, *Highlights, Facts, and Figures*, 21, 40–42; *San Francisco Chronicle*, May 25, 1987, p. 1.

The weekend the bridge opened in May 1937 there was a Grand Labor Ball at the Civic Auditorium in San Francisco. The proceeds went to the families of the men killed building the span. There was also a memorial service on the bridge for the total of eleven men who had perished during construction. Children from every school in the city cast flowers into the water. With the children were representatives from all the unions that had worked on the bridge and family members of those who had died. *Labor Clarion*, June 4, 1937, pp. 1–2. A plaque dedicated to the memory of the eleven fallen workers was erected on the bridge as well. It was blessed by religious leaders in July. *San Francisco Chronicle*, July 16, 1937, p. 1.

15 By 1987 Lambert operated seven sightseeing boats out of Pearl Harbor and was invested in fishing and hotel businesses. Adams, *Heroes*, 349. Lambert was visiting San Francisco from Hawaii for the fiftieth anniversary of the opening of the Golden Gate Bridge when I interviewed him.

16 Lambert's ideas about politics and unions run counter to those of many labor activists, as does the thinking about changing voting patterns that Fred Divita and John Urban attested to. But such sentiments were often shared by other workers over the decades following the 1930s, a political shift that has continued to vex dedicated laborites for years.

8. AL ZAMPA: LEGEND

1 The union's full name now is International Association of Bridge, Structural, Ornamental, and Reinforcing Iron Workers. Local 377 can trace its Bay Area origins back to the 1890s. In the period Zampa was describing, the union experienced a resurgence as part of the labor movement's Depression Decade recovery from its decline in the 1920s. "Structural and Ornamental Iron Workers Local No. 377," in San Francisco Building and Construction Trades Council, *Commemorating 100 Years of Excellence*, 70. Two Northern California locals of the ironworkers' union had roles in the 1930s Bay Bridge and Golden Gate Bridge construction projects: Local 377 of San Francisco and Local 378 in Oakland. The dispatching of ironworkers to jobs on the Golden Gate Bridge went through the Local 377 union hall. Thanks to Dick Zampa, Al Zampa's son, for helping to clarify and reorder this paragraph, which is hard to follow in the transcript of Isabelle Maynard's 1986 interview with Zampa on which this chapter is based.

2 The original Bay Bridge's foundations were deeper than any previously built. Dillon, DeNevi, and Moulin, *High Steel*, 16.

3 The first Carquinez Bridge across the Carquinez Strait connected the California towns of Crockett and Vallejo. Located thirty miles northeast of San Francisco, it was constructed by the American Toll Bridge Company between 1923 and 1927. Zampa got his start as an ironworker on that job in 1925 when he was twenty. He passed away in 2000 after a long life as a celebrated bridge builder. When the third of three Carquinez bridges opened in 2003, it was named the Alfred Zampa Memorial Bridge in his honor. It is the only American bridge named for a construction trades worker. John V. Robinson, *Al Zampa and the Bay Area Bridges* (Charleston, SC: Arcadia Publishing, 2005), 7–9, 33, 125–126, and *Spanning the Strait*, 1–21. Both of Robinson's books contain numerous stunning and informative bridge construction photos, many taken by him. For supplementary photos of the 1927 Carquinez Bridge under construction, see Harvey Schwartz, *Union Carpenters, Navy Town: The First 100 Years of Local 180, United Brotherhood of Carpenters and Joiners of America, in Vallejo, California, 1899–1999* (Vallejo, CA: UBCJA, 1999), 8–10.

4 *Camelback* refers to the side-view image of bridge structures like the five built on the eastern crossing of the original Bay Bridge. The shape of these spans is reminiscent of a camel's back.

5 By this time, in mid-1936, Zampa had worked on the Bay Bridge for at least two and a half years. Robinson, *Al Zampa*, 53; Adams, *Heroes*, 279. On Zampa's life and career, in addition to Robinson's work, see Misha Berson, "Fingerprints on Steel: Bridge Working Ace Al Zampa's Life above Water," *Image*, May 10, 1987, reprinted

in Napa-Solano Building and Construction Trades Council, *Celebrating 100 Years of Union History, 1899–1999* (Benicia, CA: Napa-Solano Building and Construction Trades Council, 1999), 24–26; Joseph A. Blum, "Building Bridges," *New Labor Forum* 12 (2003): 49–57.

6   The top and bottom chords are the top and bottom horizontal steel members of a truss. A stringer is a longitudinal beam installed to ultimately help support a bridge deck. See MacDonald and Nadel, *Golden Gate Bridge,* 106.

7   Zampa's fall occurred in October 1936. At this point in the construction process, there was no deck surface beneath him. That would not be completed until early the next year. Cassady, *Spanning the Gate,* 38–39, 107.

8   Zampa's back was broken in four places. He had fallen into a section of the safety net that was above hard ground and had not yet been properly tightened. Adams, *Heroes,* 279; van der Zee, *The Gate,* 164.

9   By the end of construction, nineteen men had fallen into the net and survived. Dillon, DeNevi, and Moulin, *High Steel,* 132; Starr, *Golden Gate,* 134.

10 As part of the fiftieth anniversary of the completion of the Golden Gate Bridge's construction, in 1987 Steve Zeltzer and the Bay Area Labor Video Project produced a film about the bridge's workers and their unions. As a tribute to those who died building the span and to those who survived falls, the Video Project titled the movie *Half Way to Hell.* Robinson, *Spanning the Strait,* 19–20.

11 John V. Robinson, an experienced ironworker himself, wrote of Zampa: "His near fatal fall from the Golden Gate Bridge in 1936 and membership in the 'Halfway to Hell Club' made him newsworthy. His recovery and return to work on other Bay Area bridges made him legendary." Robinson, *Al Zampa,* 9. In 1987, Isabelle Maynard's interview with Zampa became the basis for a successful play based on the ironworker's life and work. Titled *The Ace,* it was performed that year in San Francisco. Stacey Palevsky, "China-Born Author Isabelle Maynard Dies at 78," *The Jewish News Weekly of Northern California,* July 27, 2007; Robinson, *Spanning the Strait,* 18–19.

12 A sandhog is a construction worker who labors in underground excavation. Since the late nineteenth century, for an example, New York's sandhogs have become famous for working on dangerous and demanding projects like the Brooklyn Bridge, the city's many major tunnels, and New York City's subways. Local 147 of the Laborers' International Union of North America, which has represented New York City tunnel diggers for years, is widely known as NYC Sandhogs 147.

13 Workers constructed the second Carquinez Strait Bridge between 1955 and 1958. Robinson, *Al Zampa,* 83; Robinson, *Spanning the Strait,* 15.

14 Dick Zampa went on to become general organizer and then vice-president of the Iron Workers International, which serves as the union's national-level umbrella organization. Robinson, *Spanning the Strait,* 15. By 2013 four generations of Zampa family members had become ironworkers.

15 The Bay Bridge's west-side span is actually made up of two suspension bridges joined at a common anchorage. At 4,200 feet, the Golden Gate Bridge's suspension bridge main span is longer than each of the Bay Bridge structure's two 1936 suspension parts. See Dillon, DeNevi, and Moulin, *High Steel,* 16, 77.

16 Zampa's interesting take here, of course, is from the technical perspective of a veteran bridge builder, not a non-construction person who might primarily appreciate the Golden Gate Bridge's geographical setting, apt color, and graceful suspension system.

17 In 1986, when this interview was done, it understandably might not have been clear to Zampa that American unions were in the early stages of a long-term decline.

18 As the fiftieth anniversary of the opening of the Golden Gate Bridge approached in the mid-1980s, Zampa was lionized by an assortment of journalists, television producers, and other media people as the unofficial ambassador to the Bay and Golden Gate bridges. Robinson, *Spanning the Strait,* 16–17.

9. MARY ZITA FELCIANO AND PATRICIA DEWEESE: NURSES

1 The reference here is to the motherhouse of the Sisters of Mercy for California and Arizona. The motherhouse was founded twenty miles south of San Francisco at Burlingame, California, in the mid-1920s to serve as the Catholic order's West Coast administrative center. St. Mary's Hospital of San Francisco itself dates from 1857. Sister Mary Zita Felciano took her vows as a Sister of Mercy in 1930. Telephone interview, Sister Marilyn Gouailhardou, archivist, Sisters of Mercy, Burlingame, CA, May 30, 2014.

2 Slim Lambert, who is the subject of chapter 7, and Oscar Osberg, the two injured survivors of the net accident of February 17, 1937, were both treated at St. Mary's Hospital. The eight men might have been brought to St. Mary's another day. Adams, *Heroes,* 296; van der Zee, *The Gate,* 281.

3 The nineteenth-century Welsh surgeon and orthopedic medicine pioneer Hugh Owen Thomas invented the splint named after him. Its introduction into common use during the early twentieth century was credited with dramatically reducing the mortality rate of patients with femur fractures. Modified and improved over time, the Thomas splint's basic design was still in use during the early years of the twenty-first century.

10. WALTER VESTNYS AND JOYCE "BIG J" HARRIS: MAINTENANCE IRONWORKERS

1 The Teamster-affiliated Chauffeurs' Union Local 265 received its charter in 1909. It was quite active in San Francisco through the 1970s. Teamsters Local 85 dates back to 1901 and the important City Front Federation strike in San Francisco of that year. Robert Edward Lee Knight, *Industrial Relations in the San Francisco Bay Area, 1900–1918* (Berkeley: University of California Press, 1960), 212; David F. Selvin, *Sky Full of Storm: A Brief History of California Labor* (Berkeley: Institute of Industrial Relations, University of California, 1966), 21–26; Issel and Cherny, *San Francisco, 1865–1932,* 86–88. See also Robert McClure Robinson, "A History of the Teamsters in the San Francisco Bay Area, 1850–1950," unpublished PhD dissertation, University of California, Berkeley, 1951.

2 On high-tensile bolts superseding rivets in bridge construction during the 1950s and 1960s, see John Reincke, "The Turn of the Nut," *Mates: Materials and Technology Engineering and Science* 36 (October 1989): 1–2.

3 The designation B & O refers to an ironworker's backing-out punch. It resembles a hammer but features a round eye on one side of its head that fits around the end of the rivet.

4 A hickory-stripe shirt is a black-and-white vertically striped garment made of heavy material. Frisco jeans were sturdy black denim pants that withstood hard

use well. Both items were favored by Bay Area industrial workers between the 1930s and the 1960s.

5 John Francis "Jack" Shelly was then the mayor of San Francisco. Cherny and Issel, *San Francisco*, 76–78.

6 Unfortunately, over time the bridge has become known for the large number of people using it to commit suicide. During the 1960s, there were about thirty suicides a year. As of 2009, more than thirteen hundred Golden Gate Bridge suicides had been recorded, but the actual total was probably higher. MacDonald and Nadel, *Golden Gate Bridge*, 105–117; Starr, *Golden Gate*, 165–176.

7 The district, founded in 1928 as the Golden Gate Bridge and Highway District, changed its name slightly in 1969 to reflect added obligations. To ease traffic on the bridge, in 1970 the district began offering ferry service through a special division. Currie, *Highlights, Facts, and Figures*, 3–4, 59, 85.

8 Vestnys held his post as head of the ironworkers' apprenticeship program in San Francisco for more than thirty years. "Walter Vestnys Death Notice," *San Francisco Chronicle*, September 18, 2011.

9 Tongue Point in Astoria, Oregon, is the location of the Job Corps vocational training center.

10 Harris's son, Dontrelle Willis, grew up to become a standout Major League Baseball pitcher. He was National League Rookie of the Year in 2003 while playing for the World Series champion Florida Marlins. Two seasons later he won a Major League high twenty-two games, was the runner up for the National League Cy Young Award, and took home the Warren Spahn trophy as the best left-handed pitcher in baseball. Harris, who remarried, also has a second son, Walter. Robert Andrew Powell, "Dontrelle Willis, Please Phone Home," *New York Times*, May 11, 2005; Gwen Knapp, "Willis's Mother Is a Kick: Former Ironworker Inspires, Captivates," *San Francisco Chronicle*, July 22, 2005; Mike Berard, "Belated Meeting: Willis Has Cordial Reunion with Father after 19-Year Absence," *Sun Sentinel* (Denver, CO), August 22, 2003.

11 Harris was encouraging women to enter the trades even before she took this job. See Dave Donelson, "It's Dirty Work, and These Women Gotta Do It," *Christian Science Monitor*, January 6, 2003. In 2014, using her maiden name, Joyce Guy, she served as a staff member at the West Oakland Job Resource Center, an organization dedicated to helping local residents train for and find employment in the building and construction trades.

12 The Bay Area's 1967 San Mateo to Hayward Bridge underwent seismic retrofitting in 2000 and lane expansion in 2003.

FURTHER READING

Several good books have been written about various aspects of the Golden Gate Bridge. Those who want to read more will find the list below helpful in locating some of the best and most available volumes in libraries, bookstores, or online. Many of the books noted are ones I found to be especially useful in preparing this text.

Adams, Charles F. *Heroes of the Golden Gate*. Palo Alto, CA: Pacific Books, 1987. A history focused on the leading personalities and politics behind the bridge construction project, with useful descriptions of workers interspersed throughout.

Brown, Allen. *Golden Gate: Biography of a Bridge*. Garden City, NY: Doubleday, 1965. An early classic about the bridge's construction, including discussions of its political history and its record of suicides committed from its heights.

Bunting, Eve. *Pop's Bridge*. Orlando, FL: Harcourt, 2006. A short, illustration-driven children's book that looks at the Golden Gate Bridge's construction through the eyes of a high-steel worker's adolescent son.

Cassady, Stephen. *Spanning the Gate: The Golden Gate Bridge*. Rev. ed. Santa Rosa, CA: Squarebooks, 1986. A history of the bridge's construction with emphasis on its technical aspects, this book includes instructive photographs and quotes from workers.

Chester, Michael. *Joseph Strauss: Builder of the Golden Gate Bridge*. New York: G. P. Putnam's Sons, 1965. Written for young readers, this brief biography describes Strauss's early life and his long career as a bridge engineer.

Currie, Mary C. *Highlights, Facts, and Figures of the Golden Gate Bridge, Highway, and Transportation District*. 6th ed. San Francisco: Golden Gate Bridge, Highway, and Transportation District, 2009. A compilation of recent information on the bridge, this volume includes photographs and informative historical material.

Dillon, Richard, Donald DeNevi, and Thomas Moulin. *High Steel: Building the Bridges across San Francisco Bay*. Berkeley, CA: Celestial Arts, 1979. A history of the construction of the San Francisco–Oakland Bay Bridge and the Golden Gate Bridge, driven largely by historical photographs.

Dyble, Louise Nelson. *Paying the Toll: Local Power, Regional Politics, and the Golden Gate Bridge*. Philadelphia: University of Pennsylvania Press, 2009. A sobering scholarly analysis of how since the 1930s the managers of the Golden Gate Bridge, Highway, and Transportation District have often pursued their own personal agendas at the public's expense through cultivating political alliances and influencing policy decisions.

Fireman, Janet, and Shelly Kale. "Bridging the Golden Gate: A Photo Essay." *California History* 89, no. 4 (2012): 3–40. The only article-length publication cited on the list, this lavishly illustrated portrayal of the bridge's history and construction appeared in a major journal and should be readily available in libraries.

Golden Gate National Parks Conservancy. *Building the Golden Gate Bridge: Courage, Ingenuity, Vision* (San Francisco: Golden Gate National Parks Conservancy and Golden Gate Bridge, Highway, and Transportation District, 2012). A collection of photos from the district's archives.

Horton, Tom. *Superspan: The Golden Gate Bridge.* San Francisco: Chronicle Books, 1983. A brief yet helpful summary of the bridge's historical origins, the politics that predated its construction, and its building process.

Lewis, Karen R. *Building the Golden Gate Bridge: A Directory to Historical Sources.* San Francisco: Labor Archives and Research Center, San Francisco State University, 1989. An annotated guide to primary source material on the bridge that will help any researcher, this bound 76-page catalog is available at LARC and other libraries.

MacDonald, Donald, and Ira Nadel. *Golden Gate Bridge: History and Design of an Icon.* San Francisco: Chronicle Books, 2008. The building of the bridge from the perspective of an architect who redesigned parts of the span in later years, this publication includes unique hand-drawn illustrations.

Merritt, Anne. *Historic Photos of the Golden Gate Bridge.* Nashville, TN: Turner Publishing, 2008. A photo essay featuring the construction of the bridge and the May 1937 celebration of the official opening of the span to traffic.

Robinson, John V. *Al Zampa and the Bay Area Bridges.* Charleston, SC: Arcadia Publishing, 2005. Al Zampa's wide-ranging career as a high-steel bridge builder depicted through text and photos.

———. *Spanning the Strait: Building the Alfred Zampa Memorial Bridge.* Crockett, CA: Carquinez Press, 2004. A photo-driven chronicle of the building of the third bridge connecting Crockett and Vallejo, California, with valuable information on Al Zampa's life and career.

Schock, James W. *The Bridge: A Celebration—The Golden Gate Bridge at Sixty, 1937–1997.* Mill Valley, CA: Golden Gate International, 1997. A history of the bridge's construction in large format accompanied by photos, this volume includes highlights from the annual reports of the Golden Gate Bridge, Highway, and Transportation District covering 1937 through 1996.

Starr, Kevin. *Golden Gate: The Life and Times of America's Greatest Bridge.* New York: Bloomsbury Press, 2010. A helpful overview of the politics and building of the bridge by the dean of California historians, who emphasizes his personal admiration for the span's architectural achievement and beauty. The epilogue quotation is from page 126.

van der Zee, John. *The Gate: The True Story of the Design and Construction of the Golden Gate Bridge.* New York: Simon and Schuster, 1986. An in-depth history of the bridge's history, politics, and construction, this book brought to light the often overlooked contributions of the engineer Charles A. Ellis to the span's spectacular success.

INDEX

Page references in italics indicate illustrations or material contained in their captions.

International Association of Bridge, Structural, Ornamental and Reinforcing Iron Workers, 159n30; apprentice programs of, 63, 127, 128, 138–39; Divita and, 30; Drake as president of, 30; resurgence of, 170n1; Zampa (A.) as member of, 118, 127, 129; Zampa (D.) and, 171n14

International Brotherhood of Electrical Workers (IBEW), 86–88, 166n17, 166n18

International Longshore and Warehouse Union (ILWU), 7

international orange, 11, 162n21

International Union of Elevator Constructors (IUEC), 32–33, 35, 41–42, 160n2

interviews: author's methodology, 8–9; as full life histories, 6–7; history of, 7–8; subjects of, 7

Irish immigrants, 34, 160n6

ironworkers, 3, 7, 21, 28–29, 44, 49, 49–57, *51*, *55*, 161n7

ironworkers' union, 30

Isaacs, Louis M., 159n20

Italian immigrants, 5, 15, 16–17, 34, 75–76, 117, 121, 131, 157n4, 160n6

J

Japan, 71

Jenkins, Elinor ("Cotton"), 115

Jews, 34

J. H. Pomeroy Company, 28, 156n14

job categories: cable spinners, 7, 60, 63–68, *64*, *67*; electricians, 7, 75, 78–88, *85*; elevator builders, 7, 32, 35–40, *37*, 160n7; field engineers, 7, 15, 22–24; laborers, 7, 90, 96–97, 101–3; labor foremen, 7, 105, 108–9, *111*, 169n4, 169n12; maintenance ironworkers, 137, 140–43, *142*, 146–47; paint scrapers, 7, 15, 17–21, *20*, 160n7. *See also* ironworkers

Job Corps, 138, 143–44

John A. Roebling's Sons Company, 65, 67–68, *70*, 77, 79, 82, 84, 156n14, 164n9, 165n2

Jorgensen, Frank, 36–37

jumpers, 141, 173n6

K

Kentfield (CA), 75

Korean War, 138

Kreiter, Jo, 7–8

L

Labor Archives and Research Center (LARC; San Francisco State University), 6, 7–8

laborers, 7, 90, 96–97, 101–3

Laborers' Union, 94–95, 100, 103, 167n7, 168n14

labor foremen, 7, 105, 108–9, *111*, 169n4, 169n12

labor history, 4

ladders, 19, 21, 78

Lake Washington Floating Bridge, 29, 159n31

Lambert, Elinor Jenkins, 115

Lambert, Evan ("Slim"): as accident survivor (1937), 6, 13, 98–99, 105, 109–14, 166n10, 167n13; Adams and, 97; Alaskan cannery work of, 105, 106–7; author's interview with, 7; Bay Bridge work of, 105, 107; as cowboy, 105, 106, 107; education, 106; family background, 105–6; hospital treatment of, 172n2–3 (Ch. 9); impact of bridge career on, 116; injuries sustained by, 167n13, 168n2, 169n10; as laborer, 100; as labor foreman, 7, 105, 108–9, *111*, 169n4, 169n12; marriage of, 115; nicknames of, 106; political views of, 116, 170n16; post-bridge career of, 105, 114–16, 170n15; as union member, 116

latrines, 49

layoffs, 25, 49, 57, 102–3, 128

lead poisoning, 53, 162n19

Letterman, Chuck, 25

Letterman, Slew, 25, 28

Lettuce League (baseball league), 40

Lindros, Charles, 13

liquor, 56

Lithuanian immigrants, 60–61, 162–63n1

Noren, John: author's interview with, 7, 32; as baseball player, 34–35, 40, 160n5; birth of, 32, 33; education, 33; as elevator builder, 7, 32, 35–40, 37, 160n7; family background, 32; impact of bridge career on, 43; marriage of, 41; political views of, 41; post-bridge career of, 32, 40–43; retirement of, 43; as union member, 41–42; wages made by, 36

Noren, John (father), 32–33
Noren, Signe, 33
Norman, Jack, 13, 112
Northwestern Pacific Railroad, 45–47
Norton, Joshua, 9
Norwegian immigrants, 32–33
nurses, 130–36, 136

O

Oakland (CA), 41, 90, 143, 147
O'Brien, Nancy, 134
Occupational Safety and Health Act (1970), 161n9 (Ch. 2)
Occupational Safety and Health Administration (OSHA), 39, 161n9 (Ch. 2)
Old River Bridge, 122
Olson, Elmer, 58
oral history, 6, 8–9, 156n12
Oregon, 60
Oregon City (OR), 61
Osberg, Oscar, 166n10, 167n13, 172n2 (Ch. 9)
O'Shaughnessy, Michael, 9

P

Pacific Bridge Company, 96, 100, 156n14, 168n14, 169n4
Pacific Coast Baseball League, 34
Pacific Coast maritime strike (1934), 6, 62, 139, 160n4, 166n18, 167n8
Pacific Gas and Electric Company, 138, 144
paint scrapers, 7, 15, 17–21, 20, 160n7
Panafon, 130, 134
Pea Ridge (AR), 90–92
Pearl Harbor, Japanese attack on (1941), 29, 115

Pile Drivers, Bridge, Wharf and Dock Builders Union, 103–4, 118, 129, 168n20
Pisa (Italy), 16
Pitt River Bridge, 58, 162n23
Polish immigrants, 5
Pomeroy, James H., 28, 29, 30
Portland (OR), 61
Portuguese immigrants, 130, 131
Postal Telegraph (San Francisco, CA), 45
punkin', 71

Q

quittings, 18, 125–26

R

racial prejudice, 34–35, 145–46
railroad, narrow-gauge, 100, 108–9, 168n17
raincoats, 68, 84
raising gangs, 21, 50, 162n15
Raymond Concrete Pile Company, 156n14
Reagan, Ronald, 129
Reconstruction Finance Corporation, 168n19
Redding (CA), 74
Red Hill (Honolulu, Hawaii), 30
Redwood Empire, 3
Reed, Ed, 25
Republican Party, 74, 116
respirators, 162n19, 166n15
Richmond–San Rafael Bridge, 158n6
Rickey, Branch, 34, 160n5
riggers, 159n19
Ritchie, Donald A., 8–9
rivet busters, 140
rivet catchers, 158n14
riveters, 19, 21, 25, 26–28, 50, 125
rivet forges, 71, 158n14, 161n12
riveting crews, 162n15
riveting guns, 50
riveting hammers, 15, 18
rivets, 27–28, 50, 158n14
Robinson, Jackie, 160n5
Robinson, John V., 170n3, 171n11
Rock Diamond (CA), 139

United States Army Air Corps, 11
United States Army Corps of Engineers, 159n32
United States Coast Guard, 71, 75, 80, 111, 166n10
United States Marine Corps, 44
United States Senate, 165n21
United States Supreme Court, 163n4
United States War Department, 9
University of California–Berkeley, 7, 15, 17, 157n1
University of California–Davis, 7
University of Illinois, 10
Urban, John: accidents witnessed by, 71–72; author's interview with, 7, 60; as cable spinner, 7, 60, 63–68, 64, 67; education, 61; family background, 60–61; injuries sustained by, 70–71; pier work of, 68–71; political views of, 62–63, 74, 165n21, 170n16; post-bridge career of, 73–74; retirement of, 74; at Roebling party, 68, 70; social activities, 72–73; as union member, 72; wages made by, 63, 73; as whistle punk, 61–62

V

Vallejo (CA), 170n3
Van der Zee, John, 155n2
vane wrenches, 52
Vestnys, Bert, 7, 137–38, 139–40
Vestnys, Walter, 7, 137, 138–39, 140–43, 144–45

W

wages: of apprentices, 63; of divers, 94; of electricians, 82; of elevator builders, 36; of engineers, 22; of ironworkers, 57, 63, 73, 126; of laborers, 22, 57, 92, 95; of non-union warehouse workers, 167n1; of riggers, 22
Wagner Act (1935), 163n4
Waikiki (Hawaii), 115
Washington, Lake, 29, 159n31
Washington State, 28–29, 44
Watsonville (CA), 40, 133–34
weather concerns: cold, 26, 36, 56, 101;

fog, 54, 82, 83; ice, 86, 101; rain, 57, 68, 82, 101, 125; storms, 12, 68, 158n15; unpredictability of, 65–67, 83–84, 140; wind, 36, 39, 48, 57, 80, 84, 101, 125
Westclox watches, 161n3
Western Washington College (Bellingham, WA), 106
Westinghouse, 41–43
whirley crane, 165n4
whistle punks, 61–62, 163n2
Widenback, Homer, 36
women: as ironworker wives, 7, 53, 57–58, 59; as maintenance ironworkers, 7, 138, 143–47, 147; as nurses, 7, 130–36, 136; omission of, from bridge histories, 7, 49
Women in Apprenticeship, 143
workers' compensation, 120, 132–33
Works Progress Administration (WPA), 10, 31, 160n33
World's Fair (San Francisco; 1939), 114–15
World War II, 29–30, 41, 73, 104, 115, 126, 137–38, 159n32

Y

Yakima (WA), 45
Yerba Buena Island, 22, 158n16
YMCA (San Francisco, CA), 64
Yosemite National Park, 9

Z

Zampa, Al: Bay Bridge work of, 117, 118, 119, 170–71n5; as boxer, 124; bridge named after, 117, 170n3; children of, 123, 126–28; death of, 170n3; education, 121, 123; impact of bridge career on, 124, 171n16; injuries sustained by, 117, 119–21, 171nn7–8; as ironworker, 118–19, 124–26, 170n3; marriage of, 121; Maynard's interview with, 7, 117, 171n11; media coverage of, 172n18; political views of, 129; post-bridge career of, 126–29; as sandhog, 122–23, 129; Strauss as viewed by, 3, 124–25; as union member, 118, 127, 129; wages made by, 126; workers' compensation received by, 120–21

Current
CONTROVERSIES

Police Training and Excessive Force

Other Books in the Current Controversies Series

Police Training and Excessive Force

Pete Schauer, Book Editor

GREENHAVEN
PUBLISHING

Published in 2018 by Greenhaven Publishing, LLC
353 3rd Avenue, Suite 255, New York, NY 10010

Copyright © 2018 by Greenhaven Publishing, LLC

First Edition

Articles in Greenhaven Publishing anthologies are often edited for length to meet page
requirements. In addition, original titles of these works are changed to clearly present
the main thesis and to explicitly indicate the author's opinion. Every effort is made to
ensure that Greenhaven Publishing accurately reflects the original intent of the authors.
Every effort has been made to trace the owners of the copyrighted material.

Cover image: davidkrug/Shutterstock.com

Library of Congress Cataloging-in-Publication Data

Names: Schauer, Peter J., editor.
Title: Police training and excessive force / Pete Schauer, book editor.
Description: New York : Greenhaven Publishing, [2018] | Series: Current
  controversies | Audience: Grade 9 to 12. | Includes bibliographical
  references and index.
Identifiers: LCCN 2017034163| ISBN 9781534502376 (library bound) | ISBN
  9781534502437 (pbk.)
Subjects: LCSH: Police training--Juvenile literature. | Police
  brutality--Juvenile literature.
Classification: LCC HV7923 .P65 2018 | DDC 363.2/32--dc23
LC record available at https://lccn.loc.gov/2017034163

Manufactured in the United States of America

Website: http://greenhavenpublishing.com

Contents

Chapter 4: Do We Need to Change the Way We Train Police?

Yes: Police Training Must Evolve

No: Current Police Training Standards Are Adequate

Foreword

"Controversy" is a word that has an undeniably unpleasant connotation. It carries a definite negative charge. Controversy can spoil family gatherings, spread a chill around classroom and campus discussion, inflame public discourse, open raw civic wounds, and lead to the ouster of public officials. We often feel that controversy is almost akin to bad manners, a rude and shocking eruption of that which must not be spoken or thought of in polite, tightly guarded society. To avoid controversy, to quell controversy, is often seen as a public good, a victory for etiquette, perhaps even a moral or ethical imperative.

Yet the studious, deliberate avoidance of controversy is also a whitewashing, a denial, a death threat to democracy. It is a false sterilizing and sanitizing and superficial ordering of the messy, ragged, chaotic, at times ugly processes by which a healthy democracy identifies and confronts challenges, engages in passionate debate about appropriate approaches and solutions, and arrives at something like a consensus and a broadly accepted and supported way forward. Controversy is the megaphone, the speaker's corner, the public square through which the citizenry finds and uses its voice. Controversy is the life's blood of our democracy and absolutely essential to the vibrant health of our society.

Our present age is certainly no stranger to controversy. We are consumed by fierce debates about technology, privacy, political correctness, poverty, violence, crime and policing, guns, immigration, civil and human rights, terrorism, militarism, environmental protection, and gender and racial equality. Loudly competing voices are raised every day, shouting opposing opinions, putting forth competing agendas, and summoning starkly different visions of a utopian or dystopian future. Often these voices attempt to shout the others down; there is precious little listening and considering among the cacophonous din. Yet listening and considering, too, are essential to the health of a democracy. If controversy is democracy's lusty lifeblood, respectful listening and careful thought are its higher faculties, its brain, its conscience.

Current Controversies does not shy away from or attempt to hush the loudly competing voices. It seeks to provide readers with as wide and representative as possible a range of articulate voices on any given controversy of the day, separates each one out to allow it to be heard clearly and fairly, and encourages careful listening to each of these well-crafted, thoughtfully expressed opinions, supplied by some of today's leading academics, thinkers, analysts, politicians, policy makers, economists, activists, change agents, and advocates. Only after listening to a wide range of opinions on an issue, evaluating the strengths and weaknesses of each argument, assessing how well the facts and available evidence mesh with the stated opinions and conclusions, and thoughtfully and critically examining one's own beliefs and conscience can the reader begin to arrive at his or her own conclusions and articulate his or her own stance on the spotlighted controversy.

This process is facilitated and supported in each Current Controversies volume by an introduction and chapter overviews that provide readers with the essential context they need to begin engaging with the spotlighted controversies, with the debates surrounding them, and with their own perhaps shifting or nascent opinions on them. Chapters are organized around several key questions that are answered with diverse opinions representing all points on the political spectrum. In its content, organization, and methodology, readers are encouraged to determine the authors' point of view and purpose, interrogate and analyze the various arguments and their rhetoric and structure, evaluate the arguments' strengths and weaknesses, test their claims against available facts and evidence, judge the validity of the reasoning, and bring into clearer, sharper focus the reader's own beliefs and conclusions and how they may differ from or align with those in the collection or those of classmates.

Research has shown that reading comprehension skills improve dramatically when students are provided with compelling, intriguing, and relevant "discussable" texts. The subject matter of these collections could not be more compelling, intriguing, or urgently relevant to today's students and the world they are poised to inherit. The anthologized articles also provide the basis for stimulating, lively, and passionate classroom debates. Students who are compelled to anticipate objections to their own argument and identify the flaws in those of an opponent read more carefully, think more critically, and steep themselves in relevant context, facts, and information more thoroughly. In short, using discussable text of the kind provided by every single volume in the Current Controversies series encourages close reading, facilitates reading comprehension, fosters research, strengthens critical thinking, and greatly enlivens and energizes classroom discussion and participation. The entire learning process is deepened, extended, and strengthened.

If we are to foster a knowledgeable, responsible, active, and engaged citizenry, we must provide readers with the intellectual, interpretive, and critical-thinking tools and experience necessary to make sense of the world around them and of the all-important debates and arguments that inform it. We must encourage them not to run away from or attempt to quell controversy but to embrace it in a responsible, conscientious, and thoughtful way, to sharpen and strengthen their own informed opinions by listening to and critically analyzing those of others. This series encourages respectful engagement with and analysis of current controversies and competing opinions and fosters a resulting increase in the strength and rigor of one's own opinions and stances. As such, it helps readers assume their rightful place in the public square and provides them with the skills necessary to uphold their awesome responsibility—guaranteeing the continued and future health of a vital, vibrant, and free democracy.

Introduction

> *"The problems arising from the*
> *mistreatment of citizens by police*
> *officers, commonly termed police*
> *brutality, is aggravated by two*
> *factors: the tendency of many citizens*
> *to exaggerate its extent, and the*
> *frequency with which most police*
> *officials minimize its significance."*
>
> —Hubert G. Locke

Many young children growing up around the world are taught to trust the police, and to always go to a police officer if they are lost or in trouble—but that age-old advice is now questionable, due to the headline-grabbing conflicts police officers have engaged in over the past decade. The training of police officers, and other various officers of the law, has always been subject to examination, but with shootings and killings at the hands of police heavily publicized by the mainstream media, scrutiny has intensified.

Whether that excessive media coverage is deserved or overkill is up for debate, but in this day and age—with social media putting the latest breaking news at everyone's fingertips—it should be expected that events of this nature receive more news coverage, faster. Is it just that increased access to coverage makes it feels as though more citizens are killed by police officers than in the past? Are the numbers really rising—and are a majority of those citizens killed of African American descent?

There is no question that the Black Lives Matter movement has helped shed light on policing and the use of excessive force.

The movement began after the death of seventeen-year-old Trayvon Martin at the hands of George Zimmerman, who was not an officer of the law. From that point on, the movement only became stronger—more widely known following the deaths of Michael Brown in Ferguson, Missouri, and Eric Garner in New York City, with both deaths involving the police. Ultimately, these events have put police training and the use of excessive force under a microscope.

This book takes a look at the controversies surrounding police violence and law enforcement training. Chapter 1 provides an overview of what excessive force is, and then explores if the use of excessive force is as common as it seems to be—analyzing data around the issue, but also looking at how the media can often exploit situations to make them look larger or worse than they may really be. Next, Chapter 2, evaluates whether excessive force is reasonable or warranted in some cases. Are there life-and-death situations where an officer was threatened by a suspect and was forced to take lethal action, or is it never justified to use lethal force? From there, Chapter 3 questions if the use of excessive force has become a larger problem in the current day than it was previously, say in the 1980s. Again, the media comes into play, as we look at whether excessive force really has increased in the last five to ten years, or if media coverage has just become more readily accessible.

Finally, the book concludes with Chapter 4, which raises the ultimate question of if change should be made to the way that police officers are trained—based on all of the data, facts, and analysis revolving around the use of violence in today's police force. Takeaways from *Current Controversies: Police Training and Excessive Force* include learning how police officers are trained, gaining information and statistics on excessive force and when it is justified, and ultimately becoming more educated on how the media portrays the police.

Is Excessive Force as Common as We Think It Is?

Overview: Only Transparency Will Reveal the Truth About Excessive Force

John Whihbey and Leighton Walter Kille

John Whihbey is an assistant professor of Journalism and New Media at Northeastern University in Boston, MA. Leighton Walter Kille is a former assistant arts editor at the Boston Globe *who also serves as a research editor for Journalist's Resource.*

Allegations of the use of excessive force by U.S. police departments continue to generate headlines more than two decades after the 1992 Los Angeles riots brought the issue to mass public attention and spurred some law enforcement reforms. Recent deaths at the hands of police have fueled a lively debate across the nation in recent years.

In a number of closely watched cases involving the deaths of young black men, police have been acquitted, generating uproar and concerns about equal justice for all. On Staten Island, N.Y., the July 2014 death of Eric Garner because of the apparent use of a "chokehold" by an officer sparked outrage. A month later in Ferguson, Mo., the fatal shooting of teenager Michael Brown by officer Darren Wilson ignited protests, and a grand jury's decision not to indict Wilson triggered further unrest. In November, Tamir Rice was shot by police in Cleveland, Ohio. He was 12 years old and playing with a toy pistol. On April 4, 2015, Walter L. Scott was shot by a police officer after a routine traffic stop in North Charleston, S.C. The same month, Freddie Gray died while in police custody in Baltimore, setting off widespread unrest. The policeman in the South Carolina case, Michael T. Slager, was charged with murder based on a cellphone video. In Baltimore, the driver of the police van in which Gray died, Caesar Goodson, was charged with second-degree murder, with lesser charges for five other officers. There have been no indictments in the earlier cases.

These follow other recent incidents and controversies, including an April 2014 finding by the U.S. Department of Justice (DOJ), following a two-year investigation, that the Albuquerque, N.M., police department "engages in a pattern or practice of use of excessive force, including deadly force, in violation of the Fourth Amendment," and a similar DOJ finding in December 2014 with regard to the Cleveland police department. In March 2015, the DOJ also issued a report detailing a pattern of "clear racial disparities" and "discriminatory intent" on the part of the Ferguson, Mo., police department.

As the *Washington Post* reported in July 2015, a pervasive problem that is only now beginning to be recognized is the lack of training for officers dealing with mentally ill persons, a situation that can often escalate to violent confrontations.

The events of 2014-2016 have prompted further calls by some police officials, politicians and scholars for another round of national reforms, in order to better orient "police culture" toward democratic ideals.

Two sides, disparate views

Surveys in recent years with minority groups—Latinos and African Americans, in particular—suggest that confidence in law enforcement is relatively low, and large portions of these communities believe police are likely to use excessive force on suspects. A 2014 Pew Research Center survey confirms stark racial divisions in response to the Ferguson police shooting, as well, while Gallup provides insights on historical patterns of distrust. According to a Pew/*USA Today* poll conducted in August 2014, Americans of all races collectively "give relatively low marks to police departments around the country for holding officers accountable for misconduct, using the appropriate amount of force, and treating racial and ethnic groups equally." Social scientists who have done extensive field research and interviews note the deep sense of mistrust embedded in many communities.

Numerous efforts have been made by members of the law enforcement community to ameliorate these situations, including promising strategies such as "community policing." Still, from a police perspective, law enforcement in the United States continues to be dangerous work—America has a relatively higher homicide rate compared to other developed nations, and has many more guns per capita. Citizens seldom learn of the countless incidents where officers choose to hold fire and display restraint under extreme stress. Some research has shown that even well-trained officers are not consistently able to fire their weapon in time before a suspect holding a gun can raise it and fire first; this makes split-second judgments, even under "ideal" circumstances, exceptionally difficult. But as the FBI points out, police departments and officers sometimes do not handle the aftermath of incidents well in terms of transparency and clarity, even when force was reasonably applied, fueling public confusion and anger.

In 2013, 49,851 officers were assaulted in the line of duty, with an injury rate of 29.2 percent, according to the FBI. Twenty-seven were murdered that year.

FBI Director: No "reliable grasp" of problem

How common are such incidents of police use of force, both lethal and nonlethal, in the United States? Has there been progress in America? The indisputable reality is that we do not fully know. FBI Director James B. Comey stated the following in a remarkable February 2015 speech:

> Not long after riots broke out in Ferguson late last summer, I asked my staff to tell me how many people shot by police were African-American in this country. I wanted to see trends. I wanted to see information. They couldn't give it to me, and it wasn't their fault. Demographic data regarding officer-involved shootings is not consistently reported to us through our Uniform Crime Reporting Program. Because reporting is voluntary, our

data is incomplete and therefore, in the aggregate, unreliable.

I recently listened to a thoughtful big city police chief express his frustration with that lack of reliable data. He said he didn't know whether the Ferguson police shot one person a week, one a year, or one a century, and that in the absence of good data, "all we get are ideological thunderbolts, when what we need are ideological agnostics who use information to try to solve problems." He's right.

The first step to understanding what is really going on in our communities and in our country is to gather more and better data related to those we arrest, those we confront for breaking the law and jeopardizing public safety, and those who confront us. "Data" seems a dry and boring word but, without it, we cannot understand our world and make it better.

How can we address concerns about "use of force," how can we address concerns about officer-involved shootings if we do not have a reliable grasp on the demographics and circumstances of those incidents? We simply must improve the way we collect and analyze data to see the true nature of what's happening in all of our communities.

The FBI tracks and publishes the number of "justifiable homicides" reported by police departments. But, again, reporting by police departments is voluntary and not all departments participate. That means we cannot fully track the number of incidents in which force is used by police, or against police, including non-fatal encounters, which are not reported at all.

Without a doubt, training for police has become more standardized and professionalized in recent decades. A 2008 paper in the *Northwestern University Law Review* provides useful background on the evolving legal and policy history relating to the use of force by police and the "reasonableness" standard by which officers are judged. Related jurisprudence is still being defined, most recently in the 2007 *Scott v. Harris* decision by the U.S. Supreme Court. But inadequate data and reporting—and the challenge of uniformly defining excessive versus justified force— make objective understanding of trends difficult.

A 2015 report conducted for the Justice Department analyzed

394 incidents involving deadly police force in Philadelphia from 2007-2014. It found that "officers do not receive regular, consistent training on the department's deadly force policy"; that early training among recruits is sometimes inadequate in regard to these issues; that investigations into such incidents are not consistent; and that officers "need more less-lethal options."

For perhaps the best overall summary of police use-of-force issues, see "A Multi-method Evaluation of Police Use of Force Outcomes: Final Report to the National Institute of Justice," a 2010 study conducted by some of the nation's leading criminal justice scholars.

Available statistics, background on use of force

The Justice Department releases statistics on this and related issues, although these datasets are only periodically updated: It found that in 2008, among people who had contact with police, "an estimated 1.4% had force used or threatened against them during their most recent contact, which was not statistically different from the percentages in 2002 (1.5%) and 2005 (1.6%)." In terms of the volume of citizen complaints, the Justice Department also found that there were 26,556 complaints lodged in 2002; this translates to "33 complaints per agency and 6.6 complaints per 100 full-time sworn officers." However, "overall rates were higher among large municipal police departments, with 45 complaints per agency, and 9.5 complaints per 100 full-time sworn officers." In 2011, about 62.9 million people had contact with the police.

In terms of the use of lethal force, aggregate statistics on incidents of all types are difficult to obtain from official sources. Some journalists are trying to rectify this; and some data journalists question what few official national statistics are available. The Sunlight Foundation explains some of the data problems, while also highlighting databases maintained by the Centers for Disease Control (CDC). The available data, which does not paint a complete national picture, nevertheless raise serious questions, Sunlight notes:

According to the CDC, in Oklahoma the rate at which black people are killed per capita by law enforcement is greater than anywhere else in the country. That statistic is taken from data collected for the years 1999–2011. During that same time period, Oklahoma's rate for all people killed by law enforcement, including all races, is second only to New Mexico. However, Oklahoma, the District of Columbia, Nevada and Oregon are all tied for the rate at which people are killed. (The CDC treats the District of Columbia as a state when collecting and displaying statistics.) In Missouri, where Mike Brown lived and died, black people are killed by law enforcement twice as frequently as white people. Nationwide, the rate at which black people are killed by law enforcement is 3 times higher than that of white people.

As mentioned, the FBI does publish statistics on "justifiable homicide" by law enforcement officers: The data show that there have been about 400 such incidents nationwide each year. However, FiveThirtyEight, among other journalism outlets, has examined the potential problems with these figures. News investigations suggest that the rates of deadly force usage are far from uniform. For example, Los Angeles saw an increase in such incidents in 2011, while Massachusetts saw more officers firing their weapon over the period 2009–2013.

The academic community has also provided some insights in this area. A 2008 study from Matthew J. Hickman of Seattle University, Alex R. Piquero of the University of Maryland and Joel H. Garner of the Joint Centers for Justice Studies reviewed some of the best studies and data sources available to come up with a more precise national estimate for incidents of nonlethal force. They note that among 36 different studies published since the 1980s, the rates of force asserted vary wildly, from a high of more than 30% to rates in the low single digits. The researchers analyze Police-Public Contact Survey (PPCS) data and Bureau of Justice Statistics Survey of Inmates in Local Jails (SILJ) data and conclude that an estimated 1.7 percent of all contacts result in police threats or use of force, while 20 percent of arrests do.

A 2012 study in the *Criminal Justice Policy Review* analyzed the patterns of behavior of one large police department—more than 1,000 officers—and found that a "small proportion of officers are responsible for a large proportion of force incidents, and that officers who frequently use force differ in important and significant ways from officers who use force less often (or not at all)." A 2007 study in *Criminal Justice and Behavior,* "Police Education, Experience and the Use of Force," found that officers with more experience and education may be less likely to use force, while a review of case studies suggests that specific training programs and accountability structures can lower the use of violence by police departments.

A 2016 working paper from the National Bureau of Economic Research (NBER) came to a conclusion that surprised some observers. Across the U.S., though blacks are 21.3 percent more likely to be involved in an altercation with police where a weapon is drawn, the researchers found no racial differences in police shootings: "Partitioning the data in myriad ways, we find no evidence of racial discrimination in officer-involved shootings. Investigating the intensive margin—the timing of shootings or how many bullets were discharged in the endeavor—there are no detectable racial differences."

Researchers continue to refine analytical procedures in order to make more accurate estimates based on police reports and other data.

Characteristics of suspects

A widely publicized report in October 2014 by ProPublica, a leading investigative and data journalism outlet, concluded that young black males are 21 times more likely to be shot by police than their white counterparts: "The 1,217 deadly police shootings from 2010 to 2012 captured in the federal data show that blacks, age 15 to 19, were killed at a rate of 31.17 per million, while just 1.47 per million white males in that age range died at the hands of police."

Research has definitively established that "racial profiling" by law enforcement exists—that persons of color are more likely to be stopped by police. FBI Director James Comey's 2015 comments are again relevant here:

> [P]olice officers on patrol in our nation's cities often work in environments where a hugely disproportionate percentage of street crime is committed by young men of color. Something happens to people of good will working in that environment. After years of police work, officers often can't help but be influenced by the cynicism they feel.
>
> A mental shortcut becomes almost irresistible and maybe even rational by some lights. The two young black men on one side of the street look like so many others the officer has locked up. Two white men on the other side of the street—even in the same clothes—do not. The officer does not make the same association about the two white guys, whether that officer is white or black. And that drives different behavior. The officer turns toward one side of the street and not the other. We need to come to grips with the fact that this behavior complicates the relationship between police and the communities they serve.

While the cases of Rodney King in 1991 and Amadou Diallo in 1999 heightened the country's awareness of race and policing, research has not uniformly corroborated the contention that minorities are more likely, on average, to be subject to acts of police force than are whites. A 2010 paper published in the *Southwestern Journal of Criminal Justice* reviewed more than a decade's worth of peer-reviewed studies and found that while many studies established a correlation between minority status and police use of force, many other studies did not—and some showed mixed results.

Of note in this research literature is a 2003 paper, "Neighborhood Context and Police Use of Force," that suggests police are more likely to employ force in higher-crime neighborhoods generally, complicating any easy interpretation of race as the decisive factor in explaining police forcefulness. The researchers, William Terrill of Northeastern University and Michael D. Reisig of Michigan State University, found that "officers are significantly more likely to use higher levels of force when encountering criminal suspects in high crime areas and neighborhoods with high levels of concentrated disadvantage independent of suspect behavior and other statistical controls." Terrill and Reisig explore several hypothetical explanations and ultimately conclude:

> Embedded within each of these potential explanations is the influence of key sociodemographic variables such as race, class, gender, and age. As the results show, when these factors are considered at the encounter level, they are significant. However, the race (i.e., minority) effect is mediated by neighborhood context. Perhaps officers do not simply label minority suspects according to what Skolnick (1994) termed "symbolic assailants," as much as they label distressed socioeconomic neighborhoods as potential sources of conflict.

In studying the Seattle and Miami police departments, the authors of the 2010 National Institute of Justice report also conclude that "non-white suspects were less likely to be injured than white suspects … where suspect race was available as a variable for analysis. Although we cannot speculate as to the cause of this finding, or whether it is merely spurious, it is encouraging that minority suspects were not *more likely* to be injured than whites."

Use of Tasers and other "less lethal" weapons

A 2011 report from the National Institute of Justice, "Police Use of Force, Tasers and Other Less-Lethal Weapons," examines the effectiveness and health outcomes of incidents involving CEDs (conducted energy devices), the most common of which is the Taser. The report finds that: (1) Injury rates vary widely when officers use force in general, ranging from 17% to 64% for citizens and 10% to 20% for officers; (2) Use of Tasers and other CEDs can reduce the statistical rate of injury to suspects and officers who might otherwise be involved in more direct, physical conflict—an analysis of 12 agencies and more than 24,000 use-of-force cases "showed the odds of suspect injury decreased by almost 60% when a CED was used"; and (3) A review of fatal Taser incidents found that many involved multiple uses of the device against the suspect in question.

A 2011 study, "Changes in Officer Use of Force Over Time: A Descriptive Analysis of a National Survey," documents trends in the use of non-lethal force by law enforcement officers (LEAs). The results indicate that CED use has risen significantly (to about 70% of LEAs), while baton use is down to 25% in 2008. "CED use was ranked among the most-used tactics from 2005 to 2008," the scholars conclude. "Excessive-force complaints against LEAs, internally generated, have more than doubled from 2003 to 2008. Officer injuries varied little from 2003 to 2008, but they are still only about half as common as suspect injuries. Also, only 20% of LEAs collect injury data in a database, complicating future research."

Potential impact of body cameras

Video recordings of interactions between the police and the public have increased significantly in recent years as technology has improved and the number of distribution channels has expanded. Any standard smartphone can now make a video—as was the case in the Walter L. Scott shooting—and dash-mounted cameras in police cars have become increasingly common.

The mandatory adoption of body cameras by police has been suggested to increase transparency in interactions between law-enforcement officials and the public. A 2014 study from the U.S. Department of Justice, "Police Officer Body-Worn Cameras: Assessing the Evidence," reviews available research on the costs and benefits of body-worn camera technology. The author, Michael D. White of Arizona State University, identified five empirical studies on body cameras, and assesses their conclusions. In particular, a year after the Rialto, Calif., police department began requiring all officers to wear body cameras, use of force by officers fell by 60% and citizen complaints dropped by nearly 90%. The searcher notes:

> The decline in complaints and use of force may be tied to improved citizen behavior, improved police officer behavior, or a combination of the two. It may also be due to changes in citizen

complaint reporting patterns (rather than a civilizing effect), as there is evidence that citizens are less likely to file frivolous complaints against officers wearing cameras. Available research cannot disentangle these effects; thus, more research is needed.

The studies also noted concerns about the cost of the required devices, training and systems for storing video footage; potential health and safety effects; and especially privacy concerns, both for citizens and the police. In April 2015, a bill being considered in the Michigan State legislature would exempt some body-camera footage from the state's Freedom of Information (FOI) laws. Those who spoke in favor of the law included a conservative Republican legislator and an ACLU representative.

Public opinion and media

The coverage of such incidents by mass media has been studied by researchers, some of whom have concluded that the press has often distorted and helped justify questionable uses of force. Finally, survey data continue to confirm the existence of undercurrents of racism and bias in America, despite demonstrable social progress; a 2014 Stanford study shows how awareness of higher levels of black incarceration can prompt greater support among whites for tougher policing and prison programs.

Excessive Force Runs Rampant in the United States

Abbie Carver

Abbie Carver is a 2017 graduate of the Michigan State University College of Law. She served as associate editor of the International Law Review and was also a teaching assistant for Civil Procedure and for Legal Research and Writing.

This year, allegations of police violence and use of excessive force have generated many disturbing headlines.[1] So far this year, 807 people have been shot and killed by police officers.[2] Although there is no federal database that reports police violence,[3] studies suggest that in 2015, police killed a total of 1,152 people in the U.S.[4] Many of these cases involved questionable deaths of young black men.[5] For example, in August of 2014, teenager Michael Brown was fatally shot by an officer in Ferguson, Missouri.[6] In November 2014, twelve year old Tamir Rice was shot by Cleveland, Ohio police when he was playing with a toy pistol.[7]

Neither police officers in these cases were indicted.[8] In the United States, it is possible for an officer to be sued for an intentional tort; negligence; a violation of the Civil Rights Act - 42 U.S.C. sec. 1983; and be charged under both state and federal criminal codes. Id. However, despite the persistent problem of police officers' excessive use of force, courts continue to avoid second-guessing police actions and only sanction severely egregious misconduct.[9]

American police are 18 times more lethal than Danish police and 100 times more lethal than Finnish police.[10] In addition, American police kill significantly more frequently than police in France, Sweden and other European countries.[11] Paul Hirschfield, a scholar of sociology and criminal justice studied

"Why Do U.S. Police Officers Use More Excessive Force Against Civilians Than Many European Countries and What Can Be Done?," by Abbie Carver, Michigan State University College of Law International Law Review, December 13, 2016. Reprinted by Permission. Abbie Carver, Michigan State International Law Review.

police violence in both Europe and the United States and attempted to identify the root causes of the high rates of police lethality in the U.S.[12] First, Hirschfield suggests that most state laws in the U.S. make it relatively easy for adults to purchase guns; therefore, American police are "primed to expect guns."[13] Unsurprisingly, the study found that American civilians armed with weapons (even non-lethal weapons) were more likely to be killed by police. [14] However, the availability of weapons is not unique to the United States; although knife violence is a persistent problem in England, British police only killed one person wielding a knife in 2008 (who happened to be a hostage-taker).[15] Hirschfield also suggests that pervasive racism in the United States makes civilians more vulnerable to police violence.[16] However, many studies conducted in the U.S. over the past few years have suggested that racism is not the cause of pervasive police violence—that violence equally applies to all American races.[17] Regardless of the cause of fear, these findings suggest that police officers use excessive force when they fear civilians' use of violence.[18]

Hirschfield also found that more than one fourth of deadly force victims in the U.S. were killed in small towns, although only 17 percent of the U.S. population lives in these towns.[19] In Europe, small towns and cities employ municipal police who are generally unarmed and lack arrest authority.[20] In some countries, such as Britain, Ireland, Norway, Iceland and New Zealand, officers are unarmed when they are on patrol.[21] "'The practice is rooted in tradition and the belief that arming the police with guns engenders more gun violence than it prevents.'"[22] In contrast, British police officers have considered themselves to be guardians of citizens, who should be easily approachable; 82% of British police do not want to be armed.[23] Hirschfield believes that part of the problem is that the United States fosters police cultures that emphasizes bravery and aggression.[24]

Some activists have argued that gun control laws in the United States should encourage disarmament of both United States citizens and law enforcement, modeled after many European countries.

[25] However, "[m]ost experts agree, however, that it would be counterproductive to suddenly disarm U.S. police officers without addressing the origins of crime."[26]

In the alternative, the United States could adopt a more stringent deadly force standard. In 1989, the United States Supreme Court deemed it constitutionally permissible for police to use deadly force when they reasonably perceive imminent and grave harm. [27] Only 38 American states have laws regulating police and the use of deadly force and almost all of the laws are as permissive as the Supreme Court precedent.[28] In contrast, European countries must conform to the European Convention on Human Rights, which requires all signatories to permit deadly force only when "absolutely necessary" to achieve a lawful purpose.[29] Specific laws in each European country may require additional, more stringent standards; for example, Finland and Norway require police to obtain permission from a superior officer before shooting anyone.[30]

While working towards laws that disarm both citizens and police, the United States may benefit from passing legislation permitting police officers to use deadly force only when absolutely necessary—just as required by the European Convention on Human Rights.

Footnotes

1. John Wihbey & Leighton Walter Kille, Excessive or reasonable force by police? Research on law enforcement and racial conflict, Journalist's Research, http://journalistsresource.org/studies/government/criminal-justice/police-reasonable -force-brutality-race-research-review-statistics (last updated July 28, 2016).

2. Fatal Force, Washington Post, https://www.washingtonpost.com/graphics /national/police-shootings-2016/ (last updated Nov. 6, 2016).

3. Anna Almendrala, Be Wary Of Studies That Deny Racial Bias In Police Shootings, Huffington Post (July 27, 2016), http://www.huffingtonpost.com/entry/police -shootings-studies-racial-bias_us_5796f2d8e4b02d5d5ed2b4aa.

4. 2015 Police Violence Report, Mapping Police Violence, http:// mappingpoliceviolence.org/2015/ (last visited Nov. 6, 2016).

5. Id.

6. Wihbey & Kille, supra note 1.

7. Id.

8. Id.

9. Id.; Jack Ryan, Overview of Police Liability, Legal & Liability Risk Management Institute, http://www.llrmi.com/articles/legal_update/liabilityoverview.shtml (last visited Nov. 6, 2016).

10. Paul Hirschfield, Why American Cops Kill So Many Compared To European Cops, Huffington Post (Nov. 30, 2015), http://www.huffingtonpost.com/entry /american-cops-lethal_us_565cde59e4b079b2818b8870.

11. Id.

12. Id.

13. Id.

14. Id.

15. Id.

16. Id.

17. See id.

18. See id.

19. Id.

20. Id.

21. Rick Noack, 5 countries where most police officers do not carry firearms — and it works well, Washington Post (July 8, 2016), https://www.washingtonpost.com/ news/worldviews/wp/2015/02/18/5-countries-where-police-officers-do-not-carry-firearms-and-it-works-well/.

22. Id.

23. Id.

24. Hirschfield, supra note 8.

25. Noack, supra note 17.

26. Id.

27. Hirschfield, supra note 8

28. Id.

29. Id.

30. Id.

Police Officers Who Use Excessive Force Aren't Disciplined

Steven Rosenfeld

Steven Rosenfeld is the author of multiple books on elections and covers national political issues for AlterNet.

Handcuffed teenagers beaten bloody with guns. Unarmed people shot and killed in their cars. Cops firing guns carelessly into busy streets. Mentally ill people tasered in ambulances. Supervisors refusing to challenge a brutal status quo.

These examples didn't come from the New York City Police Department or Ferguson, Missouri, where the killing of unarmed black men by white cops has created a national outcry over institutional racism and excessive force. They were from Ohio, where the U.S. Department of Justice just finished an investigation and report on abusive and often unconstitutional policing by Cleveland Division of Police between 2010 and 2013. They were compiled before November 22, when a rookie officer shot and killed a 12-year-old African-American boy, Tamir Rice, for waving a toy gun around on a playground.

The DOJ's findings raise big questions. It's not just how widespread is the problem of excessive force and a corresponding lack of accountability. The harder questions include what can be done to change police culture, reverse many out-of-control tactics, and instill a belief across entire forces that restraint and accountability protect cops and civilians.

"We found that field supervisors are failing in some of the most fundamental aspects of their responsibilities—reviewing and investigating the uses of force of the officers under their command, and correcting dangerous tactical choices that place

"15 Reasons America's Police Are So Brutal," by Steven Rosenfeld, Alternet, December 06, 2014. Reprinted by Permission.

the officer and others at risk," Mayor Frank Jackson said of the report, underscoring systemic problems.

When releasing the report, U.S. Attorney General Eric Holder announced the DOJ would work with Cleveland under a consent decree and a federal court will oversee reforms. But a decade ago, the DOJ also investigated police abuses in Cleveland and found similar patterns surrounding excessive force. The city's police pledged reforms would come—yet the department's nasty status quo obviously has resurfaced.

"The voluntary reforms undertaken at that time did not create the systems of accountability necessary to ensure a long-term remedy to these issues," the DOJ's new report said. "More work is necessary to ensure that officers have the proper guidance, training, support, supervision, and oversight to carry out their law enforcement responsibilities safely and in accordance with individuals' constitutional rights."

That summation describing needed reforms typifies today's political rhetoric surrounding the crisis in militarized American policing. The DOJ report didn't say what explicit steps needed to be taken. But it did describe how deeply embedded excessive force was among Cleveland's police, what was wrong and broken in their culture and police procedures, and what was missing and needed to change.

That unvarnished look reveals how hard it will be to reform out-of-control departments, whether in Cleveland, Staten Island, Ferguson, or elsewhere. Here are 15 excerpts from the DOJ's Cleveland report showing how deeply embedded police brutality is, and why recent political rhetoric promising solutions barely scratches the surface.

1. The Street Cops Are On Their Own: "We found that CDP officers too often use unnecessary and unreasonable force in violation of the Constitution. Supervisors tolerate this behavior and, in some cases, endorse it. Officers report that they receive little supervision, guidance, and support from the Division, essentially leaving them to determine for themselves how to perform their difficult and dangerous jobs."

2. Excessive Force Is Expected and Covered Up: "These incidents of excessive force are rooted in common structural deficiencies. CDP's pattern or practice of excessive force is both reflected by and stems from its failure to adequately review and investigate officers' uses of force; fully and objectively investigate all allegations of misconduct; identify and respond to patterns of at-risk behavior; provide its officers with the support, training, supervision, and equipment needed to allow them to do their jobs safely and effectively; adopt and enforce appropriate policies; and implement effective community policing strategies at all levels of CDP."

3. Using Maximum Force Has Become Routine: "For example, we found incidents of CDP officers firing their guns at people who do not pose an immediate threat of death or serious bodily injury to officers or others and using guns in a careless and dangerous manner, including hitting people on the head with their guns, in circumstances where deadly force is not justified. Officers also use less lethal force that is significantly out of proportion to the resistance encountered and officers too often escalate incidents with citizens instead of using effective and accepted tactics to de-escalate tension.

"We reviewed incidents where officers used Tasers, oleoresin capsicum spray ("OC Spray"), or punched people who were already subdued, including people in handcuffs. Many of these people could have been controlled with a lesser application of force. At times, this force appears to have been applied as punishment for the person's earlier verbal or physical resistance to an officer's command, and is not based on a current threat posed by the person. This retaliatory use of force is not legally justified. Our review also revealed that officers use excessive force against individuals who are in mental health crisis or who may be unable to understand or comply with officers' commands, including when the individual is not suspected of having committed any crime at all."

4. Police Don't Know How To De-escalate: Officers "too often fire their weapons in a manner and in circumstances that place innocent bystanders in danger; and accidentally fire them, sometimes fortuitously hitting nothing and other times shooting people and seriously injuring them. CDP officers too often use dangerous and poor tactics to try to gain control of suspects, which results in the application of additional force or places others in danger. Critically, officers do not make effective use of de-escalation techniques, too often instead escalating encounters and employing force when it may not be needed and could be avoided."

5. Top Cops Don't Want To Hear About It: "Force incidents often are not properly reported, documented, investigated, or addressed with corrective measures. Supervisors throughout the chain of command endorse questionable and sometimes unlawful conduct by officers. We reviewed supervisory investigations of officers' use of force that appear to be designed from the outset to justify the officers' actions. Deeply troubling to us was that some of the specially-trained investigators who are charged with conducting unbiased reviews of officers' use of deadly force admitted to us that they conduct their investigations with the goal of casting the accused officer in the most positive light."

6. Top Cops Will Ignore Worst Abuses: "Many of the investigators in CDP's Internal Affairs Unit advised us that they will only find that an officer violated Division policy if the evidence against the officer proves, beyond a reasonable doubt, that an officer engaged in misconduct—an unreasonably high standard reserved for criminal prosecutions and inappropriate in this context. This standard apparently has been applied, formally or informally, for years."

7. Most Cops Face No Disciplinary Threats: "Discipline is so rare that no more than 51 officers out of a sworn force of 1,500 were disciplined in any fashion in connection with a use of force incident over a three-and-a half-year period. However, when we examined CDP's discipline numbers further, it was apparent that in most of those 51 cases the actual discipline imposed was for procedural violations such as failing to file a report, charges were dismissed or deemed unfounded, or the disciplinary process was suspended due to pending civil claims. A finding of excessive force by CDP's internal disciplinary system is exceedingly rare."

8. The DOJ Found These Problems Before. "CDP's systemic failures are such that the Division is not able to timely, properly, and effectively determine how much force its officers are using, and under what circumstances, whether the force was reasonable and if not, what discipline, change in policy or training or other action is appropriate. The current pattern or practice of constitutional violations is even more troubling because we identified many of these structural deficiencies more than ten years ago during our previous investigation of CDP's use of force."

9. Police View Their Beats as War Zones: "Instead of working with Cleveland's communities to understand their needs and concerns and to set crime-fighting priorities and strategies consistent with those needs, CDP too often polices in a way that contributes to community distrust and a lack of respect for officers—even the many officers who are doing their jobs effectively. For example, we observed a large sign hanging in the vehicle bay of a district station identifying it as a "forward operating base," a military term for a small, secured outpost used to support tactical operations in a war zone. This characterization reinforces the view held by some—both inside and outside the Division—that CDP is an occupying force."

10. Harassment, Unprovoked Searches Routine: "Some CDP officers violate individuals' Fourth Amendment rights by subjecting them to stops, frisks, and full searches without the requisite level of suspicion. Individuals were detained on suspicion of having committed a crime, with no articulation or an inadequate articulation in CDP's own records of the basis for the officer's suspicion. Individuals were searched "for officer safety" without any articulation of a reason to fear for officer safety. Where bases for detentions and searches were articulated, officers used canned or boilerplate language. Supervisors routinely approved these inadequate reports."

11. Using Tasers Routine and Never Questioned: "The [Cleveland] Plain Dealer [newspaper] also reported that, between October 2005 and March 2011, CDP officers used Tasers 969 times, all but five of which the Division deemed justified and appropriate (a 99.5% clearance rate which one police expert said "strains credibility"). The Plain Dealer analyzed similar CDP force data in 2007 and found that supervisors reviewed 4,427 uses of force over four years and justified the force in every single case."

12. The CDP Stonewalled DOJ Investigators: "We note that CDP's inability to produce key documents raises serious concerns regarding deficiencies in the Division's systems for tracking and reviewing use of force and accountability-related documents… CDP did not, for example, produce deadly force investigations that occurred after April of 2013 despite multiple requests. CDP was not able to produce some 2012 use of less lethal force reports until more than a year after our initial request for documents and failed to provide a justification for this delay."

13. CDP Didn't Want to Be Accountable: "CDP's inability to track the location of critical force-related documents is itself evidence of fundamental breakdowns in its systems and suggests that any internal analysis or calculation of CDP's use of force is likely incomplete and inaccurate. It also suggests that CDP does not accept that they are accountable for documenting and explaining their decisions in such matters to civilian leadership, the City, and the community as a whole."

14. Arrest Reports Cover Up Use Of Force: "Our review of a sample of 2012 arrest records for persons charged with resisting arrest suggests that some uses of force are not being reported. For the months of February, June and August 2012, there were 111 resisting arrest incidents, and for seven of these—over six percent—CDP acknowledges that no use of force report can be located… The inability to produce Taser firing histories compounds our concerns about the reliability of the data and undermines the assertion that Taser uses have declined."

15. There Are No Clear Policies on Using Force. "Police departments must ensure appropriate training in how and when to use force, and provide the supervision necessary for sufficient oversight of officers' use of force. Departments must also provide their officers clear, consistent policies on when and how to use and report force. Departments must implement systems to ensure that force is consistently reported and investigated thoroughly and fairly, using consistent standards…

"CDP fails in all of these areas, and this has created an environment that permits constitutional violations. It has also created an atmosphere within CDP in which there is little confidence in the fairness of the disciplinary process—a lack of confidence which extends from the rank and file all the way to the highest levels of the Division and City leadership."

No Quick or Easy Solutions

The DOJ report on excessive force by Cleveland's police is very revealing. It shows how deeply embedded the culture of abusive policing is, how resistant police departments are to changing, and how the problem is not just what weapons are used by police, but how many officers want to operate with impunity and a military mindset.

These aren't the conclusions of community activists protesting about police brutality and the institutional racism of white officers shooting unarmed black men. These conclusions come from the highest-ranking federal law enforcement officials, who had to use their political power to force the Cleveland Department to open up its records and files.

The DOJ's observation that many of the same problems of excessive force are back more than 10 years after a similar federal investigation and settlement suggests that reforming America's runaway police departments is going to be incredibly difficult. Despite public protests, there's little evidence that police themselves want to change from within.

The Police Need to Be Held Accountable

Amnesty International

Founded in 1961, Amnesty International is a nongovernmental organization that focuses on human rights around the world.

Hundreds of men and women are killed by police each and every year across the United States. No-one knows exactly how many because the United States does not count how many lives are lost. The limited information available however suggests that African American men are disproportionately impacted by police use of lethal force. While the majority of the unarmed African Americans killed by police officers are men, many African American women have also lost their lives to police violence. Police officers are responsible for upholding the law, as well as respecting and protecting the lives of all members of society. Their jobs are difficult and often dangerous. However, the shooting of Michael Brown in Ferguson, Missouri and countless others across the United States has highlighted a widespread pattern of racially discriminatory treatment by law enforcement officers and an alarming use of lethal force nationwide.

Indeed, just 10 days after Michael Brown was fatally shot in Ferguson, Missouri, on August 9, 2014, St. Louis police officers shot and killed a young black man, Kajieme Powell, 25, who was reportedly holding a knife. Police claims that he was brandishing a knife were not borne out by the available video footage of the shooting. Some of the individuals killed by police in the United States include the following: Rekia Boyd, an unarmed 22-year-old black woman was shot and killed by a Chicago police officer on March 21, 2012; Eric Garner, a 43-year-old black man, died after being placed in a chokehold by New York Police Department officers after being approached by an officer who attempted to arrest

"Deadly Force: Police Use of Lethal Force in the United States," Amnesty International, June 18, 2015. Reprinted by Permission.

him for selling loose, untaxed cigarettes on July 17, 2014; Ezell Ford, 25, an unarmed black man with a history of mental illness, was shot and killed by Los Angeles police officers on August 11 2014; Tamir Rice, a 12-year-old black boy, was shot and killed by officers in Cleveland, Ohio while playing in a park with a toy gun on November 22, 2014; Walter Scott, a 50-year-old unarmed black man, was fatally shot in the back after a traffic stop for a broken light on his car in North Charleston, South Carolina on April 4, 2015; and Freddie Grey, a 25-year-old black man, died from a spinal injury after being taken into police custody in Baltimore, Maryland, on April 19, 2015. These are all cases that have received national media attention; however, there are many more including Hispanic and Indigenous individuals from communities across the country who have died at the hands of the police.

The use of lethal force by law enforcement officers raises serious human rights concerns, including in regard to the right to life, the right to security of the person, the right to freedom from discrimination and the right to equal protection of the law. The United States has a legal obligation to respect, protect and fulfill these human rights and has ratified the International Covenant on Civil and Political Rights and the International Convention on the Elimination of All Forms of Racial Discrimination, which explicitly protects these rights.

One of a state's most fundamental duties which police officers, as agents of the state, must comply with in carrying out their law enforcement duties, is to protect life. In pursuing ordinary law enforcement operations, using force that may cost the life of a person cannot be justified. International law only allows police officers to use lethal force as a last resort in order to protect themselves or others from death or serious injury. The United Nations (UN) Basic Principles on the Use of Force and Firearms provide that law enforcement officials shall not use firearms against persons except in self-defence or the defence of others against the imminent threat of death or serious injury, and that, in any event, "intentional lethal use of firearms may only be made when strictly unavoidable in order to protect life." Furthermore, international law enforcement standards require that force of any kind may be used only when there are no other means available that are likely to achieve the legitimate objective. If the force is unavoidable it must be no more than is necessary and proportionate to achieve the objective, and law enforcement must use it in a manner designed to minimise damage or injury, must respect and preserve human life and ensure medical aid are provided as soon as possible to those injured or affected.

> "States are required to respect and to protect the right to life… The police in any society will at some point be confronted with a situation where they have to decide whether to use force and, if so, how much. Enacting an adequate domestic legal framework for such use of force by police officials is thus a State obligation, and States that do not do this are in violation of their international obligations."
>
> – UN Special Rapporteur on extrajudicial, summary or arbitrary executions

The first step to securing the right to life, according to the UN Special Rapporteur on extrajudicial, summary or arbitrary executions, is the establishment of an appropriate legal framework for the use of force by the police, which sets out the conditions under which force may be used in the name of the State and ensuring a system of responsibility where these limits are transgressed. Furthermore, the UN Special Rapporteur notes that, "The specific relevance of domestic law in this context stems from the fact that the laws of each State remain the first line and in many cases effectively the last line of defence for the protection of the right to life, given the irreversibility of its violation. National and local laws play an important role in defining the understanding by law enforcement officials and the population alike of the extent of the police powers, and the conditions for accountability. As such, there is a strong need to ensure that domestic laws worldwide comply with international standards. It is too late to attend to this when tensions arise."

Amnesty International reviewed US state laws—where they exist—governing the use of lethal force by law enforcement officials and found that they all fail to comply with international law and standards. Many of them do not even meet the less stringent standard set by US constitutional law. Some state laws currently allow for use of lethal force to "suppress opposition to an arrest"; to arrest someone for a "suspected felony"; to "suppress a riot or mutiny"; or for certain crimes such as burglary. A number of statutes allow officers to use lethal force to prevent an escape from a prison or jail. Others allow private citizens to use lethal force if they are carrying out law enforcement activities. Amnesty International found that:

- All 50 states and Washington, DC, fail to comply with international law and standards on the use of lethal force by law enforcement officers;
- Nine states and Washington, DC, currently have no laws on use of lethal force by law enforcement officers; and
- Thirteen states have laws that do not even comply with the lower standards set by US constitutional law on use of lethal force by law enforcement officers.

Many of the nationwide protests in the wake of recent police killings have demanded accountability and international law requires it. All cases of police use of lethal force must be subject to an independent, impartial and transparent investigation and if the evidence indicates that the killing was unlawful, the police officer responsible should be criminally prosecuted. However, accountability for police use of lethal force is severely lacking in the United States. The officer's own police agency usually conducts the investigation before handing the case over to the local prosecutor for review, who, depending on the jurisdiction, either convenes a grand jury or decides directly whether to file charges against the officer. The fact that investigations are handled internally and that prosecutors have to maintain good working relationships with the police as well as fulfill their duty to investigate and prosecute police use of lethal force, has led to calls being made for independent investigations and prosecutors. While this report only examines whether specific accountability measures are provided for in a state's use of lethal force statute, Amnesty International has previously documented concerns with oversight mechanisms in the United States and the need for independent and effective oversight bodies to be established.

Another concern related to accountability is the overly broad statutes governing the use of force, in particular the use of lethal force: If the facts of the case established during an investigation indicate that police used lethal force despite officers having other – less harmful – options at hand to counter a threat or that there was no threat to the life of officers or members of the public at all, this would have to be considered as a violation of international human rights law and standards and – in cases where it has resulted in death – an arbitrary deprivation of life under international law. However, if statutes allow for a use of lethal force below the threshold and outside the strict criteria established by international law, then such statutes actually prevent holding law enforcement officials accountable for violations of human rights.

The majority of deaths at the hands of police are the result of an officer using a firearm. The pervasiveness of firearms among the general population in the US means that officers have to be prepared for the worst when confronting a suspect. An unexpected movement can be mistaken as someone reaching for a firearm even if the suspect is unarmed. However, any use of a firearm – i.e. a weapon designed to kill – by law enforcement must be regulated by specific provisions of the law, establishing a more specific set of rules than for other forms of use of force, and should only be authorized when there is no other way of protecting against a serious threat of death or serious injury.

A key concern in recent cases involving firearms has been the number of shots fired by officers. Michael Brown, for instance, was shot six times, and Kajieme Powell was shot nine times. The firing of so many shots in an urban environment would often be reckless and puts bystanders at risk, and indicates an intentional lethal use of a firearm which under international law and standards may only ever be employed when strictly unavoidable to protect life.

There are a wide range of "less lethal" weapons and other tools available for use in law enforcement which carry less risk of death and injury than that inherent in police use of firearms. However, it should also be recognized that these so-called "less lethal" weapons can also result in serious injury and sometimes death. For example, at least 540 people in the United States died after being shocked with Tasers from 2001 through 2012. Also, even without the use of weapons, as recent cases have demonstrated, chokeholds or other forms of physical force can also be deadly. As such, any other type of force that implies likelihood or high risk of death must also be subject to the same strict restrictions and only be allowed for the purpose of preventing death or serious injury.

While this report focuses on the use of lethal force by law enforcement officers in the United States – that is, principally the use of firearms – an overall change in approach to all aspects of use of force by law enforcement is needed, as at present, police consider use of force to be a normal part of policing operations rather than the exception. International standards clearly require that force should not be used by law enforcement officials unless there are no other means available that are likely to achieve the legitimate objective. If the use of force is unavoidable, it must be the minimum amount of force necessary to achieve the objective, and the use of lethal force should only be used as a last resort; if the use of force is unavoidable, they should minimize damage and injury and ensure those affected receive prompt medical and other assistance. International standards also emphasize the need for law enforcement to use other means before resorting to the use of force, and to be trained in alternatives to the use of force, including the peaceful settlement of conflicts, understanding of crowd behavior, and skills of persuasion, negotiation and mediation.

What is urgently needed is a nationwide review and reform of existing laws, policies, training and practices on police use of lethal force, as well as a thorough review and reform of oversight and accountability mechanisms. As this demonstrates, one of the steps that needs to be taken is for state laws to be thoroughly reformed or, in some cases, replaced with new laws to ensure that police are not permitted to use lethal force except where it is necessary to protect against an imminent threat of death or serious injury.

The Media Fuels Antipolice Sentiment

Alexa Morelli

Writer Alexa Morelli has written for the Odyssey Group and PoliceOne.com. She studied journalism and sports management at the University of Arizona.

O ver the past few years, a lot has been happening in our country. We have a new terrorist organization that is influencing our own citizens to commit armed jihad right here on American soil and race relations are worse than they've been since the civil rights movement of the 50s and 60s. Then we have Donald Trump, a billionaire businessman, and reality TV star is currently leading in the Republican primary polls for the 2016 GOP presidential candidate. These are just a few of the significant changes in American culture.

The way America's citizens view law enforcement has also changed. There have always been people who feel disdain towards police officers and their profession (queue N.W.A.s hit song "F*** the Police," originally released in 1988). But today it seems that the publics distrust of police officers has spread far and wide. Many people wonder why that is. There seems to be a significant number of people who blame law enforcements use of heavy-handed tactics combined with cries of racism when it comes to everything from traffic stops to arrests to incarceration. So why has this not been brought to the attention of the general public until somewhat recently? Why are there entire protests, sit-ins and hunger strikes being dedicated to this issue so suddenly? Why are good police officers now being accused of crimes just for doing their jobs? There is a relatively simple answer to these questions.

The culprit to blame for the American people's negative view of police officers is the media.

"The Media's War on Police Officers," by Alexa Morelli, Odyssey Media Group, Inc, December 24, 2015. Reprinted by Permission.

This analysis will consist of three parts. First, a general analysis of the relationship between the media and law enforcement and how they affect each other is necessary. Secondly, a discussion on how the media has changed the way it reports on crime and justice in recent years and examples of this. Finally, how the changes the media has made in the way they report about law enforcement officers and their activity have changed the way Americans view and treat police officers.

The problem with blaming the media for this is that media is a very broad term. The media that this analysis refers to is mostly the mainstream media. Its the big news stations, CNN, NBC, ABC and Fox News. Its the newspapers like the *New York Times, Washington Post, Chicago Tribune,* and so on. Its journalists in general. It is people that the public trusts and that they have a long-standing relationship with. When it comes to reporting on a police officers violence or misconduct, the reporters often make the races of the police officer and the victim an important part of their story. They bury important facts about the actual cases and they fail to remain objective. If Americans could hear what happened, stating purely the facts of the case while leaving race and opinion out of it, they would be more likely to have a different opinion about the situation, or, at least, be able to form their opinion without the influence of the media. But reporters do not do this. This relates back to Rawls's Justice Theory. If the reporters were being fair and doing their job the way they are supposed to, they would use Rawls's Veil of Ignorance. If the mainstream media did this, things might be different.

The relationship between law enforcement and the media is an important one because they depend on each other.

Crime, justice, and the media have to be studied together because they are inseparable, wedded to each other in a forced marriage where they cohabitate in a fascinating, if raucous relationship, Ray Surette wrote in his novel, *Media, Crime and Criminal Justice.*

The media and crime and justice have this type of dependent relationship because crime and justice are a large percentage of what the media is reporting on. This doesn't always have to do with police officers, but cops play an important role in American society, therefore, they must play an important role in American media and journalism. Because of this, the media can directly affect law enforcement, and they do so by being able to shape the attitudes that people have towards them.

Scholars have long noted the importance of the media in shaping citizens attitudes about crime and justice Kathleen Donovan reported. Many studies have been done on this, making it hard for anyone to argue against.

Furthermore, reporters have changed the way they talk about police officers. They bring more attention than ever to anything negative done by someone in the law enforcement profession while leaving positive stories out of the line-up. CNN contributor, Eliott McLaughlin is one of these reporters. In his article entitled "We're not seeing more police shootings, just more news coverage," he tries to give police officers a bad name. He says that police have been killing innocent black people for years and it is now finally being brought to the nation's attention. But he has no facts or statistics to back this up. In fact, his only source is Robert Bogle, the president and CEO of the *Philadelphia Tribune*, an African American newspaper. He does not interview anyone in the law enforcement profession or anyone with an opinion different than his own. But he does make an important point.

The headlines make it feel as if the country is experiencing an unprecedented wave of police violence, but experts say that isn't the case," McLaughlin said. "Were just seeing more mainstream media coverage.

This is important because it shows that whether someone likes the police or not, everyone can agree that police violence is being brought to our attention more than ever before. Journalists like McLaughlin have started what some people call a hate campaign against police officers.

The seeds of this hate campaign were planted as early as 2009, when, without caring about the facts, President Obama publicly lashed out against a white police officer for arresting Professor Henry Louis Gates, a black Harvard professor. This officer did nothing wrong, Nolte said.

While bringing up how President Obama has influenced the start of this hate campaign brings forward an entirely different topic to analyze, this instance is important because the president went after this police officer for simply doing his job. The police officer was responding to a 9-1-1 call made about the residence. He arrested Gates, even though he was innocent because this is something police officers do all the time. Police officers do this because it is in their job description. It is not their job to arrest the guilty, only a court can determine that. It is their job to arrest possible suspects. The public's view of police officers only got worse after this controversy.

Things were ratcheted up a notch in early 2012 after George Zimmerman, a Florida community watchman, shot and killed Trayvon Martin, Nolte said.

Things took off from there. Suddenly the media was reporting on police officers and how they were racist because of the way the media reported on this case. Many Americans blame the police for Zimmerman being found not guilty even though the police are not the ones who determined this, a jury did. Heather Mac Donald, the Thomas W. Smith fellow at the Manhattan Institute for Policy Research, a public policy think tank in New York City, testified on criminal justice and the deincarceration movement earlier this year.

Mac Donald is also a writer for *City Journal*, and had this to say in her testimony, "The most poisonous claim in the dominant narrative is that our criminal justice system is a product and a source of racial inequity."

The problem with the media calling police officers racists is that the American people are starting to believe that police officers actively seek out black people to arrest or harass them. But, Mac Donald reported prison statistics that there has actually been an increase in white people imprisoned in the last few years, not black people. According to police reports and FBI data, of the roughly 800 people killed by a police officer this year, half were white, and only a quarter were black. This data proves that although the media makes it seem like cops are only shooting unarmed black people, this is not the case. Ninety-five percent of those people killed were for justifiable reasons while only five percent were either undetermined or have the possibility of being because of an illegal action taken by the officer. The media has chosen to either not report on this data at all or bury it beneath the few stories about police injustices. Other than changing the way they report on police officers, the media has made a few other changes due to the rise of citizen journalists and the popularity of social media.

Social media is a topic for a whole other analysis on this subject, but it cannot be left out of this discussion and neither can people who use social media forums to be a new kind of journalist that America has never had before. Because journalism is not a cut and dry profession such as being a doctor or lawyer, really anyone can claim to be a journalist without a certificate or degree. It's very easy for people to start a blog or make a Facebook page or Twitter profile about something they are passionate about and present it to people as truth. It does not matter if they have anyone or anything to back up their claims because, in this day and age, Americans will believe a lot of what they read on the internet. It sounds outrageous to some people, but it is true. Because these people are not actual professionals working for an organization, they set their own ethical guidelines.

This brings forth a whole new set of problems because a lot of these citizen journalists have joined the hate movement of police officers and post anything online to support their claims that police officers are racist and unethical. An even bigger problem brought on by this is that sometimes the mainstream media chooses to interview these people or quote them in their reporting as a source. Because a lot of citizen journalists don't fact check and the mainstream media doesn't take the time to fact check what they are saying, many Americans choose to believe them and their false claims. And the biggest problem of all, the reason this analysis is so important, is the fact that the American people are using this information and acting on it.

Its not easy to prove that the media has changed American's thoughts about police officers because thoughts are much less concrete than actions. But negative thoughts lead to negative actions.

According to the FBI, the number of police officers killed in the line of duty nearly doubled from 27 to 51 between 2013 and 2014. That is nearly one murdered police officer a week during 2014, which was also a little over a year after the mainstream media began its coordinated hate campaigns to demonize America's law enforcement officers, Nolte reports.

This statistic provides a look at the negative affects the media's new way of reporting about law enforcement has had. The number of police officers killed in the line of duty was steadily declining for years. The only variable factor in the last few years has been the media's emphasis on reporting on cases like the Zimmerman case, Ferguson, Brown and so on—cases where police officers either did their job correctly and were not charged rightly so, or were charged because they were an unethical cop and person. This has given cops a bad name overall and has made them less likely to do their job efficiently and stay safe while they do it.

To conclude, it is important to analyze whether or not there is a solution to this madness. In McLaughlin's interview with Bogle, Bogle suggested a solution, video. Many police officers are now being required to wear video cameras on their person so that they have evidence of whether or not they used proper tactics.

Body-worn cameras hold tremendous promise for enhancing transparency, promoting accountability, and advancing public safety for law enforcement officers and the communities they serve," Attorney General Loretta Lynch told MSNBC writer, Will Femia.

In addition to this, black protest groups are encouraging Americans to use their camera phones to record any instances of police violence whether they are the victim or a bystander.

FBI director James Comey discourages this saying, "scrutiny of police conduct and the threat of exposure through 'viral videos' has generated a chill wind blowing through American law enforcement over the last year."

Even Bogle, a police hater admitted, most of the time there's video, it demonstrates the officer did the right thing.

So maybe the video is the solution. No matter what, though, video evidence will not change the media and put an end to their hate campaign. That is something they have to do on their own. In order for the media to reverse what they have done something they will day admit that they have to do, they need to embrace Rawls's theory. They need to leave race, gender, income level and so on, out of the discussion when it comes to reporting on crimes and law enforcement. In an ideal world, race would not be something that makes our mind think differently about someone or something they did. We would purely judge people on their character. So maybe that is the solution to this problem, and if so, then that is up to the generations and journalists of the future.

Police Forces Face Challenges on All Sides

J. Christian Adams

J. Christian Adams is an attorney who worked in the Department of Justice Civil Rights Division under the administration of President George W. Bush, and the New York Times *bestselling author of* Injustice: Exposing the Racial Agenda of the Obama Justice Department.

T he Black Lives Matter movement must guard against becoming an advocacy arm of gangsters and criminals. A recent pistol-whipping of a police officer in Birmingham, Alabama, occurred because police around the country are becoming too afraid to act like police. Portraying criminals as victims and the police as criminals will foster an atmosphere of lawlessness and criminality that will harm every American, particularly those hardest hit by crime.

Janard Cunningham is lucky to be alive. Pulled over by an Alabama police officer for erratic driving, Cunningham exited his vehicle during the traffic stop, aggressively approached the police officer and delivered a debilitating sucker punch to the officer's head.

When any police officer is debilitated by a criminal's blow to his head, it's a life or death moment. Threatening deadly force against an attacker is perfectly reasonable. Even using deadly force to terminate the attack might be justified. But thanks to the fashionable demonization of police officers driven by activists and their enablers in the media, that's not what happened next.

Instead, Cunningham seized the stunned officer's firearm and pistol whipped him senseless. The officer said he didn't defend himself because of fear of what the media and the activists would do to him. "A lot of officers are being too cautious because of what's

"Forget Criminals, Police Now Fear Activists and the Media," by J. Christian Adams, the National Interest, August 22, 2015. Reprinted by Permission.

going on in the media," the unnamed police officer told CNN. "I hesitated because I didn't want to be in the media like I am right now. It's hard times right now for us."

When police officers fear Al Sharpton more than they fear a gangster with a gun, the country has arrived at a dangerous moment.

But Jared Cunningham wasn't alone in his depravity that day. Bystanders joined in. Emboldened by the fashionable hatred of the police, the onlookers didn't render aid to the bleeding officer, instead they snapped photos.

The photos posted on social media show a police officer face down on the concrete. Others show him covered in blood. Priorities, I suppose.

Naturally, the gruesome photos went viral, especially among the anti-police crowd.

"Pistol whipped his ass to sleep," one Facebook user wrote. The photos were passed around Twitter with hashtags such as #FDAPOLICE replacing (or joining) #BlackLivesMatter for a time.

I doubt very much the well-meaning supporters of the Black Lives Matter movement want much attention for their more zealous co-marchers. They've decided to ride this tiger and will find it very difficult to get off, no matter how many police end up hurt or killed.

The Black Lives Matter movement should be careful. In the end, they will lose everything when mainstream America sees more stories of police officers being shot and photos of bloodied detectives. Given a choice between thugs and cops, Americans will ultimately take the side of the police. When it seems the thugs have scored too many scores, Americans will lose all sympathy for those criticizing the police.

But something even more incendiary is in play. The truth is that civil society and domestic tranquility aren't givens. In fact, over the course of history, they are often the exceptions. Violent gangsters acting out is a characteristic of human experience as old as time. It is a dark tendency that systems of law and traditions of order are designed to oppose. When the acts of violent gangsters begin to intermingle with political movements, the risks multiply.

Simply put, the anti-police movement has elements which are both grotesquely violent and other elements which are explicitly political. There doesn't seem to be much effort of the latter to disown the former.

The violent acting in the name of political has always been one of the most dangerous threats to civil society. The danger exists even when the violent purport to act for the cause. Those who advocate for or praise the violence have also fulfilled an essential role historically to aid this menace.

What could be the reason that the movement to "reform" police departments doesn't seem to have the will to jettison every nook and cranny of the violent wing of the movement? I refer to both the overtly violent as well as those who delight in the use of violence against the police. Do the more mainstream and peaceful elements of the Black Lives Matter crowd relish the energy for the cause the nastier allies provide? Or is it merely a delight in payback? After all, on social media, that wicked view of payback is easy to find, as it was in response to the events in Alabama.

You can't find much criticism of this odd, informal and increasingly nasty confederation of police "reformers" among most media. In fact, some media are more likely to criticize anyone who draws attention to the violent side of the anti-police cause than they are likely to dwell on the more uncomfortable trends in the movement.

Doing anything else might expose too much, and trigger a mighty backlash by mainstream America to the growing thuggery on our nation's streets. When that thuggery starts to borrow slogans and memes of an organized, and heretofore, lionized cause, that backlash might not be far off.

CHAPTER 2

Is Excessive Force
Ever Justified?

Overview: There Is a Place for Use of Deadly Force

Eric Tucker

Eric Tucker covers the Justice Department for the Associated Press in the Washington, DC, area.

WASHINGTON — The law gives police officers latitude to use deadly force when they feel physically endangered, but there's far less legal flexibility when it comes to opening fire at fleeing individuals. Here's a look at legal issues raised by Saturday's police shooting in South Carolina in which video recorded by a bystander shows a black man being shot in the back and killed as he runs away.

Is there a federal legal standard to judge the appropriateness of police use of force?

Yes. The Supreme Court held in a 1989 case, Graham v. Connor, that the appropriateness of use of force by officers "must be judged from the perspective of a reasonable officer on the scene," rather than evaluated through 20/20 hindsight.

That standard is designed to take into account that police officers are frequently asked to make split-second decisions during fast-evolving confrontations, and should not be subject to overly harsh second guessing. The Justice Department cited that legal threshold last month when it declined to prosecute former Ferguson, Missouri police officer Darren Wilson in the shooting death last summer of an unarmed black 18-year-old.

Can police officers shoot at fleeing individuals?

Only in very narrow circumstances. A seminal 1985 Supreme Court case, Tennessee vs. Garner, held that the police may not shoot at a fleeing person unless the officer reasonably believes that

"When Can Police Use Lethal Force Against a Fleeing Suspect?" by Eric Tucker, NewsHour Productions LLC, April 8, 2015. Reprinted by Permission.

the individual poses a significant physical danger to the officer or others in the community. That means officers are expected to take other, less-deadly action during a foot or car pursuit unless the person being chased is seen as an immediate safety risk.

In other words, a police officer who fires at a fleeing man who a moment earlier murdered a convenience store clerk may have reasonable grounds to argue that the shooting was justified. But if that same robber never fired his own weapon, the officer would likely have a much harder argument.

"You don't shoot fleeing felons. You apprehend them unless there are exigent circumstances—emergencies—that require urgent police action to safeguard the community as a whole," said Greg Gilbertson, a police practices expert and criminal justice professor at Centralia College in Washington state.

Gilbertson said he thought the video of the shooting of Walter Scott in North Charleston, South Carolina, was "insane" given what he said was the apparent lack of justification.

Though the legal standard has been established, courts continue to hear cases involving use of force against fleeing felons under a variety of circumstances. Just last year, the Supreme Court sided with police officers who were sued over a high-speed, two-state chase in Arkansas that ended with the deaths of the fleeing driver and his passenger.

In cases where police officers are not supposed to use deadly force against a fleeing person, what should they do?
Each case involving a suspect who flees the police, whether in a car or on foot, poses a balancing test for an officer, said Chuck Drago, a police practices expert and former Oviedo, Florida, police chief.

"Am I creating more of a danger by chasing this person than if I let this person stay at large?" Drago said. "Especially in a vehicle pursuit, is it worth risking everyone on the road to catch this guy?"

In a pursuit on foot, the more reasonable option might be to call for backup, including perhaps with a police dog, so that other officers can set up a perimeter and trap the suspect, Drago said.

In the South Carolina case, the former lawyer for the North Charleston officer, Michael Slager, said Monday that Slager felt threatened and had fired because Scott was trying to grab his stun gun—an older model that would have had to have been manually reloaded. But if the stun gun was on the ground at the time Scott fled, Drago said, then "there is no longer a threat. The threat is gone."

There's also no indication on the video that after the physical encounter between the men, where the officer has said he believed Scott had tried to get ahold of his stun gun, that he shouts any instructions.

Is there a role for federal involvement in the investigation?
The FBI and the department's Civil Rights Division are working together to examine the case. Though the officer faces a state murder charge in South Carolina, the federal government will be looking at the shooting for potential civil rights violations.

That means federal agents and prosecutors will be looking to establish not only that Slager killed Scott, but that the officer willfully deprived Scott of his civil rights and used more force than the law allowed.

The Justice Department often investigates police use of force, though not all investigations result in prosecution. In some cases, such as in the 1991 beating of Rodney King in Los Angeles, federal prosecutors have moved forward either with their own investigation or prosecution after the conclusion of a state case.

Context Is Key: Police Are Human and Often Forced to Act

Kazu Haga

Kazu Haga is a Kingian Nonviolence trainer based in Oakland, California, who works with youth, incarcerated populations, and activists. He is also the founder and coordinator of East Point Peace Academy.

It's okay mommy…. It's okay, I'm right here with you…"

Those were the words of four-year-old Dae'Anna, consoling her mother Lavish Reynolds after she witnessed the police shoot and kill her boyfriend Philando Castile.

Those words are now scarred into the psyche of America, much like words that came before it: "Hands up, don't shoot." "I can't breathe." "It's not real."

If you haven't realized that the system of policing isn't working for the black community, you haven't been paying attention. Just hours after the killing of Alton Sterling, a four-year-old child witnessed someone getting shot and bleeding out while she sat in the backseat. The system didn't work for her, her mother or for Philando Castile. The system didn't work for Alton Sterling, or for Mike Brown, or for Freddie Gray or for countless others.

But here's something we miss in this climate of police violence: the system of policing isn't working for those working in law enforcement either. It doesn't serve anyone.

When I watched the video taken by Lavish Reynolds, I was blown away by the cool and calm demeanor in her voice and how it was offset by the complete panic in the voice of the officer. His was filled with fear.

And why wouldn't it be? Behind that trigger lies a man who just took the life of another man in front of a child. I've worked with enough people in prison, as well as veterans who have taken the lives of others, to know that no human being is immune to the fear, guilt and shame that comes with the taking of another's life.

The system of policing is one that relies on violence, fear, repression and a colonizer mentality. But the individuals who are employed to enforce that mentality are human beings with a human psyche, just like any other. It's silly to assume that these men and women aren't impacted by the violence they witness and participate in every day. No human being can participate in the levels of heightened violence that police are engaged in without being affected by it.

The tragedy in Dallas is a response from a people within a community that has lived with that fear and violence for generations. If you belong to a community that is constantly facing murder, incarceration and dehumanization, it should come as no surprise when members of that community decide that they have had enough and react with violence. It is tragic, yet should not be surprising if you can see their perspective. Similarly, just because police experience that violence from "the other side," it should not surprise us that it may affect them in similar ways, and that they may similarly react with outbursts of violence.

Martin Luther King, Jr. wrote that "the white man's personality is greatly distorted by segregation, and his soul is greatly scarred." He said that the work of defeating segregation was for the "bodies of black folks and the souls of white folks." He understood that to be a white supremacist, to hold hatred in your heart for so many and to inflict violence on others destroys your soul.

Others have written about the history of policing in the United States — especially in the South — and its roots in the slave patrol. So it should come as no great leap to consider that participating in policing in 21st century America could scar one's soul.

This is not about being an apologist for the individuals responsible for the killing of black life. It is not about comparing the suffering of black communities to that of law enforcement. But in nonviolence, we know that if you don't understand the perspective of those who you are in conflict with, you do not understand the conflict. You do not need to agree with, excuse or justify the other's perspective, you simply need to understand it so you can see the complete picture.

And part of the picture looks like this: Cops are human. They work for an institution with historical ties to slavery and a long legacy of racism. They are indoctrinated in a culture of "us vs. them," of doing "whatever is necessary so you get home," of fear, distrust, and dehumanization of those deemed as being on "the other side." They are taught to fear for their lives. They are trained almost exclusively in tactics of violence and repression. They are sent into situations of conflict every day with those limited tools, into communities where they are playing out tensions that have been brewing for hundreds of years.

Looking at that picture, no one should be surprised at incidents of police violence, and we should all understand that to some extent, it is rooted in the spiritual and emotional degradation that results from being immersed in such a violent institution.

I've been thinking lately about Eric Casebolt, the officer who responded to a call at a pool party in McKinney, Texas and proceeded to throw a young girl onto the ground and point his gun at other teenagers.

Casebolt should have been fired immediately, and his record should follow him everywhere, preventing him from ever having employment as a cop or even as a security guard.

If we look more into the history of that conflict, the story of Casebolt's own trauma begins to emerge. The pool party was the third call that he attended to that day. His first was a suicide where he witnessed a man blow his head off in front of his family, and had to console the family. Immediately after, he was called to another attempted suicide, where he had to talk a young girl down from jumping off a ledge — also in front of her family. By the time he reached the pool party, he was an emotional wreck.

Again, that's not to excuse his actions as an individual. But understanding that context and perspective also allows us to point our fingers at the larger culprit: a system of policing that didn't care enough about Casebolt's mental health that they couldn't even give him the rest of the day off. A culture of machismo that doesn't give space for cops like Casebolt to grieve or process what he just went through.

When the system comes together to defend cops like Casebolt, their defense of him is a smokescreen. The system doesn't care about any individuals — the individuals are dispensable. It is trying to distract us from the fact that the system itself is corrupt. If the system truly cared about the people who work in the system, it would create fundamental changes to stop the killings of black people, thereby decreasing the chances of retaliatory killings like the ones in Dallas.

But for us, the more we focus our anger on the individual who pulled the trigger, the more we are letting the system off the hook. And the more the system defends the individual, the more we want to see him or her locked up, as if they are the problem. Hook, line and sinker.

Individual accountability requires healing, and a space for the perpetrator of the harm to feel remorse for their actions. I've learned over time that people can't empathize with the pain that they caused until their own pain and story has been honored. So, can we build a movement that honors the pain of the officers, creates spaces to help them see the pain that they cause, and — following the example of former Baltimore officer Michael Wood — allows them to defect from a system that doesn't serve them either?

And can we hold that level of compassion without pacifying our righteous indignation towards a system that doesn't value human life? How do we build a fierce and powerful resistance movement that addresses the individual and the system? What does it look like to hold individuals accountable with compassion, and systems accountable with indignation?

#AltonSterling, #PhilandoCastile and #Dallas are sobering reminders that violent institutions are causing human death on all sides. And until we find justice for all people, their spirits will be with us, nudging us to answer those questions.

Civilians Can Use Deadly Force, Too

Robert Farago

Robert Farago is the founder and publisher of a website called the Truth About Guns (TTAG). His writing experience stems from his time as a news writer for WBRU-FM in Providence, RI.

Your legal right to use deadly force (i.e. shoot someone) varies from state to state. This article gives you some basic guidelines on the legal use of deadly force. What you are about to read is not legal advice. I am not a lawyer. After you finish here, Google "deadly force YOUR STATE HERE" and read your state's law. If you have any questions or concerns, contact your local NRA chapter. Take a Use of Deadly Force class. Do not call the police. Just as they have no legal obligation to protect you (true story) they have no legal obligation to give you accurate legal advice. OK, so, we begin with another disclaimer . . .

At the end of the proverbial day, if you shoot someone, a number of people will decide whether or not you were legally justified in doing so. The police will decide whether or not to arrest you. A District Attorney/Prosecutor will decide whether or not to charge you with a crime. Should the incident proceed to trial, a judge or jury will decide whether or not you had a legal right to fire your weapon.

In most states, juries use the "reasonable person" standard to determine guilt or innocence. Would a reasonable person in the same circumstances fire their weapon? We're talking the totality of circumstances here. Considerations include your age, weight, height, sex, physical health and life experience; the bad guy(s) age, height, sex, appearance and actions; the type of threat (weapons?); the reason for the threat (robbery? rape? knockout game?). The

"A Closer Look at a Big Question: When Can You Legally Shoot Someone in Self-Defense?" by Robert Farago, Thetruthaboutguns.com, March 13, 2015. Reprinted by Permission.

exact situation as it unfolded: who, what, when, where and why. Everything. All of it.

Regardless of the reasonable person standard, you should know your state's rules for the legal use of deadly force. You should have these rules clear in your mind before you pick up your gun. If you know when you can bring our weapon to bear on the bad guy or guys, you will do so with less doubt and more confidence. If you know when you can't shoot, you'll keep your powder dry and avoid a whole lot of legal, moral and financial trouble down the line. Maybe . . .

Generally speaking, lethal force is permissible when you or other innocent life face an imminent, credible risk of death or grievous bodily harm, and imminence is imminent. Let's start at the end of that sentence and work our way to the beginning.

"Imminence is imminent"

People use the word "imminent" to describe something they think is about to happen. "I could tell the bad guy was about to attack me from the way he looked at me and his racial slurs." So "the attack was imminent." Nope. The word "imminent" means something quite specific when it comes to armed self-defense. It means an attack in the process of happening. Hence the codicil "and imminence is imminent." You weren't thinking someone was about to attack you. They were in the act of attacking.

Even if it's a group of previously convicted criminals revving their Harleys and shouting that they're going to gut you like a fish, even if it's a blood-soaked knife-wielding maniac waving a knife in the air, you can't shoot them until they begin their attack.

OK, you can. As I said above, it's up to the police, prosecutor, judge or jury to decide if your use of lethal force was justified. They may or may not make allowances for your state of mind. Even so, the mental tripwire for the using your firearm should be "I'm being attacked." You may have the legal right to "stand your ground," but up to that point, escape and evade are your two best friends.

"Death or grievous bodily harm"

If someone attacks you with a pillow, you are not at risk of death or grievous bodily harm. Unless you're lying in a bed and they're using the pillow to try to smother you. If someone pinches you, you are not at risk of death or grievous bodily harm. Unless they're "pinching" your testicles with a pair of pliers. If someone slaps you, you are not at risk of death or grievous bodily harm. Unless they're slapping you with brass knuckles.

See how that works? The possibility of suffocation, broken bones, head injuries, stab wounds, gunshot wounds – they all count as grievous bodily harm. Bumps and bruises don't. It's simple common sense, really. Unless it isn't . . .

You, reasonable person that you are, may have had good reason to think you were in danger of death or grievous bodily harm when you fired your weapon, but actually weren't. Very much. If at all. Or were you? How bad was that fight when you pulled your gun – or how bad was it going to get? (See: use of force continuum.)

What if someone enters your house to rob it but they don't actually attack you? Is that cause enough to shoot them? What if they're carrying a gun? What if you warn them to leave and they don't? What if you don't warn them and lay in wait and then shoot them? It's a legal grey area or, if you prefer, a minefield.

That said, in most but not all jurisdictions, your home is your castle; invaders are viewed as an inherent lethal threat (hence "the castle doctrine"). When you use your firearm outside the home, things can get awful hinky, legally speaking. For example, some states apply the castle doctrine to your car or place of business. Some don't.

Either way, this raises an important point: just because you can shoot someone legally doesn't mean you should. Unless the threat of death or grievous bodily harm is completely clear, you may want to escape, evade or, perhaps, brandish your weapon as a warning.

[Note: some states allow the use of lethal force for other reasons, such as preventing kidnapping, theft or arson. Check your state's laws.]

"Credible threat"

If a 10-year-old boy points a pen knife at you from twenty feet away, that's not a credible threat of death or grievous bodily harm (nor is imminence imminent). If a bad guy steps out of the shadows right in front of you with a kitchen knife aimed at your heart, that is. If someone points a gun at you intending to do you harm (as opposed to, say, sweeping you with their muzzle at a gun range), that's a credible threat. It all comes down to how likely the threat is to be successful if you don't stop it by deploying lethal force.

Again, your opinion on the matter is subject to the authorities' and jury's opinion under the "reasonable person" standard. Again, they will base their decision on the totality of the circumstances surrounding the defensive gun use. And again, that determination varies according to state law and the local culture. Remember: there are states where you have a so-called "duty to retreat." These states are likely to have a high standard for what constitutes a credible threat. And imminence. And grievous bodily harm.

"Innocent life"

If you're minding your own business, you are the innocent party. You are legally allowed to use lethal force to stop an imminent, credible threat of death or grievous bodily harm—provided imminence is imminent, subject to the usual caveats and official second-guessing. Same goes if someone else is minding their own business when they face an imminent, credible threat of death or grievous bodily harm, and imminence is imminent. You are legally allowed to use lethal force to stop the threat against them—subject to the usual caveats and official second-guessing.

While you have an excellent idea of when you're innocent (e.g., not starting a fight), using your gun to protect "other innocent life" is fraught with danger. Let's say you see a woman being attacked by two men. The violence is severe and she's screaming rape. You shoot the attackers to save the victim's life. Only the "attackers" were undercover police trying to arrest a perp. Good luck with that. By the same token, let's say you shoot a Stop 'N Rob clerk thinking he was a robber (they'd switched places during the robbery). That's not going to go well for you, either.

The best bet is to refrain from using lethal force unless you've seen the whole incident from its inception. In fact, I'd like to end this article with a simple warning: shooting a bad guy or guys can create enormous disruption to your life; morally, spiritually, financially, socially and legally. It may not, but it can.

If you face an imminent, credible threat of death or grievous bodily harm and imminence is imminent, chocks away— remembering that some state laws on lethal force impose a duty to retreat. If, however, you can find a way not to use lethal force and avoid injury to yourself or other innocent life, that's your best option. In any case, know the law on lethal force in your state and do your best to avoid stupid people in stupid places doing stupid things. That is all.

Excessive Force Knows No Bounds

Martin Kaste

Martin Kaste is a correspondent on NPR's national desk, covering law enforcement and privacy as well as news from the Pacific Northwest. He's been with National Public Radio since 2000.

The Justice Department has released a scathing report that accuses the Chicago Police Department of systematic use of excessive force.

SCOTT SIMON, HOST:
The U.S. Justice Department has released a scathing report that accuses the Chicago police of systematic use of excessive force. The report is the Obama administration's final significant action in its campaign for police reform. NPR's law enforcement correspondent Martin Kaste joins us now. Martin, thanks so much for being with us.

MARTIN KASTE, BYLINE: You're welcome.

SIMON: Let's remember the background. What exactly has the Justice Department said about Chicago police?

KASTE: Well, this report comes after that really controversial shooting of the young black man named Laquan McDonald. He was shot back in 2014. When the video finally came out, it looked as though he was fleeing police at the moment he was shot. And the outrage caused by that video triggered the Justice Department to do this investigation. And after about a year of investigating, the DOJ is now saying that excessive force happens too much, that the Chicago Police Department uses deadly force and other kinds of force, such as the use of Tasers, too frequently in cases often where it's not justified. And they say the police department doesn't do an adequate job investigating those uses of force, disciplining officers or training them.

SIMON: What concrete effect could a report like this have on the everyday function of the police department?

KASTE: Well, that's where the whole question of the timing of this report really becomes important because normally, at least over the last eight years or so, a report like this would have been the first step in the Justice Department's pressure on a local police department to reform. The report would be sort of a public shaming, which would then set things up for the city to enter into negotiations to set up what's called a consent decree. And what a consent decree is is basically a legally binding plan for reform with a federal judge monitoring the process. They don't have one of those yet in Chicago. They basically ran out of time. And it's not clear right now whether the new administration when President Trump takes office will be interested in having one. The nominee to run the Justice Department, Jeff Sessions, has expressed some skepticism over the past about consent decrees. He says sometimes they could, in his words, smear a whole police department because of the misdeeds of a few officers.

SIMON: Chicago's Mayor Emanuel has made a point of starting reforms in training and police oversight. Do they really need a consent decree with the federal government?

KASTE: Well, reformers say that historically those noble intentions in many big cities that have had these problems - those noble intentions kind of fade away over time, that the pressure against reform is pretty intense. This is how the U.S. attorney in Chicago, Zach Fardon, put it yesterday.

(SOUNDBITE OF ARCHIVED RECORDING)

ZACH FARDON: The problems that we discovered are long-standing, in some cases decades old, and prior efforts at reform in Chicago's history, there have been many. They have not gotten the job done.

KASTE: So reformers would say without that extra pressure from a federally enforced consent decree reforms don't happen. I should point out that the mayor, Mayor Rahm Emanuel, has said he wants to enter into a binding consent decree, but he says he can't negotiate the Trump administration side of that. If they're not interested, it may not happen.

SIMON: Yeah. What's been the reaction from the Chicago Police Department, especially when we take a look at the enormous increase in shootings and murders over the last year and the accusation against the police that they haven't been patrolling as vigorously as they used to?

KASTE: Well, Chicago cops have really low morale right now, and that's something even this report talks about. And when you talk to regular cops, many of them say they think that surge in violence is in part because of all the criticism they've been undergoing for the last few years, that they've been told to basically hold off on some basic kinds of street enforcement because they're worried about the backlash. And they say that that's emboldened those young people who carry guns to go ahead and shoot each other. That's not a narrative that the current Justice Department buys into, but there's a chance that the next administration would see their point.

SIMON: NPR's Martin Kaste, thanks so much.

KASTE: You're welcome.

Law Enforcement Needs Fundamental Changes

Irving Joyner

Irving Joyner has been a professor at the North Carolina Central University School of Law since 1982, and from 1984–1992, he served as the associate dean.

In recent months, the nation has witnessed several killings of African-American individuals by White police officers and a White security guard. These include the recent killings of Oscar Grant in California, Trayvon Martin in Florida, Eric Garner in New York, Michael Brown in Missouri, and Tamir Rice in Ohio. In each case, the established criminal justice process failed to evidence a serious intent to prosecute the offending officers, sparking vocal nationwide protests. Had civilians committed the same acts as these officers, they would have been prosecuted for a criminal offense.

In most cases, the protests that arose after these deaths were immediate, in large part because many African Americans and people of color have seen close family members or friends become the victims of police misconduct. Indeed, misconduct is an issue of epic proportions in minority communities. In the vast majority of these cases, law enforcement and prosecutorial officials have failed or simply refused to pursue criminal charges against the offending police officers. In those few cases where prosecutors have brought criminal charges, district attorneys have not vigorously pursued the cases and they have generally not produced guilty verdicts.

This failure of justice is not a recent issue. I vividly recall the shooting death of my 17-year-old cousin in LaGrange, N.C., when I was seven years old. My cousin Bobby Joyner was murdered by a White police officer on a Wednesday night as he walked home from choir rehearsal. He was shot in the driveway of the all-White

"The Police, the Law, and the Unjustified Use of Force," by Irving Joyner, Scalawagmagazine, July 8, 2015. Reprinted by Permission.

high school, where he bled to death. After he died, his body was dragged across the street and placed under the bedroom window of a White woman's home; the window screen was slit with a knife in an attempt to make it appear that Bobby was breaking into her home. An African-American garbage collector was awakened from his home and directed to cover the puddle of blood in the school driveway with dirt. As soon as the sun rose the next morning, family members took pictures of the murder scene, which clearly showed the covered-up blood puddle and visible tracks where the body had been dragged through the dirt and grass and placed under the window of the house.

In 1952, there were no federal laws to protect African Americans or enable prosecutions against White police officers. In those days, during Jim Crow, you could not expect White police departments to arrest or charge any White person for crimes against African Americans. Nor could you expect a White prosecutor to prosecute a White person for committing a crime against an African American. The law, then and now, grants prosecutors complete authority to determine who will be prosecuted, and no one can interfere with that power. It is also important to remember that in 1952, there were very few African-American police officers, and perhaps no African-American prosecutors, anywhere in this country.

Therefore, despite the best efforts of my grandfather and other town leaders, their organized campaign to obtain an investigation was ignored. Instead, they immediately became the target of police intimidation and harassment. Their experience illustrated the stubborn reality, almost 100 years after Dred Scott v. Sanderford, that African Americans had no legal rights that White governmental officials were required to respect or acknowledge.

In 2015, a time when there are civil rights laws on the books and many police departments and prosecutors' offices are racially integrated, you would not expect the responses to police killings of African Americans to meet the same fate as in 1952. But the failure to investigate is the same today as it was then—except now it is a national problem.

The simple explanation for this problem is that this nation's laws are deliberately designed to protect police officers from prosecution for misconduct. This protection has served to embolden police officers in contact or confrontations with African Americans and other minorities.

An examination of North Carolina law shows why there are very few prosecutions. North Carolina's laws are no isolated phenomenon—the vast majority of states rely on a similar scheme. With respect to the officer authorization to use force, most State laws simply say that police officers are privileged to use force against civilians. Under the North Carolina statute, a police officer is justified in using physical force upon a person when, and to the extent that, the officer reasonably believes it necessary to prevent the escape or make the arrest of a person who the officer reasonably believes has committed a criminal offense. In addition, the officer is justified in using force to defend himself or a third person from what he reasonably believes to be the use or imminent use of physical force while making an arrest.

The basic notion is that the officer is authorized to use force when in the officer's judgment, he reasonably believes that the force used is necessary to effect an arrest or to discharge an authorized duty. This subjective standard differs from an objective standard where the officer's conduct is measured against what a reasonable, well-trained police officer, acting appropriately, would have done under similar circumstances. Pursuant to this subjective standard, when the officer believes that he or a third person is in danger of harm, he can, under the law, use any amount of force which that officer believes is necessary to overcome the danger or harm threatened. In determining the amount of force to be used, the officer may consider all of the surrounding circumstances, including the nature of the perceived offense, the person's reputation, the words or actions used by the person and whether he is armed or suspected of being armed.

Where a police officer uses fatal force, the controlling statutory standard is similar. A police officer is justified in using deadly or fatal force when it appears to the officer to be reasonably necessary to defend himself or a third person from what the officer reasonably believes to be the use or imminent use of deadly physical force. In addition, the officer can use fatal force to effect an arrest or prevent the escape of a person who the officer reasonably believes is attempting to escape by the use of a deadly weapon, or to prevent the escape of a person from custody imposed upon him as a result of a felony conviction. In the landmark case of *Tennessee v. Garner*, the United States Supreme Court declared it unconstitutional for a police officer to use fatal force for the sole purpose of apprehending a person suspected of committing a crime. However, that Court did affirm an officer's use of fatal force if it was necessary to prevent an escape where the suspect posed a significant threat of death or serious bodily injury to the officer or to a third person.

These statutory authorizations place the officer on an elevated scale of protection from prosecution that civilians do not enjoy. Officers are trained to understand how much authority they have, and they understand that courts are going to extend the benefit of the doubt to them unless an officer has abused his authority. The authorization for an officer to use reasonable force to complete an arrest is not intended to serve as a justification for willful, malicious, or criminally negligent conduct; nor does it authorize the officer's use of "excessive" force. Yet, in practice, it has been used to justify police killings. The mere fact that a person has committed a crime—or appears to the officer to have committed a crime— does not authorize a police officer to kill him. Even when the person resists arrest, this does not automatically justify an officer's use of fatal force, since resisting does not always involve physical threats and assaultive conduct. Clearly, the fact that the person is an African American or another racial minority member does not justify an officer's decision to kill that individual. The critical test is whether the person is engaged in actual conduct, at that moment, which places the officer or a third person in imminent danger of serious bodily injury or death. This determination is based upon the "totality of the circumstances," which always focuses on exactly what the person is doing to endanger the personal safety of the officer or a third party.

Many people are under the mistaken impression that a person must willingly and immediately submit to police authority whenever the police officer makes contact with them. As a matter of law, unless a police officer has obtained a reasonable suspicion to detain a person or probable cause to arrest a person, no lawful authority can be asserted over any individual. In the absence of reasonable suspicion or probable cause to believe that the person is engaged in criminal conduct, a police officer has no legal authority to interfere with a person's movements.

This lawful expectation leaves room for any person to dissent or resist police conduct directed toward them. Although it is not the case in most states, in North Carolina, a person has the authority to resist an unlawful arrest. However, even in North Carolina, an individual never knows when an illegal arrest is occurring and acts at their peril in choosing to resist an arrest. Individuals are expected to raise all legal challenges to an arrest or an officer's use of force in court. However, this assumes the individual is alive to make it to court and is represented by an attorney who can gather witnesses to provide factual information that supports the challenge.

The laws regarding the use of force do not favor civilians over police officers. Police officers abuse their legal authorization to the use of force, which aligns with an aggressive, militarist policing culture and style that is deliberately designed to deter individual resistance. These aggressive practices demonstrate forceful conduct in order to convince civilians that they should not resist the police. Often times, officers will even engage in "swarm" tactics where they use as many officers and weapons as possible to convince people that they are overpowered or can be overpowered. Consequently, individuals are pushed out of positions where they can observe what is occurring or are prevented from recording the events. Using this strategy, police officers are able to isolate individuals who have been targeted for a police operation from others who might serve as eyewitnesses or who could lodge an on-the-spot protest of inappropriate conduct.

Where a police officer uses any degree of force, fatal or non-fatal, against an individual, it is not necessary that the person was actually armed, dangerous or presently engaged in the commission of a crime in order to justify the officer's conduct. The United States Supreme Court has determined that a reasonable belief by the officer that force was necessary, even if based on a mistake of fact or of the applicable law, is sufficient to satisfy the constitution. Based on the North Carolina statute, as long as the officer himself reasonably believed that the person posed a threat or danger of serious bodily injury or death, he would be justified in using fatal force.

Moreover, prosecutors, who work closely with individual officers, are not inclined to prosecute police officers for their aggressive use of power. Moreover, a prosecutor's decision not to prosecute cannot be reviewed or reversed by anyone. At the next election, voters can vote in a new prosecutor, but there is no legal authority that can compel a prosecutor to pursue criminal charges against a police officer. On the other hand, if the prosecutor decides to prosecute an officer, a grand jury must also affirm that decision. To further compound this lack of oversight, there is no independent or meaningful complaint process or redress apparatus within local police departments. In fact, the filing of a misconduct complaint with the Internal Review Unit usually will intensify the complaining party's persecution and harassment.

Finally, the courts have created a "qualified immunity" status for police officers. With "qualified immunity," the law protects an officer against civil rights claims, except in those very rare cases where the particular conduct committed by the officer violates clearly established law. If those particular facts or law have not been previously found to be illegal through some judicial adjudication, the officer is protected from a civil rights lawsuit even being filed. Under "qualified immunity," most legal challenges never go to trial and escape an adjudication based upon the legal merits. By the same token, prosecutors enjoy "absolute immunity" from a civil rights claim for the refusal to investigate a police misconduct claim or to prosecute the offending police officer. Even where a legal claim against a police officer survives the "qualified immunity" barrier and is allowed to go to trial, it can take years and huge amounts of money before a final verdict is rendered.

In order to deal with police misconduct, it is necessary to make fundamental changes to the laws, authority, and procedures which presently protect police officers and enable them to use indiscriminate physical force against individuals. Anything short of a comprehensive change of the laws regularly used to justify the unjustified killings of African Americans and other racial minorities will achieve no more than spitting in the wind. As such, efforts to alter and bring about fundamental change of the police culture and its use of force will continue to frustrate people.

As a beginning proposition, fundamental changes should include:

A change in the legal standard that authorizes the use of force—from the police officer's subjective judgment to that of an objective, reasonably well-trained officer;

1. The creation of an independent civilian review board that has the ability to review all police misconduct, has subpoena power, is staffed by trained professionals and can administer discipline for police misconduct and improper training;

2. The provision of authority for the state attorney general to appoint a special prosecutor to investigate and prosecute wrongful death claims;

3. Requirements that police officers reside in the cities or towns where they are employed;

4. Requirements of written permission for police officers to search a person's residence or automobile where a search warrant has not been previously issued;

5. Requirements of the use of car and body cameras while

officers interact with individuals, and of discipline for those officers who fail to use these devices;

6. Requirements of psychological examinations for all officers, bi-annual re-evaluations, and the administration of mental assessments after an officer has been involved in a fatal force incident;

7. Requirements that all officers and administrators to successfully participate in ongoing racial sensitivity and conflict resolution training every five years, more often if needed;

8. An insistence that police departments become more racially and culturally diverse across each administrative level;

9. A re-examination of the question of who controls the police, and placement of the police under the authority of a citizen commission.

The reforms listed above represent a mere starting point and should not be viewed as exhaustive. It is important to understand that modern-day police authority and the use of force have no constitutional origin or justifications. Rather, they has been created by statutes and endure only by public consensus. As presently used, the powers of the police have grown to the extent that they dwarf the constitutional rights and protections which citizens enjoy. As such, the legal limits of this authority should be re-examined.

Police Officers Have Incentives to Engage in Misconduct

Jonathan Blanks

Jonathan Blanks is a research associate in the Cato Institute's Project on Criminal Justice and also serves as the managing editor of PoliceMisconduct.net. His research focuses on law enforcement practices, overcriminalization, and civil liberties.

During any given criminal case, certain facts in police testimony that appear to be banal or happenstance—such as the placement of a hand or someone dropping a bag of drugs—seem reasonable when taken by themselves.

But looking at police testimony in similar cases, if some facts continue to appear in case after case, an observer may come to a disquieting conclusion: police are lying.

"Testilying" is the colloquial term for the police practice of lying on official documentation or in court under oath (i.e., perjury). Typically, testilying is used to justify searches in drug cases that would otherwise be deemed illegal.

The exclusionary rule, established in *Mapp v. Ohio* (1961), states that evidence gathered from a search that violates the Fourth Amendment cannot be used in court against a defendant. If, however, a police officer testifies that he saw the drugs dropped into plain view, he has probable cause—and thus, legal permission—to conduct a search without a warrant.

Some criminal justice observers think it may be the most common manifestation of police misconduct.

Alex Kozinski, now-chief judge of the U.S. Court of Appeals for the Ninth Circuit once said, "It is an open secret long shared by prosecutors, defense lawyers and judges that perjury is widespread among law enforcement officers." Many commentators in the legal

"Reasonable Suspicion: Are Police Lying in Use of Force Cases?" by Jonathan Blanks, Cato Institute, January 7, 2015. Reprinted by Permission.

community agree, though there is no consensus about what to do about it.

The repeat players in the criminal justice system naturally recognize testimony they hear over and over again. Unless drug dealers magically became klutzier after Mapp, there is strong reason to believe so-called dropsy testimony has become a widespread and illegal institutional work-around to the Fourth Amendment.

Perjury—lying in court under oath—is a crime in any circumstance, whether in a misdemeanor drug trial or a capital murder case. Police officers are very rarely charged with perjury in any type of case, despite testilying's ostensible pervasiveness. If testilying is as common as some believe, and police feel immune to perjury prosecutions, the incentive to lie to defend themselves or a colleague in a use-of-force case must be very strong.

Testilying in drug cases strongly suggests police are acutely aware of the evidentiary rules and procedural demands placed on them by legislators and the judiciary. As I noted in my last piece, officers operate with wide discretion within the boundaries of those demands.

In use-of-force cases particularly, giving broad leeway to police officers makes a lot of sense. Unlike members of the public who are free—if not demanded, in some cases—to flee dangerous situations, police officers are tasked to run toward danger for the sake of the citizenry. Police are forced to make split-second judgments on dangers to themselves and others when dealing with a potentially dangerous suspect.

Officers are human and therefore make honest mistakes, and thus the justice system should provide them with a modicum of protection when they make errors that reasonable people would make given the same circumstances.

But just as any power may lead to abuse, so may legal privileges, even those granted with the best of intentions.

The two most prominent Supreme Court cases in use-of-force authority are *Tennessee v. Garner* (1985) and *Graham v. Connor*

(1989). These two cases indeed provide ample protections for police officers with regard to the use of force.

Edward Garner was a teenager fatally shot by Memphis police while fleeing officers after commission of a burglary. In *Tennessee v. Garner*, the Supreme Court held that lethal force may not be used to stop a suspect simply to prevent him from fleeing. The Court writes:"Where the suspect poses no immediate threat to the officer and no threat to others, the harm resulting from failing to apprehend him does not justify the use of deadly force to do so....A police officer may not seize an unarmed, nondangerous [sic] suspect by shooting him dead....[I]f the suspect threatens the officer with a weapon or there is probable cause to believe that he has committed a crime involving the infliction or threatened infliction of serious physical harm, deadly force may be used if necessary to prevent escape, and if, where feasible, some warning has been given." Tennessee v. Garner, 471 U.S. 1 (1985), 9-12.

Notably, the Garner decision exposed the government to litigation for the officer's unreasonable use of force. The Court noted that Garner, being an unarmed young teen of slight physical build who was fleeing police, could have posed no imminent threat to police or others and therefore the use of lethal force was clearly unreasonable.

In Graham, the Court goes further to describe what is and is not a Fourth Amendment violation as a result of excessive force. Perhaps as a surprise to some readers, there is no right against excessive force as such, but rather courts must make after-the-fact determinations of whether seizures (i.e., violence used by police to arrest or detain a suspect) before trial are unreasonable and thus violate the Fourth Amendment. Therefore, even though the officers involved in Graham handcuffed and roughly threw an innocent man suffering insulin shock into a squad car saying, "Ain't nothing wrong with the motherfucker but drunk. Lock the son of a bitch up," the Court ruled his perfectly legal but suspicious behavior—running into and out of a convenience store—led the police officers to reasonably believe that a crime may have been committed and his detainment, however aggressive, was therefore legal.

Simplifying, then, these cases taken together lay out the standards for what is expected of police officers in use-of-force encounters and how their actions should be judged after the fact. Garner outlines the specific conditions that may obviate the prohibition on the use of lethal force against a suspect: the suspect must pose an immediate threat to the officer or the public; be armed and/or dangerous; must threaten the officer with a weapon; or had committed a crime causing serious physical harm. Additionally, when possible, the officer should warn the suspect before opening fire. Graham dictates that any actions taken by a police officer must be "objectively reasonable" given the circumstances presented to pass Fourth Amendment scrutiny.

Just as we see the fit-the-requirement nature of dropsy testimony to avoid Mapp's exclusionary rule, we may expect to see similar accounts of officer-involved shootings in regard to Garner and Graham.

Put another way, the requirements of these cases may inadvertently provide a template for officer testilying in use-of-force cases.

Sure enough, these shootings tend to include many of the following details: a description of the officer's imminent fear for his own safety; phrases such as "the suspect made furtive movements" or "charged the officer"; the suspect exhibited a superhuman resistance to nonlethal force such as physical restraint, TASER, bean-bag rounds, or even bullets; the suspect ignored repeated and explicit demands to put hands up; or the suspect "raised his weapon." In addition, some version of the phrase "he reached for his waistband," "he reached under the seat," or "he was reaching for my gun" will demonstrate the officer had reason to believe the suspect was reaching for a firearm, satisfying Garner's imminent safety requirement, even though the suspect may turn out to be unarmed.

These statements paint a picture of an officer waiting until the last possible moment and exhausting all other available means before deploying lethal force. Indeed, this is what we want our officers to do when faced with mortal danger. A recollection of facts in this way—absent proof to the contrary—is often enough to clear a police officer, given the cultural inclination to give police the benefit of the doubt and the case law currently governing use-of-force incidents.

Surely, sometimes those facts recited in these investigations are entirely true. But given the relative uniformity of testimony in case after case, it is unreasonable to believe each officer is following the guidelines time after time.

The quick-to-violence escalations we see on video of officer-involved shootings and other uses of force unambiguously confirm this. Add the continued patterns of abuse in minority communities, the resentment that treatment engenders, and the disproportionate rate at which people of color are shot by police, the numerous protests around the country demonstrate a concentrated and growing skepticism the police narratives in use-of-force incidents.

One may wonder how exactly these stories acquire such relative uniformity across jurisdictions, and whether testilying has, in fact, bled into use-of-force cases.

In his grand jury testimony, then-Ferguson police officer Darren Wilson recounted that he methodically and rationally went through the checklist of possible non-lethal defenses against his alleged attacker Michael Brown as he was in imminent fear for his own life. Perhaps that's true.

But Wilson also testified:"Yeah, just from what I have been told about the incident originally, is that you are supposed to have 72 hours before you are actually officially interviewed, recorded statement and all of that. You tend to remember more through a couple sleep cycles then what you do as soon as it happens. It is a traumatic event, a lot of details kind of come as one detail."

Police officers may receive such "cooling off" periods before giving statements in criminal or internal investigations of which they played a role. Although not codified in Missouri law, this period is just one aspect of a broader program of police protection known as "law enforcement officers' bills of rights." These bills of rights are only statutory in a handful of states, but various protections in them are operative in many jurisdictions as standard operating procedure.

Among the other benefits afforded to police officers is the right to union representation at all questioning by police authorities. This means that during this cooling off period, the officer may discuss the matter with union representatives and, presumably, they will work together to provide the best possible story for the investigators. Such a story would necessarily align with the requirements of Graham and Garner.

Whether Wilson was given this time after initial questioning as a matter of collective bargaining agreement or professional courtesy, it's fair to say most civilian shooting suspects wouldn't hear a detective say, "Go home, sleep on it for a couple days—oh, here's the number of a good defense lawyer—and come back when you get your head right."

Given all this, that Wilson's testimony about the events that led to Michael Brown's death read like a checklist of the most menacing and dangerous behavior imaginable by Brown and, alternatively, that Wilson himself calmly considered and then exhausted every possible non-lethal option before opening fire cannot be surprising.

Again, it could all be true, but the people of Ferguson have plenty of reasons to doubt it.

Positive framing of events so requires no malice, it is natural that someone and his counsel would paint his actions in the best possible light. But it is important to remember that our criminal justice system is based on an adversarial system—prosecution and defense before a neutral arbiter—and prosecutors who regularly depend on police officers as their allies in court are naturally less likely to challenge the credibility of those officers when one of them is accused of wrongdoing.

Moreover, as Garner shows, a finding against the officer further exposes the department and government to costly lawsuits, thereby increasing potential political pressure to exonerate the officer.

In short, police officers are afforded extra protections in use-of-force incidents and, additionally, are less likely to face anyone within the criminal justice apparatus who will strongly challenge their version of events. This creates an environment that implicitly tolerates inappropriate uses of force because of the diminishing likelihood of negative repercussions for those actions.

Police have a dangerous job. Undoubtedly, officers face deadly situations and can be wholly justified in their use of lethal force. And it would be going too far to say that police lawyers, unions, and prosecutors knowingly suborn police perjury.

However, the incentives in jurisdictions all over the country encourage officers to lie, not only in their day-to-day work, but also when their actions result in violence against the public.

The criminal justice apparatus has yet to seriously address police lying in most cases, let alone when police themselves are subjects of criminal investigations. Thus, police officers are incentivized to lie and their institutions are incentivized to protect their officers in use-of-force incidents.

This results in more injustice, less trust in the police, and more dead civilians.

CHAPTER 3

Is Excessive Force a Bigger Problem Now?

Overview: Things Have Changed Since the Early '90s

Nicole Flatow

Nicole Flatow is the editor of CityLab at the Atlantic. *She has also served as the associate director of communications for the American Constitution Society and the deputy editor of ThinkProgress Justice.*

Amadou Diallo. Rodney King. Timothy Thomas. Looking at where we are today in the weeks after the shooting of Michael Brown in Ferguson, Missouri, it can feel like nothing has changed in the way we police the police.

Many things haven't. Juries acquitted police. Cops got their jobs back. And brutality happened again.

Some things have gotten worse. Like police militarization.

But some things have gotten better, or are still moving toward reform in the wake of a prominent brutality incident. A history of these incidents reveals that some major recent police reforms got their start after highly publicized episodes of police violence. But it was only after years or decades and dogged, persistent community-building that some progress started to manifest.

Rodney King, 1991, Los Angeles

Videotape by a bystander captured five officers pummeling Rodney King with batons more than 50 times as he struggled on the ground outside his car. The recording immediately sparked outrage, but anger magnified when the officers who beat King were acquitted by a jury the following year. The acquittal triggered three days of violent riots during which at least 53 people died—and created immense momentum for reform. The cops in that case were ultimately held accountable, when federal prosecutors took up the case and secured convictions of four officers. And by

"What Has Changed About Police Brutality in America, from Rodney King to Michael Brown," by Nicole Flatow, ThinkProgress, September 11, 2014. Reprinted by Permission.

some measures, the LAPD was transformed in the two decades that followed.

Los Angeles was the original militarizer of police, even before the federal government started handing out left-over or used weapons, and before the height of the War on Drugs.

"The LAPD was the godfather of that kind of militaristic response," said John Jay College of Criminal Justice's Joe Domanick, author of a forthcoming book on LAPD reforms and the West Coast Bureau Chief for the Crime Report.

Los Angeles was forced to scale back in some ways after the riots, partially as a result of the Christopher Commission, created in response to the King beating to develop recommendations for reform. But initially, few of the Commission's recommendations were adopted by the city. "The Christopher Commission recommendations laid a foundation but weren't successful in bringing about reform," Domanick said.

One of the most significant reforms that did come out of the Commission was ending the policy of lifetime terms for police chiefs. The police chief who presided during that period and had overseen an era of increased militarization at the Los Angeles Police Department, Daryl Gates, was forced to resign. And thereafter, lifetime terms were over.

In the intervening years, the city took advantage of its prerogative to hire chiefs for five-year terms and then bring in someone new, in a series of chiefs who instituted some change but failed to alter the culture. Domanick said that changed when Bill Bratton became chief more than ten years later in 2002 and instituted what is known as community policing. Underlying this approach is the idea that police can rarely solve public safety problems alone, and require the input of various stakeholders to come up with solutions that might be resolved by social services or other measures instead of a heavy police hand. Bratton was hired as a reformer chief, after a series of incidents of corruption emerged known as the Rampart scandal. "He started to make a dent in the culture of occupying force," said Domanick, whose forthcoming book is titled, *Blue: The Ruin and Redemption of the LAPD.*

When Bratton arrived, the stage was set for real change because of a few other intervening developments. Five years after King's death, the city finally instituted a recommendation to create an independent inspector general to review the Department. In 1994, Congress passed provisions in the Crime Control Act meant to address police misconduct in a more systematic way, partially on the momentum of the Diallo beating. One provision gave the Department of Justice the power to bring civil suits against local police departments that exhibited a "pattern and practice" of excessive force or other constitutional violations, and the Department used that power to enter into a settlement known as a consent decree with Los Angeles.

This provision is perhaps among the most far-reaching remedies for holding entire police management structures accountable. Typically, Justice Department investigations that find constitutional violations result in agreements known as "consent decrees" that avert litigation by agreeing to federal monitoring and reforms. Common reforms include changes to police training, stronger mechanisms for complaints against officers, and improved supervision. A Vera Institute study of the first consent decree in Pittsburgh, Pennsylvania, found that use of force incidents declined after the consent decree ended, and that the city largely succeeded in meeting DOJ goals, but that citizens still perceived police as sometimes using excessive force, particularly against minorities.

It was in executing his city's consent decree that Bratton transformed the LAPD. "It is like night and day," Jeff Schlanger, who was hired to monitor the LAPD in 2001, told NBC News. As in Ferguson, what was most lost after the Los Angeles riots is what is known as "police legitimacy"—community trust in the police that underlies all of their work. Bratton instituted an era of communication and respectful interaction between individuals and police, creating a department that reflected the community and building relationships with community leaders. He even demonstrated some inclination for holding officers accountable. After a violent police response to 2007 immigration rallies in McArthur Park, Bratton announced immediate investigations and several officers were eventually demoted or fired.

But many things remained unresolved. For one thing, the mechanisms for policing the police didn't improved much. A Human Rights Watch report noted that "at risk" LAPD officers who frequently use significant force continued to act with impunity, and officers were not frequently punished for misbehavior, either internally or by the courts. For another, some tactics embraced by Bratton have created their own set of hostilities with minority communities, as a result of policies that see targeting low-level offenses in high-crime areas as key to thwarting larger crime, Domanick said.

When this policy is not implemented with constant rigor, these police stops can also lead to unnecessary police violence and even death, as in the case of Ezell Ford, shot while reportedly laying on the ground after a routine police stop for still-undisclosed reasons.

Amadou Diallo, 1999, New York City

Plainclothes officers from the New York Police Department shot street vendor Amadou Diallo just outside his Bronx apartment building after they mistook his wallet for a gun. These officers, too, were acquitted at trial.

Then-police Commissioner Howard Safir instituted some changes after weeks of protest, including adding more minority officers to the special "Street Crimes" unit whose officer had shot Diallo and requiring all officers in the unit to wear uniforms.

But Darius Charney with the Center for Constitutional Rights said these fixes were nothing more than cosmetic, and lamented that the city initiated nothing like the Christopher Commission to reform itself. Weeks later, his organization honed in on what was perceived as the real issue uncovered by the shooting—the aggressive over-use of police stops. CCR filed a lawsuit to force reform, triggering a campaign against stop-and-frisk overuse in the NYPD that is still continuing.

At the time of the police shooting, the overwhelming police presence in some minority-heavy communities was a revelation to the general public. CCR's lawsuit sought data on the numbers and types of stops. For years, production of this data was delayed even after the City Council passed a data collection law. But in 2006, outrage once again bubbled up when Sean Bell was killed by undercover cops in the wee morning hours of his wedding day, and the New York Civil Liberties Union compelled the city to release the data.

What this data revealed was that "stop-and-frisk was actually getting worse, not better," Charney said. The number of police stops had increased more than five-fold over the course of just five years, and they were just as racially skewed as they had ever been. With facts finally in hand, CCR filed a second lawsuit that resulted in a long-awaited victory when a federal judge held last year that the New York Police Department had engaged in unconstitutional racial profiling.

Even now, the court has not yet enforced that order as the police unions hold up final resolution by attempting to intervene on the appeal that Mayor Bill de Blasio has already dropped. But using the momentum of that litigation, advocates were also able to successfully campaign for new city legislation to hold police accountable. One new bill creates an inspector general to oversee NYPD. Another allows citizens to sue the police department for profiling not just based on race but also sexual orientation, religion, housing status, and other discriminatory categories.

"We have been able to I think working in tandem with advocates and organizers outside of the courtroom really make meaningful change," Charney said of the city's progress.

But progress hasn't solved many things yet. In the weeks before Brown's death, police killed Eric Garner using an illegal chokehold, after they stopped him for suspected sale of untaxed cigarettes. That death was ruled a homicide by the medical examiner.

Police accountability is still wanting in New York, with a citizen review board whose recommendations for officer discipline are often ignored by the police commissioner, and no neutral mechanism for prosecuting police. "We for many years have really pushed for a state-level agency … to prosecute crimes for municipal level police officers," Charney said, citing the inherent bias prosecutors have in favor of the police.

And as a Twitter campaign gone wrong in April demonstrated, NYPD still hasn't quite come to terms with its tainted reputation.

Timothy Thomas, 2001, Cincinnati

The big-city police departments in Los Angeles and New York have been under close watch both before and after these incidents, as they face the unique challenges and advantages of concentrated metropolitan areas. But perhaps an incident that most closely mirrors that in Ferguson is the 2001 shooting of Timothy Thomas by police that triggered riots in Cincinnati, Ohio. Thomas, a 19-year-old with an infant son, started to run when an officer approached him on the street outside a nightclub. The officer called in back-up, a chase was on, and shots were fired with almost no information about Thomas. Cops said they thought Thomas was reaching for a gun but none was ever found.

The officer in that case, too, was acquitted. But even before the verdict, community members responded to the shooting with intense riots and an economic boycott, exposing a history of racial tensions with police. Thomas was the 15th black man who died during a police confrontation in the six years before the riot. And by the time of Thomas' death, the perception was that Cincinnati faced intractable tensions between citizens and police that couldn't be fixed by yet another investigation or report. But public outrage along with federal intervention created the momentum for a different, expansive settlement in 2002 from litigation that started even before Thomas was killed. The pressure became so great that police stopped resisting, and started collaborating.

As a result of agreements involving several advocacy groups

and the Department of Justice, officers were trained on how to choose less-lethal force, and how to deal with the mentally ill and those under the influence of drugs or alcohol. They even created a mental health response team. They were not just given Tasers, but also exhaustive training on when they could use them and how. If they used a Taser, they had to document their use. And if their record didn't match what was being reported, an investigation would ensue. Cars were equipped with dash cameras. They took "community policing seriously," doing walk-throughs of neighborhoods with residents, holding community meetings, and responding to community problems with nuanced solutions. Cincinatti's police chief has so embraced the reforms in the Collaborative Agreement that he takes a copy everywhere he goes.

And one more thing. Police were actually held accountable. Mike Brickner, senior policy director of the ACLU of Ohio, said one of the persistent problems the city encountered was that a few bad actors were committing egregious acts again and again without punishment, and giving the entire department a bad name as a consequence. But after Thomas' death, a Citizen Police Review Board was formed that seemed to actually have buy-in from the police department. Officers were disciplined, given new training, or fired. Police and particularly police unions had resisted the accountability mechanisms "tooth and nail" for years before Thomas' death. But when public pressure became overwhelming, Brickner says even police unions fell in line. And in the end, many officers ended up liking the review mechanism, finding that it could be just as useful to exonerate an officer who had been wrongfully accused as to punish an officer for wrongdoing.

"I never thought I'd hear myself say this, but those riots were some of the best things that ever happened: They taught us who we are and what mattered," Kathy Y. Wilson, who for years wrote a local column called "Your Negro Tour Guide," told the *Washington Post*.

"The outcomes of the Cincinnati collaborative agreement were pretty astounding and we were really pleased with them," Brickner said. But he cautions against any reform plan that pretends there is an easy fix. "I will not pretend that this is an easy process," Brickner said. His advice to other cities: If it goes too smoothly, you're probably not really instituting change. "It takes a lot of time and a lot of hard work and there will certainly be for anyone going through a process like this moments where it's very difficult and very painful," he said.

Last month, two Cincinnati officers shot Donyale Rowe to death after he was pulled over for failure to signal. Immediately after the incident, the police chief named the officers involved and published their performance reviews. He said Rowe had a gun, and he released video of the incident from the dash cam. No tension erupted.

"Even where there is a strong intervention and things have changed significantly, I think it's unrealistic to say that there is never going to be another police problem or another issue that crops up," he said. "But I think what has changed is that there are much fewer of them." And when incidents do come up, "police also have the tools and the training and the mutual understanding of how to talk about these issues ... so that they can be quickly navigated through and done in a way that communities can agree on and live with and that they don't boil over in the way they dd in 2001."

And police accountability remains one of the most sticky problems. A 2008 *Cincinnati Enquirer* review found that while 35 police officers were fired over a 20-year period, 19 of the 25 who appealed the decision to an arbitrator got their jobs back, with heavy backing from the police union. Many of the others who didn't win faced criminal charges that made it "difficult ... or impossible" for them to get their job back.

Post-Ferguson

The city of Ferguson will have its own local reforms to consider, as the council has already passed several bills to establish a police review board, and set limits on excessive court fines and fees exposed after Brown's death. If past experience is any indication, reforming the police department is possible over the course many years and many battles.

But nationally, problems persist. "This is a very systemic problem in just about every community throughout the United States," Brickner said.

And even in communities that have seen dramatic change, there are as many holes left to be filled as there have been reforms. One is the intransigent, incredible challenge of holding police accountable. Police unions exercise strong influence over many local boards that decide whether cops get to keep their jobs. Juries tend to side with police. And the law overwhelming favors the police. UC Irvine law school dean Erwin Chemerensky, who has long followed this issue, wrote after Brown's death that "the officer who shot Michael Brown and the City of Ferguson will most likely never be held accountable in court" due to doctrines from the Supreme Court down that weigh against holding officers accountable.

Another is a culture that embraces guns. Police are given a lot of leeway to use deadly force, in many instances when the public perception is that other lesser measures might do. As CNN's Mark O'Mara noted after Brown's death, "Cops are doing the job we told them to do."

Riots in Ferguson have also exposed to America the extreme militarization of police forces that has only grown since the past waves of police shootings. And the racism in the criminal justice system persists, both overtly, and implicitly, even as more whites than ever believe the criminal justice system is no longer biased.

But there are reasons to be hopeful. For one thing, criminal justice reform is increasingly becoming a bipartisan issue. Even Rep. Paul Ryan (R-WI) became one of a growing number of congressional Republicans who have called for criminal justice reform. Domanick said he was also encouraged that there was outrage at Ferguson's police militarization across the political spectrum. For another, reform options exist that didn't before, such as body cameras for police. In fact, it is the emergence of mobile recording devices that has exposed some of the recent violent incidents—and debunked any attempts by police to skew the facts.

In the case of Ferguson, U.S. Attorney General Eric Holder has announced he will initiate an investigation of the city's "patterns and practices" in addition to the separate criminal investigation of the Brown case. In fact, Holder has taken on a new tone for the country's top law enforcer that acknowledges the United States epidemic of discriminatory and overly punitive criminal punishment.

But underlying all of this is the segregation and oppression that was unveiled in Ferguson. A Washington Post investigation last week revealed that these underlying problems still persist in Cincinnati, meaning that while police were indeed reformed, fixing the racial tensions that existed in 2001 Cincinnati is "a job unfinished." Even Cincinnati's black police chief says he fears his own son's encounters with the police.

"The cultural disconnect is very real; you have the weight of generations of abuse on African Americans," Cincinnati Police Chief Jeffrey Blackwell told the *Washington Post* after Brown's death.

"[T]he mentality is that these lives in the ghetto are not to be valued," added Domanick. "Policing and violence are only symptoms of this larger problem. We're gonna have problems. But at least we're starting to know now what works in terms of reducing crime short term and long term and what works in terms of community policing and good community relations."

Some Data Proves Excessive Force Has Increased

Celisa Calacal

Writer Celisa Calacal serves as the opinion editor of Ithaca College's award-winning student newspaper the Ithacan *and also writes for ThinkProgress and Alternet.*

This is how many people police have killed so far in 2016

The year isn't over yet, and police have already killed at least 1,023 people—many of whom were unarmed, mentally ill, and people of color.

This number comes from the *Guardian*'s police killings database, but the Killed by Police database counts 1,096 people who have died at the hands of police so far this year. The *Washington Post* reports that 908 people have been shot and killed by cops.

Going by the *Guardian*'s count, Native Americans and Black people are being killed at the highest rates in the United States. 215 Black Americans have been killed by police so far this year, at a rate of 5.38 deaths per million. February and March were the deadliest months this year, with 100 people killed by police in each month. Police have killed 32 people in December so far.

[...]

The slight discrepancies in numbers between Killed by Police and the *Guardian* reflect differences in how each outlet collects data about police killings. Killed by Police is mainly open-sourced and also relies on corporate news reports for its data on people killed by police. For its database, the *Guardian* relies on traditional reporting on police reports and witness statements, while also culling data from verified crowdsourced information using regional news outlets, research groups, and reporting projects that include Killed by Police.

"This Is How Many People Police Have Killed so Far in 2016," by Celisa Calacal, ThinkProgress, July 5, 2016. Reprinted by Permission.

There has always been a high volume of police killings, although damning videos, photos, and news reports highlight officer violence—especially against people of color—now more than ever. But what's become an even more alarming trend is the number of officers involved in these killings who receive minor to no punishment.

According to the *Wall Street Journal*, 2015 saw the highest number of police officers being charged for deadly, on-duty shootings in a decade: 12 as of September 2015. Still, in a year when approximately 1,200 people were killed by police, zero officers were convicted of murder or manslaughter, painting the picture that officers involved in killing another person will not be held accountable for their actions.

In 2016, several officers have gone to trial but none of them received jail time. Here are some of the most egregious examples of cops who haven't been penalized for killing:

William Porter, Edward Nero, and Caesar Goodwin—Baltimore, Maryland

Freddie Gray was apprehended by police during a bike patrol on April 12, 2015, when a violent arrest left him unable to walk on his own. On the way to booking, no officer put a seat belt on Gray, causing him to be thrown around the van with no help received from any of the officers. In total, there were six officers involved in his death, and three have been tried so far. But during those three trials, which spanned from December 2015 to June, none of the officers were convicted.

The trial of Officer William Porter ended in a hung jury in December, amounting to no action being taken against Porter unless a second trial scheduled for later this year finds him guilty. In May, Officer Edward Nero was declared not guilty of all criminal charges against him—second-degree assault, reckless endangerment, and misconduct in office. Nero was one of the first officers to encounter Gray during his arrest and helped load Gray into the police van, where he was not secured with a seat belt.

On June 23, the latest trial in Gray's case found Officer Caesar Goodwin not guilty of second-degree depraved heart murder, reckless endangerment, second-degree assault, and manslaughter. Goodwin drove the police van where Gray suffered the spine injury that ultimately led to his death, didn't secure the 25-year-old's seat belt, and waited to call a medic when Gray was in distress. Goodson faced the most serious charges of the six officers.

Peter Liang—New York City

In April, two months after a jury convicted him of manslaughter and official misconduct, former NYPD Oficer Officer Peter Liang was sentenced to five years probation and 800 hours of community service.

Liang is responsible for fatally shooting 28-year-old Brooklyn resident Akai Gurley last November, in the dark stairwell of a public housing building. While Liang was in the building, the rookie cop claimed he accidentally fired his gun and the bullet ricocheted off the wall before striking Gurley in the heart. Gurley was innocent of any wrongdoing and unarmed when he was killed.

During the trial, Liang claimed the shooting was accidental, but was convicted of manslaughter in February. The former officer was also convicted of official misconduct for failing to provide any sort of medical assistance to Gurley as he lay bleeding on the staircase. Following his conviction, Liang was fired from the NYPD.

Just before his sentence was handed down, the manslaughter charge was reduced to criminally negligent homicide. And despite being convicted of manslaughter, Brooklyn District Attorney Ken Thompson announced in March that jail time for Liang should be taken off the table. He recommended six months of house arrest, five years of probation, and 500 hours of community service, instead.

Liang was the first NYPD officer convicted of an on-duty shooting in the past decade.

Mark Ringgenberg and Dustin Schwarze—Minneapolis, Minnesota

In March, Hennepin County Attorney Mike Freeman announced that the two officers involved in the fatal shooting of 24-year-old Jamar Clark will not be facing any criminal charges for their actions. Clark, who was unarmed, died from a gunshot to the head when Schwarz fired his gun 61 seconds after arriving on the scene.

According to the county attorney, Clark was resisting arrest and attempted to grab Ringgenberg's gun. Despite this claim, several witnesses say that Clark was already handcuffed. Although placed on administrative leave following the shooting, both officers returned to desk duty in January.

Two weeks prior to the decision, Freeman announced that Hennepin County, including Minneapolis, will no longer use grand juries to determine whether cops involved in fatal shootings should be indicted. "I concluded that the accountability and transparency limitations of a grand jury are too high a hurdle to overcome," he said. Beginning with Clark's case, Freeman's office would decide to indict in the future.

The policy shift was made in response to pressure from Black Lives Matter activists who protested against grand jury proceedings in the Clark case.

The Poor Suffer the Most at the Hands of Police

Gabriel Black

Gabriel Black works for International Youth and Students for Social Equality, the youth and student organization of the Socialist Equality Party. He also writes for the World Socialist website.

At least 1,152 people were killed by police in the United States in 2016 according to the tracking site killedbypolice.net. While the total number of killings documented is slightly down from 2015's total of 1,208, police continued to kill at the rate of three people every day.

The number of people killed by police every year in the United States far dwarfs those killed by police in every other major advanced capitalist country. In 2015, for example, US cops killed 100 times more people than German police, despite the United States having only about four times Germany's population. Meanwhile in the United Kingdom only 14 people were killed by police in 2014.

Paul Hirschfield, a sociologist at Rutgers University, found that the US police shot and killed at a ratio of 3.42 people per million inhabitants per year. In contrast, Denmark had a ratio of 0.187; France, 0.17; Sweden, 0.133; Portugal, 0.125; Germany, 0.09; Norway, 0.06; Netherlands, 0.06; Finland, 0.034; and England and Wales, 0.016.

The overwhelming and often deadly violence meted out by American police is, among other things, an expression of the brutal and tense state of class relations in the United States. Large sections of the working class live in or near poverty with basic needs like clean water, nutritious food, a job, health care, a good place to live and an education beyond reach.

"US Police Killed More Than 1,150 in 2016," by Gabriel Black, World Socialist website, January 4, 2017. Reprinted by Permission.

The state, in turn, has responded with brute force, cutting access to basic social services and spending billions of dollars upgrading and militarizing the nation's police force. This has included the mobilization of the National Guard and the imposition of states of emergencies to quell protests against police violence in recent years.

The United States is a country where fraud, bribery, deception and outright theft, all on a massive scale, are standard business practices for the major banks and corporations. Meanwhile the working class is held to an entirely different standard, in which execution without trial by a police officer is an increasingly common punishment for the smallest of misdemeanors.

The end of the year is an opportunity to assess this mass loss of life and clarify the political issues at stake in this state sanctioned murder.

According to the *Washington Post*, which runs its own database on the number of people shot and killed by police (not just killed), 24 percent of the victims of police shootings and killings were black in 2016. That is 232 people out of 957 total shot and killed. In 2016 African Americans were shot at a rate double their percentage share of the total population.

While the media discussion around police killings and the protests by the Black Lives Matter organization has focused on the disproportionate rate at which blacks are killed by police, the largest share, 48 percent, are white.

As the World Socialist Web Site has emphasized, "Blacks are killed by police at a much higher rate than their proportion in the population, an indication that racism plays a significant role, but the number of white victims demonstrates that class, not race, is the more fundamental issue."

The exclusive focus on race by the pseudo left and the Democratic Party establishment conceals the most fundamental issue, that of class.

While the *Post* does not track the class of those killed going through each killing, though, case-by-case, one would be hard pressed to find people from the upper classes, let alone better off sections of workers and professionals, regardless of the color of their skin. Those who are killed are often from the lowest sections of the working class, and often its most vulnerable layers: the unemployed, the mentally ill, those living in the poorest neighborhoods, both rural and urban, and the homeless.

For example, of the 957 killed, 240 had clear discernible signs of mental illness—that is, 25 percent of the victims.

Of the victims, 441 were not armed with a gun, 46 percent of those killed. One-hundred seventy people were armed with a knife. And, 44 had a toy weapon of some kind. Forty-seven were neither armed nor driving a car in a way the police deemed dangerous.

Sixty-five were driving cars, causing the police to categorize the vehicle as a weapon. However, in many instances there is no evidence to show that a vehicle acted as a weapon. For example, Christian Redwine, a 17-year-old white male, was shot after a car-chase in which Redwine crashed. He was unarmed and was suspected of stealing the vehicle.

Another notable fact is that 329 of the victims were fleeing, about 34 percent of the victims.

These cumulative statistics show the willingness of police to quickly kill people who pose little to no threat to them.

Police killings should be considered in the broader context of punishment for the most vulnerable and impoverished. In the United States, over 2 million people are in federal or state prisons. Furthermore, 4.75 million are on probation or parole. This means that about 7 million people, 3 percent of the adult population, have been or are in prison.

As in the case of police killings, many of these people have been locked up for shoplifting, grand theft auto and robbery. Many others are incarcerated for drug possession and use.

While millions of destitute and hopeless people in the United States are brutally punished for relatively minor infractions, the real criminals, those in the Bush and Obama administrations responsible for wars of aggression that have cost the lives of hundreds of thousands in the Middle East, as well as the bankers who crashed the economy in 2008, have reaped the benefits of their much more serious crimes.

No amount of police training, community engagement or racial bias classes will end police killings. The deaths are born out of much more fundamental political and economic realities than what this or that police officer feels and thinks. In 2017, amidst a worsening political and economic crisis, the state will be even more ready to kill, harass and imprison the poorest section of the population.

Being Unarmed Makes No Difference

Adam Hudson

Adam Hudson is a journalist whose work has appeared in multiple media outlets, including AlterNet, Truthout, teleSUR English, the Nation.

Police officers, security guards, or self-appointed vigilantes extrajudicially killed at least 313 African Americans in 2012 according to a recent study. This means a black person was killed by a security officer every 28 hours. The report notes that it's possible that the real number could be much higher.

The report, entitled "Operation Ghetto Storm", was performed by the Malcolm X Grassroots Movement, an antiracist grassroots activist organization. The organization has chapters in Atlanta, Detroit, Fort Worth-Dallas, Jackson, New Orleans, New York City, Oakland, and Washington, D.C. It has a history of organizing campaigns against police brutality and state repression in black and brown communities. Their study's sources included police and media reports along with other publicly available information. Last year, the organization published a similar study showing that a black person is killed by security forces every 36 hours. However, this study did not tell the whole story, as it only looked at shootings from January to June 2012. Their latest study is an update of this.

These killings come on top of other forms of oppression black people face. Mass incarceration of nonwhites is one of them. While African Americans constitute 13.1% of the nation's population, they make up nearly 40% of the prison population. Even though African Americans use or sell drugs about the same rate as whites, they are 2.8 to 5.5 times more likely to be arrested for drugs than whites. Black offenders also receive longer sentences compared to whites. Most offenders are in prison for nonviolent drug offenses.

"Operation Ghetto Storm" explains why such killings occur so often. Current practices of institutional racism have roots in the enslavement of black Africans, whose labor was exploited to build the American capitalist economy, and the genocide of Native Americans. The report points out that in order to maintain the systems of racism, colonialism, and capitalist exploitation, the United States maintains a network of "repressive enforcement structures". These structures include the police, FBI, Homeland Security, CIA, Secret Service, prisons, and private security companies, along with mass surveillance and mass incarceration.

The Malcolm X Grassroots Movement is not the only group challenging police violence against African Americans. The Stop Mass Incarceration Network has been challenging the policy of stop-and-frisk in New York City, in which police officers randomly stop and search individuals for weapons or contraband. African-American and Latino men are disproportionately stopped and harassed by police officers. Most of those stopped (close to 90%) are innocent, according to the New York Civil Liberties Union. Stop Mass Incarceration also organizes against the War on Drugs and inhumane treatment of prisoners.

Along with the rate of extrajudicial killings, the Malcolm X Grassroots Movement report contains other important findings. Of the 313 killed, 124 (40%) were between 22 and 31 years old, 57 (18%) were between 18 and 21 years old, 54 (17%) were between 32 and 41 years old, 32 (10%) were 42 to 51 years old, 25 (8%) were children younger than 18 years old, 18 (6%) were older than 52, and 3 (1%) were of unknown ages.

A significant portion of those killed, 68 people or 22%, suffered from mental health issues and/or were self-medicated. The study says that "[m]any of them might be alive today if community members trained and committed to humane crisis intervention and mental health treatment had been called, rather than the police."

Forty-three percent of the shootings occurred after an incident of racial profiling. This means police saw a person who looked or behaved "suspiciously" largely because of their skin color and attempted to detain the suspect before killing them. Other times, the shootings occurred during a criminal investigation (24%), after 9-1-1 calls from "emotionally disturbed loved ones" (19%) or because of domestic violence (7%), or innocent people were killed for no reason (7%).

Most of the people killed were not armed. According to the report, 136 people or 44%, had no weapon at all the time they were killed by police officers. Another 27% were deaths in which police claimed the suspect had a gun but there was no corroboration to prove this. In addition, 6 people (2%) were alleged to have possessed knives or similar tools. Those who did, in fact, possess guns or knives were 20% (62 people) and 7% (23 people) of the study, respectively.

The report digs into how police justify their shootings. Most police officers, security guards, or vigilantes who extrajudicially killed black people, about 47% (146 of 313), claimed they "felt threatened", "feared for their life", or "were forced to shoot to protect themselves or others". George Zimmerman, the armed self-appointed neighborhood watchman who killed Trayvon Martin last year, claimed exactly this to justify shooting Martin. Other justifications include suspects fleeing (14%), allegedly driving cars toward officers, allegedly reaching for waistbands or lunging, or allegedly pointing a gun at an officer. Only 13% or 42 people fired a weapon "before or during the officer's arrival".

Police recruitment, training, policies, and overall racism within society conditions police (and many other people) to assume black people are violent to begin with. This leads to police overacting in situations involving African-American suspects. It also explains why so many police claimed the black suspect "looked suspicious" or "thought they had a gun". Johannes Mehserle, the white BART police officer who shot and killed 22-year-old Oscar Grant in January 2009, claimed Grant had a gun, even though Grant was subdued to the ground by other officers.

Of the 313 killings, the report found that 275 of them or 88% were cases of excessive force. Only 8% were not considered excessive as they involved cases were suspects shot at, wounded, or killed a police and/or others. Additionally, 4% were situations were the facts surrounding the killing were "unclear or sparsely reported". The vast majority of the time, police officers, security guards, or armed vigilantes who extrajudicially kill black people escape accountability.

Over the past 70 years, the "repressive enforcement structures" described in the report have been used to "wage a grand strategy of 'domestic' pacification" to maintain the system through endless "containment campaigns" amounting to "perpetual war". According to the report, this perpetual war has been called multiple names — the "Cold War", COINTELPRO, the "War on Drugs, the "War on Gangs", the "War on Crime", and now the "War on Terrorism". This pacification strategy is designed to subjugate oppressed populations and stifle political resistance. In other words, they are wars against domestic marginalized groups. "Extrajudicial killings", says the report, "are clearly an indispensable tool in the United States government's pacification pursuits." It attributes the preponderance of these killings to institutionalized racism and policies within police departments.

Paramilitary police units, known as SWAT (Special Weapons and Tactics) teams, developed in order to quell black riots in major cities, such as Los Angeles and Detroit, during the 1960s and '70s. SWAT teams had major shootouts with militant black and left-wing groups, such as the Black Panther Party and Symbionese Liberation Army (SLA) in 1969 and 1974, respectively. SWAT teams were only used for high-risk situations, until the War on Drugs began in the 1980s. Now they're used in raids—a common military tactic—of suspected drug or non-drug offenders' homes.

The War on Drugs, first declared by President Richard Nixon in 1971, was largely a product of US covert operations. Anticommunist counter-revolutionaries, known as the "Contras", were trained, funded, and largely created by the CIA to overthrow the leftist Sandinista government of Nicaragua during the 1980s.

However, the CIA's funding was not enough. Desperate for money, the Contras needed other funding sources to fight their war against the Sandinistas. The additional dollars came from the drug trade. The late investigative journalist Gary Webb, in 1996, wrote a lengthy series of articles for the San Jose Mercury News, entitled "Dark Alliance", detailing how the Contras smuggled cocaine from South America to California's inner cities and used the profits to fund their fight against the Sandinista government. The CIA knew about this but turned a blind eye. The report received a lot of controversy, criticism, and tarnishing of Webb's journalistic career, which would lead him to commit suicide in 2004. However, subsequent reports from Congressional hearings and other journalists corroborated Webb's findings.

Moreover, major banks, such as Wachovia (now part of Wells Fargo) and HSBC have laundered money for drug dealers. Therefore, the very threat that the Drug War claims to eliminate is perpetuated more by the National Security State and Wall Street than by low-level street dealers. But rather than go after the bigger fish, the United States has used the pretext of the "war on drugs" to implement draconian police tactics on marginalized groups, particularly poor black communities.

In 1981, President Ronald Reagan passed the Military Cooperation with Civilian Law Enforcement Agencies Act, which provided civilian police agencies equipment, training, and advising from the military, along with access to military research and facilities. This weakened the line between the military and civilian law enforcement established by the Posse Comitatus Act of 1878, a Reconstruction-era law forbidding military personnel from enforcing domestic laws. Five years later, in 1986, Reagan issued National Security Decision Directive 221, which declared drug trafficking a national security threat to the United States. This militarized the U.S. approach to drugs and overall policing. Additionally, the global war on terror and growth of the National Security State expanded this militarization of domestic police under the guise of "fighting terrorism".

The adoption of military tactics, equipment, training, and weapons leads to law enforcement adopting a war-like mentality. They come to view themselves as soldiers fighting against a foreign enemy rather police protecting a community. Nick Pastore, a former Police Chief of New Haven, Connecticut from 1990 to 1997, turned down military equipment that was offered to him. "I turned it all down, because it feeds a mind-set that you're not a police officer serving a community, you're a soldier at war," he told the New York Times. He said "tough-guy cops" in his department pushed for "bigger and more hardware" and "used to say, 'It's a war out there.'" Pastore added, "If you think everyone who uses drugs is the enemy, then you're more likely to declare war on the people." Mix this war-like mentality with already existing societal anti-black racism and the result is deadly. Black people, who, by default, are assumed to be criminals because of their skin color, become the victims of routine police violence.

The fact that a black person is killed by a police officer, security guard, or vigilante every 28 hours (or less) is no random act of nature. It is the inevitable result of institutional racism and militaristic tactics and thinking within America's domestic security apparatus.

A Decline in Interaction Leads to a Decline in Deadly Force

Steven Malanga

Steven Malanga is a published author, the George M. Yeager Fellow at the Manhattan Institute, and senior editor at the City Journal. *He writes about the intersection of urban economies, business communities, and public policy*

When Congress passed the Violent Crime Control and Law Enforcement Act in 1994, legislators mandated that the attorney general begin studying and reporting on excessive use of force by police. Soon after, the Bureau of Justice Statistics developed a series of recurring studies that measured everything from police behavior in specific situations, like traffic stops, to incidents in which police use force. Much of the data was based not on reports by local police departments, but on direct surveys of citizens, providing some 20 years of information on how the police interact with American citizens, and how those citizens see the police.

If Congress believed that this new data might provide some context and insight for national debates about the use of force by police, such as the one we're having now in the wake of grand jury decisions not to indict police officers for their role in deadly incidents in Ferguson and Staten Island, legislators were largely mistaken. After the Ferguson grand jury made its ruling, President Obama told the nation that "the law too often feels like it's being applied in a discriminatory fashion." Since the Ferguson incident involving Michael Brown and officer Darren Wilson last August, the New York Times has published stories about communities where minorities get stopped more frequently than whites, implying racial discrimination. But these stories ignore Bureau of Justice Statistics data showing that crime victims disproportionately

"What the Numbers Say on Police Use of Force," by Steven Malanga, Manhattan Institute for Policy Research, Inc, December 4, 2014. Reprinted by Permission.

identify minorities as perpetrators of crime, too. Senator Rand Paul has even used Ferguson to launch an attack on the war on drugs, saying that it puts the police in a difficult situation in dealing with the public—though drugs had little to do with the confrontation between Brown and Wilson (except as they may have influenced Brown's aggressive behavior).

Despite such pronouncements, two decades of data on police interactions with the public don't support the idea that something extraordinary is afoot, that the police are becoming "militarized" as President Obama has suggested, or that distrust between police and local communities has produced an enormous spike in conflicts. By contrast, the data show that significant crime declines have been accompanied by a leveling off and then a reduction in confrontations with the police, as reported by Americans of all races.

After the 1994 legislation passed, Justice Department researchers began exploring ways to study the issues as Congress had mandated. In 1996, they produced a preliminary report on police/citizen interactions that broadly estimated that some 45 million Americans had some type of contact with law enforcement during the preceding year. Of those 45 million, the study found, slightly more than half a million reported that the police had used force against them. This initial study, regarded as experimental, wasn't detailed enough to say much more and was subject to large margins of error, but it led to a series of more comprehensive and in-depth reports, produced from 1999 through 2011.

What's striking in the progression of these later studies is a steady decrease in the number of people having interactions with the police—from about 45 million in 2002 to 40 million in 2011—or from about 21 percent of the 16-and-older population to about 17 percent. One clear reason for the decline has been the corresponding drop in crime: the number of people reporting crimes or other problems to the police fell by about 3.6 million from a peak in 2002. More important, perhaps, was that reports of use of force by police also fell, from 664,000 in 2002 to 574,000 in a 2010 report. Those declines occurred across all races. The number of African Americans reporting that police used force against them fell from 173,000 to 130,000. Among whites, the number has dropped from a peak of 374,000 to 347,000.

Since 1999, Justice Department studies have also measured how police and citizens interact during more mundane encounters, like traffic stops—vastly expanding the data about how citizens who otherwise don't have cause to deal with the police might see their performance. In the most recent survey, in 2011, 88.2 percent of those stopped by the police said they thought officers acted properly. There were few significant distinctions by race. Nearly 83 percent of African Americans judged police behavior to be proper, for instance. The study also asked citizens whether they thought the police had stopped them for a "legitimate" reason—and here the data on race is particularly interesting. Some 80 percent of all drivers viewed their stops as legitimate, compared with 68 percent of African Americans. But the study also asked drivers to report the race of the officers who stopped them, and African Americans were just as likely to say that stops initiated by white officers were legitimate as those initiated by black officers. Similarly, white drivers saw no difference in how they were treated by white officers or black officers on this question.

Since 1994, Washington has produced other legislation meant to monitor how local law enforcement behaves. In 2000, for instance, Congress passed the Death in Custody Act, which mandated that the Justice Department collect data on deaths in local and state prisons, including data by race. These data show no startling trends that might raise flags about how those arrested and incarcerated locally get treated. Average mortality in local prisons measured per 100,000 prisoners has decreased from 151 in 2000 to 128 in 2012. Among African Americans, average mortality has dropped from 127 per 100,000 to 109.

These data are particularly instructive in the context of another series of Justice Department surveys, which ask Americans whether they have been victimized by crime. Those who say yes are then asked to identify the race of their attacker. In a 2008 survey, 58 percent of violent crime victims of identified the perpetrators as white, and 23 percent as black. That compares with a national population 74 percent white and 12 percent black. (After 2008, questions about the race of offenders disappear from the victimization data on the FBI's website.) Police frequently point to this survey and others like it to explain that stop rates and arrest rates are higher for minorities because crime rates are higher in minority areas. Victims disproportionately identify perpetrators as minority.

Still, surveys like the victimization report haven't stopped some activists from advocating a form of law enforcement that expects police stops and arrests to mirror the population at large, rather than to reflect a police response to reports of crime. In the aftermath of Ferguson, Attorney General Eric Holder said that he intended to wipe out racial profiling. But as a 1999 Justice Department study on traffic enforcement made clear, racial differences alone in stops or arrests by police "may not signal racial profiling." The study went on to clarify that "to form evidence of racial profiling," the data would also have to show that "Blacks and/or Hispanics were no more likely than whites to violate traffic laws," but were still targeted more frequently than whites. That distinction, which puts stops and arrests within the context of violations committed by a group, has been lost in much of today's media discussion on policing.

National statistics and trends, of course, don't obviate the need to investigate individual acts of force by the police, especially when they result in the death of a citizen. Clearly, even more precise, improved statistics are needed. We don't have good national data on how often police officers discharge their weapons, for example, so we don't know how that changes over time. And as the Wall Street Journal has noted, the FBI's statistics on justifiable homicides by the police nationwide are inaccurate, thanks to a lack of standards in how police departments categorize and report those incidents.

Some of the data reported by large police departments suggest that it's possible to make strides in these areas. New York City keeps detailed records about the use of guns by police officers on duty. Since 1991, the peak of crime in New York, the number of yearly shooting incidents by NYPD officers has declined by more than two-thirds, from 332 to 105. The number of individuals shot and killed by police officers has fallen from 39 to 16. Something similar might be afoot nationally, but we don't have the data to know.

Even if we did, none of this information will make much difference if politicians, activists, and the media keep ignoring it because it doesn't fit the prevailing narrative.

Portland Can Serve as an Example to Other Police Forces

Maxine Bernstein

Writer Maxine Bernstein has been covering crime, police, and law enforcement for the Oregonian *since 1998.*

A Portland Police Bureau analysis shows the bureau's use of force has dropped 35 percent since 2008, according to a four-page report released Wednesday.

The data shows there were 675 use of force incidents by Portland police in 2011, down from 1,039 in 2008.

It's not clear from the report what the bureau's use of force incidents include, but the report specifically notes that the data excludes an officer's pointing of a firearm.

It also presents a graphic that shows that 3.9 percent of arrests in 2011 involved force, down from more than 4 percent of arrests in each of the three prior years.

Portland Police Chief Mike Reese credited policy, training and supervision changes for the drop in use of force.

They include new training for sergeants on when to walk away from certain suicide calls if the person is not a risk to themselves or others; dispatchers' training to divert certain mental health crisis calls from police to the county's crisis line and their mental health workers; and increased internal police bureau reviews of officer use of force.

The report says the bureau is planning to create a "mental health crisis triage desk," but doesn't explain what services it will provide.

Bureau spokesman Sgt. Pete Simpson said the bureau's crisis intervention coordinator is trying to work out some agreement that would allow information on a caller's mental health history to

"Portland Police Release Report Showing Decline in Use of Force," by Maxine Bernstein, Oregon Live LLC, September 5, 2012. Reprinted by Permission.

be shared immediately at a new "mental health crisis triage desk." This triage desk would assist in getting a person help, rather than sending a police car out.

"Since 2008, there has been a concerted and growing effort to emphasize de-escalation tools and a confrontation management approach in community contacts to minimize the need for the use of force," the report says.

The brief report was released Wednesday as a federal investigation continues in the bureau's use of force, and as some officers and rank-and-file union leaders are questioning what the chief's standard is regarding police use of deadly force.

Reese testified last fall during fired Officer Ronald Frashour's arbitration hearing that Aaron Campbell posed no immediate threat to police before Frashour fatally shot him in the parking lot of a Northeast Portland apartment complex on Jan. 29, 2010. Reese testified that Frashour, who he fired in November 2010, didn't have a right to shoot Frashour. An arbitrator has ordered Frashour be rehired, but the city has refused, and has challenged the arbitrator's decision before the state Employment Relations Board.

"He never displayed a weapon. He didn't take any offensive action towards the officer," Reese said, of Campbell, in his sworn arbitration testimony in the Frashour firing. "We can't use force on him."

For Campbell to have posed an immediate threat, the chief testified, he would have had to take an "offensive action"—"turn toward us, pull something out, take a shooting stance."

The chief's testimony stunned Portland police rank-and-file officers, union leaders and the union's use-of-force expert, who say the chief articulated a new standard, one that's inconsistent with their training. And in the end, the arbitrator discounted the chief's stance in her March ruling, ordering Frashour be reinstated.

On Wednesday, in a prepared statement released by the bureau with the use of force report, Reese said, "The community has expressed concern over police use of force and we are hoping to highlight the enhancements the Police Bureau has made and show the use of force numbers have declined. We also want community members to know we review every use of force report and will continue to monitor the numbers."

Dan Handelman, of the police watchdog group Portland Copwatch, called the report "thin."

"It's interesting information, but I think it's too thin," said Handelman.

He said the report doesn't identify whether the use of less-lethal force is up or down or the number of police shootings has dropped. Handleman said police shootings since 2007 have increased in number, with two in 2007, four by 2011 and five or six so far this year, depending if you include the shooting by a Portland cop in Aloha earlier this year.

"This mostly looks like a fluff, PR piece," Handelman said. "We need more information to be able to have a meaningful discussion as a community."

UPDATE: [...] Portland police Sgt. Pete Simpson released further data, which was not included in the report.

The new data not included in the report breaks down use of force incidents involving the pointing of firearms, takedowns, Tasers, control holds, police Hobble restraints, pepper spray, bean bag shotgun use and batons.

It shows that officers' pointing of firearms has dropped 37 percent from 2008 through 2011, from 813 incidents in 2008 to 509 in 2011. Police takedowns had a similar drop, from 539 in 2008 to 341 in 2011, a 37 percent drop.

Taser use dropped 40 percent, according to police data - from 378 incidents in 2008 to 228 in 2011, the data shows.

Yet, pepper spray use rose 21 percent between 2008 and 2011, from 58 incidents in 2008 to 70 cases in 2011, the new data released after the report shows.

Officer-involved shootings also have risen over the last several years, the requested data shows. The bureau data shows there were six officer-involved shootings in 2010, compared to one in 2009, two in 2008, two in 2007, five officer-involved shootings and two deaths in police custody in 2006.

The Oakland Police Are Turning Over a New Leaf

Joaquin Palomino

Joaquin Palomino is a data and investigative reporter at the San Francisco Chronicle. *He has also written for outlets like* National Geographic, *the Verge, Al Jazeera America, and Reuters.*

Excessive use of force has long been a problem for the Oakland Police Department, leading to civic distrust, costly lawsuits and the nation's longest-running federal intervention.

Despite several recent officer-involved shootings, a Chronicle analysis of Oakland Police Department data shows such incidents are becoming less common. Officer-involved shootings, excessive force complaints and incidents in which officers used force have all declined precipitously over the past three years in Oakland.

Save any major slipup, the department, which has been monitored by a federal court since 2003, is expected to soon regain its autonomy. It would save the city millions and help the law enforcement agency shed its reputation as one of America's most dysfunctional.

But if history is any indication, maintaining the gains achieved under federal oversight could be just as daunting as securing them.

"We have seen improvement, but the jury is still out on whether it will be sustainable," said civil rights attorney Jim Chanin, who has helped oversee the department's reforms. "There are some positive signs that it will be, but we don't know yet."

OPD by the numbers

The Oakland Police Department averaged roughly eight officer-involved shootings per year between 2000 and 2012. There have been just six over the past 24 months, including the uptick this

"Sharp Downturn in Use of Force at Oakland Police Department," by Joaquin Palomino, Hearst Corporation, September 3, 2015. Reprinted by Permission.

summer—a decline of more than 60 percent in shootings from the prior decade's average.

Alameda County sheriff's deputies and Highway Patrol officers were involved in four shootings in Oakland over the same time frame, all of them fatal, despite having fewer cops on the streets, according to data obtained through a public records request.

A review of more than 22,000 use-of-force incidents also shows less severe altercations between police and the public are on the decline.

Between 2009 and 2014, the number of use-of-force incidents recorded by the department dropped four-fold, from 3,902 to 895. There were 49 incidents reported in July — the lowest monthly count in the reviewed time frame.

If current trends continue, aggressive interactions with the public would drop to 630 in 2015.

The falling numbers are a good indication that police-community relations are improving, according to Barry Krisberg, a UC Berkeley criminologist. "Oakland has been pretty quiet compared to the 600 bullets fired in Stockton, or some pretty horrendous lethal-force incidents in San Jose," he said.

Use-of-force complaints, which include a range of behaviors from grabbing suspects by the hair or bending their wrist to choke holds and shootings, also dipped more than 40 percent from 2013 through 2014. Grievances filed with the Citizens' Police Review Board—which investigates some excessive-force allegations — steadily declined from a high of 90 in 2009 to 15 in 2014.

Meanwhile, arrests have remained relatively steady, suggesting the positive numbers may not be the result of lax policing.

A long time coming

Along with improvements in community relations, certain crimes have also dropped. Homicides fell from 126 in 2012 to 80 in 2014. The numbers are on pace to be about the same this year. Serious crimes fell 8 percent over the same time period.

"We have had three successive years of double-digit reductions in shootings, so we're definitely having an impact," Oakland Police Chief Sean Whent said in an interview with The Chronicle. "But it's still a high-crime city and we have a lot more work to do."

The improvements have been a long time coming.

A handful of law enforcement agencies have struggled to complete federal mandates to reform, but none has been under oversight for longer than Oakland, which entered what is known as the Negotiated Settlement Agreement more than a decade ago.

Misconduct payouts

The department's difficulties have provoked ire from court-appointed monitors and some community members.

The frequency with which officers drew and pointed guns at suspects, the handling of the Occupy Oakland protests—which resulted in hefty misconduct settlements including a $4.5 million payment to an Iraq War veteran shot in the face with a tear gas canister—and inability of the department to punish bad cops were all regularly criticized by courts and city leaders.

Some feared the department would never turn a new leaf.

Things began to change, though, in 2013 after Whent was appointed chief. He ushered in new use-of-force trainings, updated foot and vehicle pursuit policies to keep officers out of dangerous situations and oversaw the full implementation of the body camera program—which has been attributed to improved interactions between police and civilians.

"Oakland needed fresh leadership and I think they got it," Krisberg said. "There's no reason to think that police-community relations, which had deteriorated so badly, could have fixed themselves."

Maintaining the gains

Oakland police still need to iron out some lingering suggestions from the federal monitors, including expanding the department's use-of-force review board, more thoroughly tracking vehicle-stop data and addressing the issue of fired cops being re-hired through arbitration. Still, the department and some civic leaders believe an end of federal oversight is on the horizon.

The prospect elicits both hope and anxiety.

"There is a long history of important reforms that, for one reason or another, simply faded away," said Samuel Walker, a criminologist at the University of Nebraska who has studied the OPD. "This has been a problem for the entire history of policing."

Anticorruption policies implemented at the New York Police Department in the 1970s helped clean up the force, but the reforms didn't last. In 1993, a special mayoral panel determined that NYPD "had failed at every level to uproot corruption," and that it "concealed lawlessness by police officers," according to the New York Times.

The San Diego Police Department exemplified best-practice policing throughout the 1980s and 1990s, Walker said, but it was recently rocked by a sexual assault scandal. Ten officers were investigated for rape, domestic violence, driving under the influence and sexual battery during a three-month span in 2011, according to a U.S. Department of Justice audit; six were ultimately arrested. More sexual assault cases piled up in 2014 and 2015.

"Community leaders in Oakland have to be diligent, they can't just say, 'The war is over,'" Walker said. "The department will be on its own, so it's up to Oakland to ensure that they don't slide back."

Some have proposed creating a police commission — a civilian board that sets policy and conducts disciplinary hearings for misconduct. In theory, a commission would add an extra layer of oversight if and when the monitors pack up.

An insurance policy

"After having spent so many millions of dollars and so much time, why would we not want to make sure there's a protection in place to keep us from losing our investment?" said Rashidah Grinage, former executive director of Oakland police watchdog group PUEBLO.

Whent thinks improvements can be cemented in without a commission.

He points to his department's 700 body cameras — roughly the same number as sworn officers — and the fact the city has set aside money for two new auditors at the Office of the Inspector General, which keeps tabs on the Police Department. He also said the department plans to make a civilian the head of internal affairs.

All should help keep the progress intact, he noted.

"That would be the biggest disaster; if we were to end the Negotiated Settlement Agreement and then all of the sudden go back to something else," Whent said. "It really is my goal that the day it ends, nobody recognizes any difference."

CHAPTER 4

Do We Need to Change the Way We Train Police?

Overview: Empathy Training May Lead to New Standards

Christopher Moraff

Christopher Moraff is a reporting fellow at John Jay College of Criminal Justice and frequently writes about policing, criminal justice policy, and civil liberties for outlets like Next City and the Daily Beast.

Yesterday, a grand jury refused to indict a member of the NYPD for asphyxiating asthmatic suspect Eric Garner in July with a "chokehold" maneuver banned by his department. In the past two weeks, a police officer in Cleveland whose record reflected he had "dismal" handgun skills gunned down a 12-year-old holding a BB gun in a Cleveland park, and autopsy results showed that a mentally ill man shot 14 times by a police officer in Milwaukee was hit in the back. In all three cases the police officer involved was white while the suspect was black.

These deaths once again press the need to address the way officers engage the public at large, and public mistrust that results from such examples is one of the reasons some police departments, from Washington state to Chicago, are making an effort to put "protect and serve" back at the forefront of policing. Philadelphia Police Commissioner Charles Ramsey might want to look to how both are taking the lead. Earlier this week, President Obama appointed Ramsey head of a national Task Force on 21st Century Policing, as part of an initiative to address the breakdown in police-community relations that has taken over the public dialogue since the August shooting of 18-year-old Mike Brown by an officer in Ferguson, Missouri.

In an interview with the Associated Press, Chief Ramsey called the task ahead of him "daunting, but ... doable."

"Can Different Training Make Police Officers Guardians, Not Warriors?" by Christopher Moraff, Nextcity, December 4, 2014. Reprinted by Permission.

Revising Police Training

In 2012, Chicago tapped a team of Yale criminologists to remodel its officer training program under a mandate from Police Superintendent Garry F. McCarthy. By January 2014, more than 8,000 Police Academy graduates had been schooled in the new curriculum—which teaches officers to be responsive, impartial, respectful and fair.

Proponents of the strategy say it not only reduces tensions between police and the community, but improves public safety by making citizens more likely to obey laws and cooperate with police.

Members of Chicago's Police Education and Training Division spent the spring and summer retraining officers in the California cities of Salinas, Oakland and Stockton and are now fanning out to other municipalities to share what they learned.

Exactly one year after Chicago finalized its new curriculum, Washington graduated its first class of police recruits through a radically modified officer training program. The goal is to put police on the street who can navigate tense situations with empathy while respecting the impact their actions have on how situations unfold.

The training strategy is the brainchild of Sue Rahr, who left her job as sheriff of King County to take over as head of the Washington State Criminal Justice Training Commission in 2012. David Bales, Rahr's deputy, says the program dispenses with military-style boot-camp elements common to many police academies in favor of coursework focused on communication and conflict resolution. In addition to traditional training in firearms and takedown techniques, recruits take courses in behavioral psychology and are encouraged to talk problems out rather than simply respond to barked orders.

"We are guided by the underlying goal of producing officers who are guardians as opposed to warriors," says Bales, who himself has more than three decades of law enforcement experience.

"The most common corresponding emotion to fear is anger, and anger does not facilitate ongoing compliance," he adds. "We teach recruits that when they mistreat people they actually may make that person more dangerous."

The program is hardly a cakewalk. In one exercise, described in an article published last year in the Seattle Times, recruits are doused twice in the face with pepper spray and asked to complete a series of tasks that frequently includes reciting the federal and state statutes governing the use of force.

Bales says the purpose of the exercise is to demonstrate to officers that they can focus, think, problem solve, defend themselves and even deescalate while under extreme duress.

"When an officer has confidence in their abilities, they are less likely to overreact out of fear," he says.

Unintended Consequences

Despite a pronounced drop in crime, technological improvements in policing and the increased professionalism of law enforcement, surveys show that "trust and confidence" in police has remained relatively unchanged (averaging about 50 percent) for four decades. New polling from Gallup shows that whites are significantly more likely to express trust in police than blacks.

At least part of the problem can be viewed as an unintended consequence of the war on drugs—which turned entire communities into de facto battlefields and a generation of young men of color into potential enemy combatants.

Reining in police militarization (another goal of the Obama administration's new proposal) is a vital first step to repairing the damage. But even the most deadly weapon is just a mindless tool. It's the attitude and character of the police officer holding it that matters.

In a statement provided to Next City, Chief Ramsey acknowledged the importance of officer behavior in informing the overall tone of police-community relations: "We as police departments have an obligation to build public trust and that starts with transparent behavior and developing police legitimacy across the board."

A report released last March by the Police Executive Research Forum, which Ramsey heads, also highlighted the critical role police "legitimacy" and the related concept of "procedural justice" play in effective law enforcement. The latter concept refers to the belief, supported by decades of scholarly research, that processes that are perceived to be fair are the most likely to generate favorable outcomes.

Criminologists such as Yale's Tom Tyler, who has spent decades studying the effect of officer behavior on law abidance, have found that citizens are more likely to gauge their interactions with police based on the perceived fairness of law enforcement rather than its effectiveness or lawfulness.

"The issue of interpersonal treatment consistently emerges as a key factor in reactions to dealings with legal authorities," Tyler writes. "[P]eople focus on cues that communicate information about the intentions and character of the legal authorities with whom they are dealing."

For instance, he cites studies that suggest members of minority groups factor how they are treated by police into determining whether they have been racially profiled. (This helps explain why policies like stop-and-frisk tend to be counterproductive).

Fewer Deadly Encounters

It hardly needs to be said that not shooting people who don't deserve to be shot is a crucial piece of the police legitimacy puzzle. Calling a shooting justified is not the same thing as calling it necessary; this has led some departments to rethink the way they train their officers in the use of deadly force.

Following the police shooting in Albuquerque last March of homeless camper James Boyd, the New Mexico Law Enforcement Academy began instructing officers to take cover and consider their options instead of immediately engaging aggressive suspects.

Two months earlier, Dallas Police Chief David O. Brown issued changes to the department's use-of-force program to require training once every quarter instead of bi-annually.

In the wake of the Mike Brown shooting, one city, Richmond, California, emerged as the poster child for the police reform movement for going five years without a single fatal shooting by its officers despite the city's long history of violent crime. Richmond Police Chief Chris Magnus credits the achievement to the expanded use of non-lethal weapons and monthly firearms training focused on accuracy and accountability.

Over the last five years, the Richmond PD has expended just eight bullets on five people. That's nearly as many bullets that Officer Darren Wilson fired into Mike Brown. (It's worth noting that Wilson's grand jury testimony also suggests that Ferguson police are given the discretion over whether to carry non-lethal weapons such as Tasers.)

On September 14th, Richmond experienced its first fatal officer involved shooting since 2007, to which the city responded with two separate investigations and a concerted community outreach effort. Both the police chief and his deputy attended the victim's funeral in civilian clothes to avoid provocation.

Chief Magnus's ability to think empathetically about his impact on the community he serves has won him high praise both inside and outside of Richmond. In September, he was summoned to Ferguson as one of two law enforcement experts tapped by the DOJ to review civil rights charges in connection with the Mike Brown killing.

As they move forward with their mission it's fair to say the members of the President's new trust-building task force can learn a lot from the experiences of forward-thinking leaders like Magnus.

The Washington State Criminal Justice Training Commission is now working with Seattle University to gauge if the department's new empathy training is having its intended effect. Deputy Director Bales says that while it may be too soon for any concrete evidence, there's no doubt in his mind that he is helping put better, more responsive police officers of the streets of his state.

"Empathy connects us to people, makes us better crisis interventionists, better investigators, better public servants and healthier, happier people," he says. "Could it be a national model? I don't know, but we will enthusiastically contribute to the discussion and the development of best practice in any way we can."

Inadequate Training Can
Only Lead to Trouble

Paul Waldman

Paul Waldman is a senior writer for the American Prospect as well as a writer for the Plum Line blog at the Washington Post *and a columnist for the* Week. *He's also a published author.*

Maria Haberfeld is a professor at the John Jay College of Criminal Justice in New York. A veteran of the Israel Defense Forces who also served in the Israel National Police, she has conducted research on police forces in multiple countries, and has also written many books on terrorism and policing, including Critical Issues in Police Training. We spoke on Friday about the events in Ferguson, Missouri, and the shooting of Kajieme Powell by St. Louis police, which was caught on video. Powell, brandishing a steak knife, approached officers, saying "Shoot me!." As reported by the Post-Dispatch, St. Louis Police Chief Sam Dotson said lethal force was permitted under department rules if a knife-wielding attacker is within 21 feet of police.

Paul Waldman: Did you think what the officers did [in Powell's shooting] was appropriate? It seems pretty clear that that's standard operating procedure.

Maria Haberfeld: Yes it is, absolutely.

PW: Are those procedures adequate to deal with those kinds of situations?

MH: The procedures are adequate; what's not adequate is the way police officers are trained. That's the problem, and this is something

"Expert: U.S. Police Training in Use of Deadly Force Woefully Inadequate," by Paul Waldman, The American Prospect, August 27, 2014. Reprinted by Permission.

I've been talking about for decades. The majority of police officers are overwhelmingly trained with a focus on the technical part of use of force, and are not trained enough in the emotional, psychological, physiological aspects of use of force. And of course, the social aspects of use of force: how this all plays later on within the community, how it impacts police-community relations.

So the use of force is not something that should stand alone. Unfortunately, in most of the training academies, it does stand alone, even if there is some rhetoric about, "Oh yes, we integrate [it] into other modules." The reality is—and I look at police training all the time, in various jurisdictions around the country and around the world—that's not the case, unfortunately.

PW: So, is most of [that training] focused on "Here's how to protect ourselves"? It seems that's the message when you hear police representatives talk about this. Their focus is, obviously, that police work is very dangerous, and if there's any kind of a threat at all, we're going to neutralize it.

MH: Yes, but how you perceive the threat is a subjective thing, and how you go about neutralizing the threat is also a subjective thing, even though they're trained around this continuum of force that allows them to go from one step to another, or skip a number of stages based on their assessment of the situation. Their assessment of the situation sometimes can be exaggerated based on their previous experience, based on what's going on in any given moment, based on the bystanders' reactions. So it's a very complicated and complex issue that cannot be just explained by: "We have the right, we are authorized, and it's our discretion."

There are a host of variables that go into things. And those variables, at least in my mind, should be constantly addressed, and not end with the police officer graduating from police academy, and then the only thing they have to do is to qualify twice a year whether or not they can still carry a weapon. But this qualifying twice a year is focused completely on the technical aspect of use of deadly force.

PW: One thing I've seen in the discussions about this is, for instance, that the police in England and Wales fire their guns only a few times in a year.

MH: Because they're not armed.

PW: So that raises a couple of questions. If most of them are not armed, what do those police do if they don't have guns, and they're confronted with a suspect who, say, has a knife?

MH: First of all, there are a few countries where police forces are not armed—Ireland would be the other one. The British police have units that are armed, and if there is a situation that would require an armed backup, then the backup is called for. But a situation like this, where they have somebody with a knife, it's a simple explanation. It goes back to training. Police forces in the U.K., in Ireland, in other countries where police forces are not armed, they have a much more extensive, in-depth training than we have. An average training in the United States is fifteen weeks. Fifteen weeks is nothing. Police forces in other countries have twice, three times as long training as we have here.

It's all about how police officers are prepared to deal with people who pose threats to them or to others. This is not something that we should save money on, but to me, that's exactly what we're doing. We are saving money on police training, saying that it's very expensive to have longer training. And I think it's irresponsible in a democratic society to say that a profession that has the authority to use deadly force, we just should shorten the training because a longer training is too expensive. Basically, what we're doing is putting a dollar sign on people's lives, both police officers and members of the public.

PW: So that means that if you're a policeman someplace else—

England, France, Germany—you're going to be trained so that you're better capable of talking that person down and getting them to put down their knife or their pipe or whatever it is that they have?

MH: No doubt in my mind, based on what I am seeing in police training in other countries, that police officers are better prepared to deal with the public over there than the ones we have here. No doubt in my mind, based on the research that I have done over the years.

PW: Do you think that a controversy like this one will make police forces around the country more likely to reexamine how they do their training?

MH: No.

PW: It won't make any difference at all?

MH: No, and I'll tell you why. Ninety percent of the police budget goes to salaries in any department. So, whatever is left is allocated to equipment and some other stuff, and nothing is left for training. The majority of police departments around the country don't have in-service training. So if you don't have the money, you're not going to re-examine.

PW: Well that's a little depressing.

MH: It is depressing. I've been writing about this for twenty years, it's very depressing to me. [Most] police departments in the United States are not NYPD or LAPD. Police departments in the United States are exactly what we're seeing—the Ferguson police department, fifty cops. This is the average size of a police department in the United States. So you can understand that a department of that size is not going to get any resources. This is very sad, and this is why I've been talking about the need to centralize law enforcement in the United States, to professionalize their response to the public, not just about use of force, but about everything.

Because policing is not just about the high-profile incidents, it's also about how they perform on a daily basis vis-à-vis the public. But this requires skills, this requires education, this requires training. An average police department, all they care about is whether you have a GED, and you didn't use drugs in the last three years. I mean, it's ridiculous. If somebody looks at this a little bit closer, then it's really scary.

PW: Is the training and the resulting way the cops deal with the public—not just about the use of force but about everything—do you think that is superior in other Western countries, too?

MH: Absolutely. I don't think, I know, because I do research with police departments in other countries, I see their training, I visit the departments, their police academies. That's what I've been doing for almost twenty years, so I know exactly that it's superior over there—not in each and every country, but the majority of police forces in democratic countries today—yes, absolutely.

Police Reform Is the Key to the Future

Norm Stamper

Norm Stamper is the former Seattle police chief, serving from 1994 to 2000. He has since authored a book about the dark side of policing.

*F*ormer Seattle Police Chief Norm Stamper knows what it is like to be at the center of a firestorm over police conduct. In 2000, when the World Trade Organization convention took over his city, Stamper's officers were criticized for their heavy-handed, and often violent, response to street protests.

Hundreds of peaceful protesters were arrested and rounded up along with those who had smashed store windows and destroyed police cars. Stamper resigned that year.

Since his resignation, Stamper has become a vocal proponent of police reform. Last month, he published "To Protect and Serve: How to Fix America's Police," which outlines his vision of police forces trained to meet national standards, gleaned from more than three decades of experience in the uniform.

Stamper says police shootings, like those of Alton Sterling and Philando Castile, are further evidence that change is urgently needed. He says the prevalence of guns in American society contributes to the distrust that has grown between the police and the communities they patrol—a point President Barack Obama addressed this weekend, speaking in response to the fatal shooting of five Dallas police officers.

Here is Stamper in his own words, as told to Kerry Shaw of The Trace.

When I heard about Dallas, I felt heartsick. I don't have a television, but I'm online a lot, and the alerts started pouring in. These were police officers, selected for the color of their skin.

The other thing that went through my mind was that this will be a huge setback to Black Lives Matter. A number of police officers

"I Ran a Big City Police Department. The Way We Train Cops to Use Lethal Force Is Broken," by Norm Stamper, The Trace, July 12, 2016. Reprinted by Permission.

around the country have been condemning the movement for months. I've even seen links from various police groups talking about how disgusting it is. They've countered with Blue Lives Matter, and that is a movement now.

So what we have is polarization, and polarization is never good. It's worse now than it was before the Dallas shootings.

I was also concerned that the shootings by police that happened before Thursday night's assassinations would get lost, and that as a country we'd forget that people are hurting and it's not just cops.

As we watch these shootings unfold, repeatedly, on a dashcam of a police car or an iPhone video, we're left with the impression that police officers do not—and this is a sweeping generalization—place sanctity on human life. They're too quick to pull the trigger. We've seen too many [shootings] that didn't have to happen, where there was minimal risk to the officer. That's causing enormous anger and terrible sadness in the African-American community and other segments of our society. Many cops are also disturbed by this, but they don't speak out as much as they should.

The Supreme Court has made it very clear that the only time a police officer can use lethal force is when your life or the life of another is at imminent risk. We have 18,000 law enforcement agencies. That's 18,000 different policies for determining imminent risk, 18,000 different sets of procedures and tactics. The room for different interpretations, even within a police station, is substantial.

Wouldn't it be nice if every cop and every citizen could know what the actual practice was for lethal force? Or for stop-and-frisk or search-and-seizure? When it comes to stopping an American on the streets, or when it comes time to pull a gun or a trigger, the standards need to be the same from coast to coast.

Right now we don't have any national standards for policing. Instead we have a patchwork of policies, with wide variation in training, supervision, and performance evaluation. I think the average citizen would be surprised to know how unsupervised one of the most delicate and dangerous jobs is.

The process of setting and enforcing the standards should be done at the federal level in conjunction with local agencies. Each agency needs to have sufficient muscle to say, "We'll certify every cop, we'll certify every agency. Oh and by the way, in extreme situations, we'll de-certify any cop or agency."

If you get de-certified as a police officer, don't even think about applying across town. You've forfeited your right to be a police officer.

In creating those standards, we'd have to reach some consistency in training. Now we typically provide many hours of firearms training but very few hours of training in de-escalation. Since Ferguson, some agencies have really bolstered their training in de-escalation, but many have not. Some are full-blown military stress academies.

If you want police officers to act like soldiers — and I'd hope that we don't, but rather as true domestic peacekeepers, partnered with their communities — then the last thing you'd do is train them under a militaristic model.

An academy should pose challenges, but those ought to be structured simulations of what police officers encounter in the real world — people pulling guns on you, knives on you, calling you names. You want police officers to be self-confident people.

We can also dramatically improve training so that a cop can understand how his body reacts in a stressful, ambiguous situation: like when there may be a gun, or when a baby has entered the scene at the same time as a gun. These are shoot/don't shoot scenarios that are likely to occur on the job. Right now we do these simulations once in training. Maybe we bring someone in a second time if they made questionable choices.

Of course, guns play a big role in all this. They put another level of pressure on police officers. Guns make it all the more evident that the next domestic violence incident or bar room brawl could have someone packing heat. Guns make police officers hyper vigilant. And a scared cop is a dangerous cop.

Fear, more than anything, distorts perception. It causes individuals to see things that aren't there. It can cause them to experience tunnel vision. They'll focus on the threat at the expense sometimes of everything around it. Often tunnel vision will not allow you to see an innocent bystander. It will not allow you to recognize that you have an opportunity to take cover, that you don't have to stand there, exposed to someone with a gun.

I am extremely disturbed by the proliferation of guns in the country, and most major city chiefs feel the same way I do.

We need true community policing. I'm envisioning a system where citizens are invited to participate in hiring and instructing new police officers. They'd also be involved in police oversight. (I avoid using the word "civilians," as it creates the mindset that police officers are soldiers.)

And, finally, we have to find a way to end the drug war. By definition, you don't fight a war without enemies. And that's what we're doing, and we're targeting people of color in wildly disproportionate numbers. And then we wonder why there's such a strain on the relationships between cops and young black men.

And you could say, "Oh, they're breaking the law." Well, so are young white men. But black men are being targeted at disproportionately higher rates.

We know prohibition didn't work, and that was very similar to the war we're now waging against illegal drugs. We've spent $1.3 trillion since Nixon declared drugs "public enemy number one" and we have incarcerated tens of millions of people—that number needs to sink in—for nonviolent drug offenses. And what do we have to show for it? Drugs are more available, more potent, and more accessible to our children. It's been a colossal failure.

Police Power Can Be a Dangerous Thing

David Rudovsky

David Rudovsky is a senior fellow at the University of Pennsylvania Law School. He teaches courses in evidence, criminal law, and criminal procedure.

As a result of recent high-profile shootings of unarmed African American civilians by police, the long simmering problem of excessive police force in the United States has sparked a national debate on policing, race, and community relations. As has been the case on repeated occasions in our nation's history, claims of unlawful or oppressive police practices have focused attention on the powers granted to law enforcement, the use of these powers against racial minorities, political activists, dissidents, and others who challenge the status quo, and on the appropriate remedial mechanisms. And although the great majority of interactions between police and civilians do not involve force or unreasonable force, video-documented incidents of excessive force have moved the debate from one of "is there a problem" to the scope of excessive force, its causes, and effective remedies.

Data collection is still inexcusably deficient in many police agencies, but the data that are available demonstrate patterns of excessive force, as well as large racial disparities in the use of force. A recent study on racial and ethnic disparities in the use of lethal police force from the years 2010 to 2014, by Dr. James W. Buehler of Drexel University, reported 2,285 deaths that resulted from police use of force. The same study found that among males who were 10 years and older, the mortality rate for African Americans and Latinos was 2.8 and 1.7 times higher respectively when compared with Whites.

Other studies have shown significantly higher rates of shootings among unarmed African Americans when compared

"The Troubling Issues Regarding Police Use of Force," by David Rudovsky, University of Pennsylvania Law School, February 27, 2017. Reprinted by Permission.

with Whites. In Philadelphia—a city that has approximately 45 percent White, 44 percent African American, and 14 percent Latino residents—80 percent of force incidents involved African-American suspects, 10 percent involved Latinos, and 9 percent involved Whites.

To be sure, more must be considered before these data can be said to show a causal relationship based on race, since other factors—such as crime rates or the dangers inherent in different suspects' reactions to police intervention—might explain the racial disparities. However, in related studies involving incarceration rates and stop-and-frisk encounters, non-racial factors have not explained similarly large racial disparities. For example, in litigation surrounding Philadelphia's stop-and-frisk practices—where the racial data were quite similar to the data on use of force—regression studies have shown that factors such as crime rates, police deployment, and social or economic conditions do not explain the racial differentials in stop-and-frisk practices.

The debate over the causes of unlawful or unreasonable police use of force has focused on the role of (1) law enforcement agencies, in terms of training, supervision, and discipline of officers; in short, on the critical issue of agency and individual accountability, (2) the courts, in terms of remedies that are (or are not) available for excessive force, both to compensate individuals whose rights have been violated and to create a system of remedial measures that have a deterrent effect, (3) civilian review agencies, and the powers of investigation and discipline that should be vested in them, and (4) prosecutors, who have the power to bring criminal prosecutions against officers who engage in the criminal use of force.

Over the years, commentators have documented systemic deficiencies in each of these agencies in controlling and remedying excessive force. In my view, although there is a need for civilian review, litigation involving systemic deficiencies in police policies and practices, and robust judicial oversight, the primary responsibility for developing practices and policies that can ensure effective, equitable, and reasonable uses of force lies with law enforcement agencies. If police departments do not address and "own" the problem, oversight by prosecutors, civilian review boards, and the courts will not provide sufficient counterweights.

Other commentators in this series have shown the reasons why criminal prosecutions, civil rights litigation, and court interventions have not been effective in controlling police violence. Criminal prosecutions are extremely rare as prosecutors must rely on police for the investigation of criminal cases and are reluctant to prosecute officers unless there is overwhelming evidence of serious misconduct. And juries often fail to convict even when the evidence is strong. Civilian review agencies are almost always without sufficient investigative, adjudicative, and disciplinary powers to effectuate departmental changes.

As for judicial intervention, the U.S. Supreme Court, through an application of a series of "judicial door closing" doctrines, has erected numerous roadblocks to effective civil rights litigation. The Court has given an extraordinarily high level of deference to officers who employ force and has interpreted the Fourth Amendment in a manner that only prohibits the most egregious use of force. As Professors Brandon Garrett and Seth Stoughton have commented, "Fourth Amendment case law is not only poorly suited for police training, but [is] actually counterproductive."

Further, the doctrine of qualified immunity protects officers from damage actions even when their actions have violated the Fourth Amendment, injunctive relief is often barred by standing principles, and except in cases of clear systemic violations of constitutional protections, police departments, municipalities, and states are immune from suit. Although some litigation reform efforts have succeeded—in particular, interventions by the U.S. Department of Justice (DOJ) Civil Rights Division—these initiatives may be in jeopardy with the change in administrations.

So, what is to be done? First and foremost, as Jonathan Smith, the former Chief of the Special Litigation Section of the Civil Rights Division of the DOJ, and others have written, real reform is not possible without the democratization of policing through community participation among those most affected by policing tactics and enhanced transparency in operations. In many ways the police are the least regulated arm of government, notwithstanding their enormous powers. Administrative law principles could be used to require a democratic process of adoption of rules and regulations that control and limit departmental use of force.

Second, police departments must engage in an in-depth review of use-of-force policies and training. For the past 50 years, with the advent of proactive policing characterized by "zero tolerance practices," aggressive stop-and-frisk policies, and a militarization of police forces, the "warrior" model of policing has become dominant.

However, with the recent attention to excessive force and racial bias, a new debate has emerged, spurred in part by the Black Lives Matter movement. In 2016, the Police Executive Research Forum, a national organization of police officials, issued recommendations on use of force that provide a "guardian" model for policing. These principles stress respect for the sanctity of human life, the need for standards for the use of force that are more restrictive than those imposed by the Constitution, force that is proportional to the dangers of the situation, de-escalation techniques, and fair, transparent, and independent investigations of the use of force.

These and other related recommendations were also made by President Barack Obama's Task Force on 21st Century Policing. The task force emphasized comprehensive data collection as a means towards greater transparency in operations, prioritizing de-escalation tactics, diversity in police ranks, internal accountability, and strong action on racial profiling. These recommendations mirror many of the provisions of consent decrees initiated by the DOJ in its investigative and litigation efforts under its "pattern or practice" authority.

Third, police training must accentuate the need for officers to refrain from escalating tactics and to develop communication and other related skills that can reduce incidents of deadly and other kinds of serious force. Many use-of-force incidents involve mentally ill persons who pose a danger only to themselves. The

Washington Post has reported that 25 percent of all fatal shootings by police are of persons suffering from serious mental illness. Police departments should establish "Crisis Intervention Teams" that are trained to respond to these incidents with tactics of patience, deliberation, and de-escalation.

Further, police policies must go beyond the highly deferential constitutional standards announced by the Supreme Court. In a recent case, San Francisco v. Sheehan, the Supreme Court missed the opportunity to adjust constitutional standards to the realities of police use of deadly force. The Court granted qualified immunity to an officer who responded to a report of a mentally disabled woman living in a group home who was threatening to hurt herself with a knife by making an unannounced intrusion into the room in which she was located. When she responded, not surprisingly, by moving towards him with the knife, he fired several times.

Notwithstanding universal agreement among policing and psychology experts that an officer in these encounters should not enter barricaded rooms and that trained negotiators should be called to de-escalate the tension, the Court determined that no clearly established Fourth Amendment rights had been violated because the officer faced the threat of serious bodily injury when he used deadly force. But if "reasonableness" is the touchstone of the Fourth Amendment, why would the Court credit the decision to use deadly force as one made in a "split-second" context and ignore the officer's responsibility in creating the danger?

Fourth, officers should be provided with less-than-lethal equipment such as safe chemical sprays and electronic control weapons like tasers—along with comprehensive training and supervision—that can be used when resistance is serious but not life-threatening, and the suspect can be safely secured without deadly force.

Fifth, to ensure proper accountability, internal investigations must be conducted with integrity, provide appropriate discipline and retraining when fault has been found, and implement a high level of transparency surrounding investigative information and decision-making. Investigators must also recognize the deleterious effects of the police "code of silence" on their adjudications. All too often, lack of accountability leads the offender and other officers to assume that breaking the rules has no consequences.

Sixth, departments must expand the use of technology that promotes accountability and transparency. Many of the recent controversial use-of-force incidents became known only through police body-worn and surveillance cameras, as well as cell phone videos. All departments should be moving to universal body and patrol car cameras, with regulations that require that these cameras function at all critical stages of police-civilian interactions.

Seventh, more attention must be paid to explicit and implicit racial bias. This concern cuts across hiring, training, and supervision of officers and should incorporate the new advances and learning with respect to the phenomenon of "implicit bias," which relates to how unconscious attitudes and perceptions may alter a person's view and understanding of other people's conduct and actions. For police, this is especially important in their assessment of the dangers posed by civilians, and in particular suspects who may pose a risk of physical danger to the officer.

There is experiential evidence of the effectiveness of new paradigms and cultures of policing. For example, due to concerns about the levels and patterns of force by officers in the Philadelphia Police Department, former Philadelphia Police Commissioner Charles Ramsey requested a study by the DOJ on the Police Department's policies, training, and investigations of use of force. The study produced a wide-ranging set of recommendations that were soon implemented by the Philadelphia Police Department. More time will be required before definitive conclusions can be drawn, but it is instructive that use-of-force patterns in Philadelphia appear to have changed in significant ways. Thus, comparing data from 2012 with 2015, the Philadelphia Police Department reported the following:

	2012	2015
NUMBER OF POLICE SHOOTING INCIDENTS	59	35
NUMBER OF SHOTS FIRED AT CIVILIANS	477	200
PERSONS KILLED BY POLICE	16	2
PERSONS INJURED BY POLICE	32	15
NUMBER OF OFFICERS FIRING AT PERSONS	104	46

The renewed debate on police use of force provides an opportunity to correct both the constitutional and operational standards in an area that poses fundamental challenges to our commitment to restraints on necessary—but widely abused—governmental powers.

De-Escalation in Dallas Is Paying Off

Naomi Martin

Naomi Martin is a staff writer at the Dallas Morning News, *where she covers government and politics. She has also covered the police in Dallas, New Orleans, and Baton Rouge.*

In a vacant school last week, two Dallas officers—one with a gun, the other a Taser—tried to talk a hulking man out of shooting himself.

The man left his guns behind and walked toward them. Stop, the cops said. He didn't.

"I'm going less lethal," an officer said. He fired his Taser.

Commanders said the outcome of the encounter, which was a staged police training drill, marked a vast change from old-school policing. They said in years past, that type of situation could've ended in a chokehold or a shooting.

Police Chief David Brown says this shift toward de-escalation is driving a sharp drop in excessive-force complaints against officers. In 2009, the year before Brown became chief, 147 such complaints were filed. So far this year, 13 have been filed—on pace to be the lowest number in at least two decades.

"This is the most dramatic development in policing anywhere in the country," Brown said in an interview Friday with The Dallas Morning News. "We've had this kind of impact basically through training, community policing and holding officers accountable."

Brown says his commanders have improved the quality of so-called reality-based training and increased required training hours for street cops over the past year. Trainers model the scenarios on real-life events recorded by officers' body cams, dash-cams, and the media.

"Dallas Police Excessive-Force Complaints Drop Dramatically," by Naomi Martin, Dallas Morning News Inc, November 2015. Reprinted by Permission.

"We can learn from what Dallas is doing," said Chuck Wexler, executive director of the Police Executive Research Forum in Washington, D.C. "That's what police departments need—they don't need training in silos: one day about the law, one day about firearms, one day about crisis intervention."

Brown believes the Dallas training has also led to a 30 percent decline in assaults on officers this year, and a 40 percent drop in shootings by police.

Slowing things down

Training instructors say they preach tactics that sometimes seem counter-intuitive to veteran officers: Slow down instead of rushing into a situation; don't approach a suspect immediately. Try to build a rapport; don't have multiple officers shout at once.

"By slowing things down, we're able to make better decisions and get more peaceful resolutions," said instructor Sgt. Anthony Greer.

Department leaders acknowledge that other factors also probably contributed to the decline in complaints, such as community engagement efforts. Also, the complaint decline coincides with street officers being outfitted with body microphones and dash-cam videos.

"The officers know they're being monitored," said Assistant Chief Tammie Hughes, who oversees internal affairs.

Excessive-force complaints have also dropped in Seattle, Birmingham, Baltimore, Portland, Ore., Paterson, N.J., and New York City.

The Dallas decline, though, seems to be among the most dramatic. The complaints dropped by 64 percent from 2009 to 2014.

Brown noted, however, that many uses of force by police are inevitable for officers to protect themselves.

Last year, two of 53 excessive-force complaints were sustained. One of those officers was fired. None of the 13 complaints filed so far this year have been sustained by investigators.

Skepticism

Several criminologists acknowledged that they were surprised by the drop in Dallas complaints, and said they would like to know more about how that happened.

"Anybody in any criminal justice research is going to be taken aback by such a dramatic swing in numbers," said Ronal Serpas, a former New Orleans police chief who is now a professor at Loyola University. But, he added, changes in training, accountability measures, and body microphones could have plausibly made a dent. "It could very well be true."

Without a formal study, there's no way to know for sure what caused the reduction in complaints, said John Worrall, a criminal justice professor at the University of Texas at Dallas.

"The marked drop between 2014 and 2015 strikes me as conspicuous and in need of an explanation," Worrall said. He said the chief's claim of training improvements could be valid, but added that "it is doubtful that such improvements could have such a pronounced effect in such a short span of time."

Alex Piquero, a fellow criminal justice professor at the university, said the complaint numbers could have also been affected by lower crime rates, citizens complaining less, and officers using less force.

Regardless, he said, the numbers appear to show a real change rather than just a random blip, because the trend "continues to go in the same direction for a sustained period of time."

But some critics expressed skepticism about Brown and his command staff's claims.

Slower 911 response times have much more to do with the drop than changes in training, which are a "smokescreen," said Ron Pinkston, president of the Dallas Police Association.

"We're not getting there in a timely manner, so the bad guys are already gone," Pinkston said. "The only complaint out there is the citizen saying, 'What took you so long?'"

Others said the reduction reflects a growing public opinion that filing a complaint is pointless.

"People don't feel that their complaints will be taken seriously, and they're right," said community activist John Fullinwider, co-founder of Mothers Against Police Brutality.

Teaching vs. testing

Reality-based training isn't new at the department, but Brown says the training has been ramped up in frequency and quality.

Officers on patrol, who respond to emergencies and therefore are most likely to use force on suspects, must complete the training every year now—twice as frequently as they used to go.

Deputy Chief Jeff Cotner, who now supervises the academy, says all patrol officers have been through the new classes. Records obtained by the *News* confirmed that a significant portion of all officers have cycled through the training in the past two years.

The academy's approach to training has changed, too, from a "testing" approach to a "teaching" one, said Executive Assistant Chief David Pughes, who oversaw reforms there last year. The scenarios now are more realistic, he said.

"You can have a reality-based training program all day long," Pughes said. "But if you're throwing people into unrealistic, no-win scenarios, you're not doing a whole lot to improve things."

Before the Ferguson, Mo., protests and unrest last year, Pughes said, much of American police training was geared toward responding to mass shootings. Officers were trained to rush ahead, find the shooter, and stop the threat to human lives immediately, which most of the time meant killing the shooter.

After Ferguson, departments rushed to add de-escalation, and Dallas beefed up its program, he said.

The training, which is held now at the old Lamar Elementary School, requires some imagination. The department is now trying to secure funding for a roughly $3 million to $4 million fake village with a gas station, school, apartment complex, and house.

"We definitely want our officers to defend themselves and we want them to go home at night," Brown said. "But we also want to avoid the controversies of a shooting that violates our deadly force policy. You do that through training."

"The Ferguson effect"

Another factor contributing to fewer force complaints could be what some law enforcement leaders call "the Ferguson effect"—the idea that officers are less likely now to confront suspects or use force because they don't want to risk being at the center of a viral incident.

But that notion is controversial among police officials. Many, including Brown, are insulted at the notion that officers would somehow abandon their duties in any way.

"Officers are still working hard and still doing their job," said Cotner. "I hear them [on the police radio] making themselves available and going toward the problem. You can't say ... there's a chilling effect."

Communities Need to Be Trained, Too

Andrew Bell & Bruce Razey

Andrew Bell has more than twenty years of experience in law enforcement and twenty-five years of experience in the US military and civilian service. He's now a criminal justice faculty member with American Military University. Bruce Razey enjoyed a thirty-year career in law enforcement, with one of his main jobs being police training.

In my 20-year police career, I [Bell] never discharged my weapon in the line of duty. However, there were several situations where I had legal justification to use a firearm, but, fortunately, my police training helped me find an alternative way to de-escalate the situation.

One such situation occurred when I was a young officer in the early 1980s. The call was to break up a high school fight. When I arrived at the scene, I pushed my way through a crowd of kids just in time to see one kid running away. When he got about 50 yards away, he turned around and came back to fight. I heard someone yell, "He's got a knife." As the 17-year-old got within about 30 yards, I could see a big butcher knife in his hand. He was now in a full sprint toward me.

When he was about 15 yards away, he started to raise the butcher knife. I still had my side-handle baton in my right hand. I dropped the baton on the ground and drew my weapon. I raised my weapon, formed a good sight picture on the kid's chest and started to pull the trigger. I thought I would cam the gun until the hammer fell. Camming is the ability to squeeze the trigger on a revolver and knowing the point where the hammer will fall striking the firing pin.

As I squeezed the trigger, my vision narrowed, sound was muffled and it seemed like time played in slow motion. Out of

"An Officer's Experience: Police Training to Reduce Use of Force Cases," by Andrew Bell and Bruce Razey, InPublicSafety.com, June 8, 2016. Reprinted by Permission.

my peripheral vision, I caught a glimpse of another kid holding my side-handle baton challenging the kid with the knife to fight. Suddenly, things seemed different. In an instant, I realized the kid with the knife was not trying to stab me, he was going after the other kid. I realized I could still take control of this without shooting, but I had to act quickly.

I holstered my revolver. Instantly, I was back in real time. I grabbed my baton away from the one kid and as I did the kid with the knife stopped dead (figuratively) in his tracks about five yards away. I looked at the kid with the knife and said, "Drop the knife." The kid threw the knife on the ground and ran in the opposite direction. Both kids were eventually apprehended and charged with disorderly conduct.

In those days, appropriate "less than lethal" weapon choices did not exist. The side-handle baton usually fell off your belt every time you ran and CS gas was seldom, if ever, used because innocent people nearby were often hit with the overspray. It wouldn't be until the late '80s and '90s when tools like the Taser, pepper spray and beanbag rounds came into play. Even then, not every officer had them.

The Importance of Combat Police Training

The only thing that stopped me from shooting that day was the combat police training I received as a young officer. Combat training is being aware of and understanding your environment and taking action based on changes to the situation. No advancements in technology or new less-than-lethal weapons will ever replace the value of combat training in teaching officers to recognize the threat and take the appropriate action. It is often the lack of proper police training and the lack of reality-based training that leads to escalation of force and unnecessary death.

Police departments across our nation spend a great deal of time and effort training their personnel to recognize when deadly force is authorized and legal. This is the proper thing to do, since departments and their employing municipalities are civilly liable for the actions of their officers. However, police departments should not stop there. In addition to honing firearms skills, marksmanship, and "shoot/don't shoot" scenarios, additional police training should be considered.

Value of Total Incident Training

Most shooting situations escalate from some other type of call for service, but many departments have little total incident training. Except for initial firearms training of officers, firearms/weapons training in isolation can be counterproductive for police. Police training officers go to the range to shoot. They go to shoot/don't shoot training to shoot. For instance, our original "edge weapons" training which included learning the "21-foot rule" left me feeling as though I must shoot or be stabbed. If officers were never taught alternatives to shooting, you can see why they would feel that shooting was their only option.

Total incident training can assist the officer to assess the totality of the situation and provide alternate methods to de-escalate a perceived or actual threat. Rather than merely relying on instinct, officers are trained to think for themselves. Officers should ask themselves, "What is really going on here?"

I can only remember attending one police training scenario when we were not supposed to shoot. The suspicious call involved a kid standing with his back to the officer who does not respond to commands. He puts his hands in his pocket and finally turns around quickly, pulling something out of his pocket. Fearing a weapon, officers often shoot (also because they're at shooting training). In his hand is a card that says, "I am a deaf-mute."

Progressive police departments that include total incident training as part of their firearms training often find themselves in a better light after an officer-involved shooting. Which sounds better? "The officer was legally authorized to use deadly force" or "The officer assessed the totality of the situation and was forced to shoot the aggressor to stop the deadly action."

Police officers are often required to make the decision to

shoot in a split second. But as the knife incident above illustrates, situations do arise when an officer has time to consider other methods to resolve the conflict.

During officer training, there are only brief discussions about the changing dynamics of a combat situation. In shoot/don't shoot training, discussions involve whether officers have the legal authority to shoot. Once it is deemed they have a green light to shoot, alternatives are seldom, if ever, discussed. Training programs must address alternatives to assist the officer during the decision-making process about whether or not to use deadly force.

Making such a decision involves in-depth training and role-playing scenarios. Police officers are paid to risk their lives, but they certainly should not be expected to take a bullet due to slow decision making. This article does not suggest that a police officer should always consider a less-than-lethal alternative in every situation.

In the knife situation outlined above, the officer would have been justified shooting the youngster. Hold on! The police officer admitted the kid wasn't trying to stab him; he was attempting to use the butcher knife on the other kid. That's true, but the officer has the responsibility to protect all lives. That includes the officer's life and the other kid's life, as well as the aggressor's life.

Using Real-Life Training Scenarios

Firearms training should include real-life situations such as the knife and deaf-mute incidents mentioned above like this to promote discussions. Officers should place themselves in these situations and think about alternative ways to resolve the threat, but only if the incident allows for ample time. Input by the firearms training staff is imperative, but officers should be encouraged to brainstorm alternative methods and actions.

Any police department, no matter how small, should have no problem identifying real-life scenarios for training and discussion. Caution should be taken, however, to avoid incidents under investigation or review. Additionally, no officer should be ridiculed or otherwise made to feel he acted improperly after using deadly force. Only the officer(s) involved in the incident were there and as long as their actions were deemed legal, their decision as to how to handle it should never be questioned by their peers.

In summary, if a police officer is justified in using deadly force, the officer should never risk his life or jeopardize the safety of others by being reluctant to do so. However, if time permits during an incident, it is important that officers seek out alternative less-than-lethal methods to help preserve life.

A word about transparency is in order. We constantly hear the public critique police shootings with such ridiculous statements such as: "The cop didn't have to kill him. He could have just shot him in the leg or something." Or: "He was only a boy, he had his whole life ahead of him." News flash! Police officers are not trained to kill people. They are trained to neutralize a person's aggressive acts. Officers are trained to shoot at the torso, the large body mass, because it's the easiest part of the body to hit. This isn't target shooting, folks.

Therefore, in addition to training police personnel, police departments would do well to train their communities. A "Citizen's Police Academy" is, in my opinion, one of the best ways of teaching the public why police officers respond the way they do. I have spoken with many citizens who have completed training offered by police departments and every one was positively enlightened by what he or she learned.

There are two basic schools of thought concerning firearms police training and police-involved shootings. The primary goal of police administrations is to prevent and/or reduce liability. The officers' major goal is to protect the citizens they serve and to come home to their families safe each night. Police departments do not have to take sides or settle for one goal or the other. Both can be achieved with appropriate and consistent police training.

Organizations to Contact

The editors have compiled the following list of organizations concerned with the issues debated in this book. The descriptions are derived from materials provided by the organizations. All have publications or information available for interested readers. This list was compiled on the date of publication of the present volume; the information provided here may change. Be aware that many organizations take several weeks or longer to respond to inquiries, so allow as much time as possible.

+Acumen
(212) 566-8821
email: courses@plusacumen.org
website: www.plusacumen.org

+Acumen is an organization that offers free and low-price courses for people who are interested in making social changes. The organization has various partners—including the US Department of Labor—who assist in helping the organization grow. All in all, +Acumen also has a network of 300,000 students within 190 different countries who are helping to make social change across the globe.

American Civil Liberties Union
125 Broad Street, 18th Floor,
New York, NY 10004
(212) 549-2500
website: www.aclu.org

The American Civil Liberties Union (ACLU) is an organization that has worked to defend the people's constitutional rights for nearly 100 years. Made up of more than 1.6 million members, the ACLU is also America's largest public interest law firm, with all 50 states being represented. The ACLU is nonprofit and non-partisan and is headquartered in New York City.

Black Lives Matter
website: www.blacklivesmatter.com

Black Lives Matter is an online forum dedicated to building a community of people to help fight against anti-black racism and to develop the necessary connections needed to end social injustice. The movement was formed in 2013 by Patrisse Cullors, Opal Tometi, and Alicia Garza and has since expanded into a national movement with chapters across the country. Various BLM chapters have been covered by the media in the last few years due to high-profile police shootings.

Black Youth Project 100
PO Box 9031
Chicago, IL 60609
(773) 940-1800
email: info@byp100.org
website: www.byp100.org

The Black Youth Project is an activist member-based organization of African American men and women between the ages of eighteen and thirty-five. The mission of the organization is to train young black individuals on social justice in hopes of ending criminalization as well as police brutality and racial profiling. BYP100 members are asked to contribute $10 per month to the organization and dedicate a minimum of three hours per week to the organization's matters.

Center for American Progress
1333 H Street
Washington, DC 20005
(202) 682-1611
website: www.americanprogressaction.org

Founded in 2003, the Center for American Progress Action Fund is a nonprofit organization that is dedicated to improving the lives of Americans through forward-thinking ideas, strong leadership, and action.

International Association of Chiefs of Police
44 Canal Center Plaza Suite 200
Alexandria, VA 22314
(703) 836-6767
website: www.theiacp.org

International Association of Chiefs of Police is an organization dedicated to advancing law enforcement through advocacy and education programs. While the organization does many things, one of its main focuses is on the training of police officers. The IACP is made up of 30,000 members throughout 146 countries around the world.

International Law Enforcement Educators and Trainers Association
8150 White Oak Avenue
Munster, IN 46321
(262) 767-1406
email: info@ileeta.org
website: www.ileeta.org

International Law Enforcement Educators and Trainers Association is an organization dedicated to the training of police officers and various arms of law enforcement. One of ILEETA's main focuses is to ensure the safety and security of citizens, while improving the understanding and communication within the communities officers serve. ILEETA holds an annual conference that more than 800 members attend.

National Association Against Police Brutality
PO Box 64170
Washington, DC 20019
(202) 749-9775
email: info@naapb.org
website: www.naapb.org

The National Association Against Police Brutality was founded by Jonathan Newton, a law student who was a former police officer, as part of community service requirements for his degree. Formed in December 2014, the entity's goals include educating citizens on their civil rights as well as assisting citizens in legal aid against those who were victimized by the police, among other things. Since its creation, the organization's website states that it's received more than eight hundred calls regarding people seeking assistance following an encounter with an unprofessional officer of the law.

National Police Accountability Project
499 7th Avenue, Suite 12N
New York, NY 10018
(212) 630-9939
email: assistant.npap@nlg.org
website: www.nlg-npap.org

The National Police Accountability Project is a nonprofit organization dedicated to protecting the civil rights of people who have encounters with law enforcement. A central mission of the NPAP is to develop accountability of police officers when violating constitutional laws. The NPAP is a project of the National Lawyers Guild, which was founded in 1937 as an alternative to the American Bar Association.

The Trace
email: info@thetrace.org
website: www.thetrace.org

The Trace is a nonprofit news organization that serves to educate its readership on gun usage and violence in America. The Trace, in partnership with a company called Slate, has built an interactive map that shows the locations of nearly 40,000 gun-related incidents, also providing information and details on the incidents. The organization not only reports on news, but also reports on potential fixes for the gun epidemic that the United States currently faces.

Bibliography

Books

Alison Behnke. *Racial Profiling: Everyday Inequality.* Minneapolis, MN: Lerner Publishing Group, 2017.

Stephen Egharevba. *Police Brutality, Racial Profiling, and Discrimination in the Criminal Justice System.* Hershey, PA: IGI-Global, 2016.

Thomas Fensch. *The Sordid Hypocrisy of to Protect and to Serve: Police Brutality, Corruption and Oppression in America.* New Century Books, 2015.

Skolnick Fyfe. *Above the Law: Police and the Excessive Use of Force.* New York, NY: Free Press, 2010.

Corinne Grinapol. *Racial Profiling and Discrimination: Your Legal Rights.* New York, NY: Rosen Young Adult, 2015.

Maria R. Haberfeld. *Critical Issues in Police Training.* Edition 1. Saddle River, NJ: Prentice Hall, 2002.

Las Vegas Review Journal. *Deadly Force: When Las Vegas Police Shoot, and Kill.* Las Vegas, NV: Stephens Press, LLC, 2011.

Alana Lentin. *Racism and Ethnic Discrimination.* New York, NY: Rosen Publishing Group, 2011.

Autumn Libal. *Discrimination & Prejudice.* Broomall, PA: National Highlights Inc., 2014.

James P. Mcelvain. *Police Shootings and Citizen Behavior.* El Paso, TX: LFB Scholarly Publishing LLC, 2008.

Seumas Miller. *Shooting to Kill: The Ethics of Police and Military Use of Lethal Force.* New York, NY: Oxford University Press, 2016.

Cliff Roberson. *Police Misconduct: A Global Perspective.* Boca Raton, FL: CRC Press, 2017.

Michael Ruth. *Police Brutality*. New York, NY: Greenhaven Publishing, 2016.

Bill Stonehem. *Police Shootings on the Rise in the United States*. Self-Published, 2016.

US Department of Justice. *The Role of Police Psychology in Controlling Excessive Force*. Washington, DC: U.S. Department of Justice, 2016.

Periodicals and Internet Sources

Michael A. Cohen. "Dallas Police Department Leads the Way in Se-escalation," *Boston Globe*, July 9, 2016, https://www.bostonglobe.com/opinion/2016/07/08/ dallas-police-department-leads-way-escalation/ pxvSK7SpFx86m3mV3UuJbI/story.html.

Camila Domonoske. "Shots in the Back, Children Tasered: DOJ Details Excessive Force by Chicago Police," NPR, January 13, 2017, http://www.npr.org/sections/thetwo-way/2017/01/13/509665735/shots-in-the-back-children-tasered-doj-details-excessive-force-by-chicago-police.

Jason Hanna and Madison Park. "Chicago Police Use Excessive Force, DOJ Finds," CNN, January 13, 2017, http://www.cnn.com/2017/01/13/us/chicago-police-federal-investigation/index.html.

Tom Jackman. "De-escalation Training to Reduce Police Shootings Facing Mixed Reviews at Launch," *Washington Post*, October 15, 2016, https://www.washingtonpost.com/local/public-safety/de-escalation-training-to-reduce-police-shootings-facing-mixed-reviews-at-launch/2016/10/14/d6d96c74-9159-11e6-9c85-ac42097b8cc0_story.html?utm_term=.14b0b4056567.

Kimberly Kindy. "New Style of Police Training Aims to Produce 'Guardians,' not 'Warriors,'" *Washington Post*, December 10, 2015, http://www.washingtonpost.com/sf/

investigative/2015/12/10/new-style-of-police-training-aims-to-produce-guardians-not-warriors/?utm_term=.b8a9e2475e31.

Wesley Lowery. "Police Chiefs Consider Dramatic Reforms to Officer Tactics, Training to Prevent So Many Shootings," *Washington Post*, January 29, 2016, https://www.washingtonpost.com/news/post-nation/wp/2016/01/29/police-chiefs-consider-dramatic-reforms-to-officer-tactics-training-to-prevent-so-many-shootings/?utm_term=.40867e3b715b.

Barbara Reynolds. "I Was a Civil Rights Activist in the 1960s. But It's Hard for Me to Get Behind Black Lives Matter," *Washington Post*, August 24, 2015, https://www.washingtonpost.com/posteverything/wp/2015/08/24/i-was-a-civil-rights-activist-in-the-1960s-but-its-hard-for-me-to-get-behind-black-lives-matter/?utm_term=.5875e1f2c49a.

Brad W. Smith and Malcolm D. Holmes. "Police Use of Excessive Force in Minority Communities: A Test of the Minority Threat, Place, and Community Accountability Hypotheses," Oxford Academic, July 24, 2014, https://academic.oup.com/socpro/article-abstract/61/1/83/1626052

Katherine Spillar. "How More Female Police Officers Would Help Stop Police Brutality," *Washington Post*, July 2, 2015, https://www.washingtonpost.com/posteverything/wp/2015/07/02/how-more-female-police-officers-would-help-stop-police-brutality/?utm_term=.492d1d3e171c.

Seth Stoughton. "How Police Training Contributes to Avoidable Deaths," *Atlantic*, December 12, 2014, https://www.theatlantic.com/national/archive/2014/12/police-gun-shooting-training-ferguson/383681/.

Phillip Swarts. "Police Need Better Training and Community Relations, Presidential Task Force Is Told," *Washington Times*, January 13, 2015, http://www.washingtontimes.com/

news/2015/jan/13/police-brutality-solutions-are-training-community-/.

Annie Sweeney. "Police 'De-escalation' Training — How It Could Help Chicago," *Chicago Tribune*, March 25, 2016, http://www.chicagotribune.com/news/ct-police-training-las-vegas-chicago-met-20160324-story.html.

Juleyka Lantigua-Williams. "How Much Can Better Training Do to Improve Policing?" *Atlantic*, July 13, 2016, https://www.theatlantic.com/politics/archive/2016/07/police-training/490556/.

Timothy Williams. "Long Taught to Use Force, Police Warily Learn to De-escalate," *New York Times*, June 27, 2015, https://www.nytimes.com/2015/06/28/us/long-taught-to-use-force-police-warily-learn-to-de-escalate.html.

Holly Yan. "States Require More Training Time to Become a Barber than a Police Officer," CNN, September 28, 2016, http://www.cnn.com/2016/09/28/us/jobs-training-police-trnd/index.html.

Index

W

Z